BRUCE K. OLSEN

# The Decadent Emperors:
## Power and Depravity
## in Third-Century Rome

# THE DECADENT EMPERORS:
## Power and Depravity
## in Third-Century Rome

George C. Brauer, Jr.

*This book was originally titled:*
The Young Emperors: Rome, A.D. 193-244

BARNES
&NOBLE
BOOKS
NEW YORK

Originally titled as *The Young Emperors: Rome, A.D. 193-244*.

This edition published by Barnes & Noble, Inc.,
by arrangement with HarperCollins Publishers, Inc.

1995 Barnes & Noble Books

ISBN 1-56619-689-2

Printed and bound in the United States of America

M 9 8 7 6 5 4 3 2 1

# ACKNOWLEDGMENTS

I am grateful to Professor Richard H. Chowen of the Department of History, University of South Carolina, for his careful reading of Chapters XIII and XXIII of this book.

G.C.B.

# ⚜ PREFACE ⚜

During much of the first half of the third century after Christ, Rome was ruled by the young. Caracalla died in 217 at the age of twenty-nine, having commanded the Empire since the death of his father in 211; his younger brother Geta, who tried to rule jointly with him, died in 212. When Elagabalus came to the throne in 218 he was fourteen years old; he died in 222. His successor Severus Alexander was thirteen at his accession but lasted until 235. Gordian III, who reigned between 238 and 244, was eighteen when he died.

This book attempts to tell the story of Caracalla, Geta, Elagabalus, Severus Alexander, and Gordian III, as well as the older persons most closely associated with them. It also attempts to show certain important characteristics of the period they lived in: a period when the full-blown Empire began to decay, when the noblest achievements of classical civilization were monuments of the past, when the old gods were gradually dying, when the Orient attracted and influenced the West immeasurably, when Christianity grew underground. It was an age of gross materialism and religious ecstasy, of high ideals and administrative irresponsibility, of intense ambition and short glory.

# ❧ CONTENTS ❧

## ❧ I ❧

# The Rise of Septimius Severus

In the year of Rome 940 or A.D. 188, when his son Bassianus was born, Lucius Septimius Severus governed a portion of Gaul. It would have been absurd to suppose that Severus would one day be proclaimed Emperor, but he himself may have hoped that this would happen; astrologers had predicted that the lady he had married a year or two before, a rich Syrian named Julia Domna, would be an Emperor's wife.

Born into a Punic family at Leptis Magna on the Mediterranean coast of Africa in 146, Severus apparently learned Latin as a second language; he always spoke it, as well as Greek, with an accent. His literary and philosophical education was completed at Athens, an academic town immersed in its own past. Much earlier he had studied law at Rome and, evidently with the help of an influential uncle, had been elevated from the equestrian, or knightly, order to senatorial rank. He occupied financial posts, or questorships, in southwestern Spain and Sardinia; assisted the proconsul, or governor, of Africa; was tribune of the people; became a praetor, or judicial magistrate; administered justice in eastern Spain as *legatus juridicus;* and commanded troops in Syria. His public life was a case of consistent rise from office to office and of valuable service to the Empire and himself. Now, as governor of Gallia Lugdunensis, he could tell his rich wife that his status was higher than ever.

He had owed prime loyalty during the early part of his career to Marcus Aurelius, the man whose reign closed what was probably the most glorious time of Roman imperial history. It was a period of over

1

eighty years of public happiness—punctuated occasionally by distant
wars against barbarians, disturbances within the provinces, and minor
tyrannical measures, but about as ideal an age on the whole as Rome
ever achieved. Under the intelligent, victorious, heroic Trajan (98–117),
the strong, restless, beauty-loving, unsatisfied Hadrian (117–138), the
benevolent, duty-conscious Antoninus Pius (138–161), and the wise
and stalwart Marcus Aurelius (161–180), the Roman world experienced expansion, prosperity, and an abundance of good things. Trajan
brought the Empire to its greatest size; Hadrian, always on the move,
visited the recesses of his dominions and attended carefully to the
problems of his non-Roman subjects; the period of Antoninus Pius was
one so undisturbed that it has almost no history. There was little terror,
whereas there had been much under earlier Emperors such as Caligula,
Nero, and Domitian; and there was as little sadness, perhaps, as possible. The cities of the provinces flourished in brilliance and beauty; men
were at peace and grew rich; some of the rich cultivated their intellects
or patronized the arts; and the poor could gaze upon splendor.

The reign of Marcus Aurelius constituted a late afternoon in all
this happiness. He did as much as a man could do, but the barbarians
became insistent, a plague tortured the Empire, and prosperity perhaps
declined to some degree. The afternoon, however, was still lovely, and
Romans of the future were to look back at the reign of the good Marcus as a golden age and were to honor his spirit more devotedly than
the spirits of most of their deified rulers.

Since Rome made no provisions for the passing on of the rule of the
Empire by direct line of descent, it was rare for a son to follow his father on the throne. However, the Emperor Commodus was the son of
Marcus Aurelius. Most inhabitants of the Empire, Roman citizens, provincials, and slaves, probably noticed very little change after he
assumed command in 180. They went on making money or sweating
for a bare subsistence, fathering or mothering children, worshipping
the old gods or finding new ones to worship, feasting together, suing
one another, cheering at the chariot races, strolling under colonnades,
recovering from illnesses or dying; and the fact that they heard stories
of horror from Rome probably made them think that the glory was
diminishing but did not unduly distress them.

Nevertheless, Commodus was not a good Emperor. Although he
was not an extremely good gladiator either, he prided himself on his

gladiatorial skill and, to a large measure, let the Empire take care of itself. He wasted the imperial treasury, killed off noble Romans, and lived licentiously.

Severus was among those citizens who were not unduly distressed. Intelligent and ambitious, he continued to rise. After his governorship of Gallia Lugdunensis he governed Sicily, and in the year 190 he was a *consul suffectus,* or honorary consul. Then Commodus put him in charge of three legions whose duty it was to defend civilization against barbarism in Pannonia, where the Danube formed the border of the Empire. The post was an extremely demanding one, and Severus executed his assignment admirably, winning sincere respect from the legions on this far frontier. It was in Pannonia, presumably, that his son Bassianus spent two years of early childhood—probably in the city of Carnuntum, Severus' headquarters. With his army around him, Severus may occasionally have remembered the prophecy that his wife's husband would become an Emperor; and, with his little boy Bassianus very much in his thoughts, he may even have dreamed of establishing a dynasty.

On the last night of the year 192 Commodus was strangled in his bath by an athlete named Narcissus. To the throne came Pertinax, a citizen of courage and probity, who had seen much military service and had governed a number of provinces. It looked as if good times were to return, but the troubles had only begun. Since the treasury was depleted, Pertinax tried to replenish it. His measures may have been somewhat extreme. At any rate, some Romans thought so. His elevation to the imperium was simply the prelude to his death. On March 28, 193, he was speared by a guard. Other guards cut off his head.

Rome had seen many days of disorder during her long lifetime, but few were as disordered as the day of Pertinax' murder. She acquired a new Emperor in a manner unexpected and shameful.

Aware that the Praetorian Guard was not disposed in his favor, Pertinax had, earlier in the day, sent to the camp of the Praetorians his father-in-law, Sulpicianus, Prefect of the City, with the injunction to keep the guards placated. Almost ten thousand in number and the prime military force in the capital, the Praetorians were at the height of their influence. They had been coddled by Commodus into a state of superb arrogance. Everybody knew that they were potential

Emperor-makers and -breakers, especially in a city where a large part of the population, quelled by twelve years of tyranny, hesitated to voice a political objection of any kind. If the Praetorians declared a man Emperor, the diffident Senate would no doubt confirm their choice; and if they rose against a man, his imperial days were probably numbered. Therefore, when Sulpicianus was shown the detached head of Pertinax, instead of wasting time sentimentalizing over his unfortunate son-in-law, he decided to buy the Empire from the Praetorians for himself. He was a rich senator; if he promised the guards enough money, they would hail him as the new chief of the Roman world.

Rumors of Sulpicianus' intention circulated throughout the city, and it soon appeared that somebody else could play the same game. There was a senator named Didius Julianus, who had governed provinces and fought barbarians. He was in his late middle age, a trifle foolish perhaps, and inordinately rich, and he had a wife who lusted to be an Empress. He hurried to the camp of the Praetorians and stood by the gates, which were closed.

Sulpicianus was still inside the camp.

The bidding began.

Messengers went between the two men egging each of them on, reporting how much the other had raised the bid. It was a profitable day for the Praetorians. Outside the camp, Rome waited.

Didius Julianus succeeded in purchasing the Empire. He apparently promised each Praetorian twenty-five thousand sesterces for it (a sestertius was worth about fifty cents).

The auction over, the soldiers admitted the new Emperor into the camp to receive their oaths of allegiance and to be presented with the imperial insignia. Then, with military pomp, standards borne proudly before them, and heads held high, the Praetorians marched Didius Julianus to the Senate.

When at a late hour he reached what was now to be his own palace, he prepared to enjoy his dinner. The menu which would have satisfied Pertinax, however, was not to his liking; it was too simple, and he made fun of it. He would show the people that he was a real Emperor by showing that he knew how to eat like one: he ordered a sumptuous supper. Then, in contempt, he evidently proceeded to play dice close to the spot where the headless body of his predecessor lay.

In remote Pannonia, Severus heard of the events at Rome. He possibly heard also that the governor of Syria, a man named Pescennius Niger whom he already knew, had been proclaimed Emperor by the legions in that part of the Empire. He decided that it was time to act. On April 14, at Carnuntum, he addressed his own soldiers—the Illyrian troops, many of them old in the service, on whom he could rely. A large number of these legionaries had served under Pertinax during the wars of Marcus Aurelius, and had admired him as much as they now admired Severus. They were in a mood to avenge the death of their brave former commander. And the Empire lay open to anyone with the cunning and the power to grab it.

Severus talked to his men of the vile assassination of Pertinax, about the auctioning off of the Empire, and of the foolish Didius Julianus who had bought it. Many of these men must have thought with anger of the proud Praetorians who had sold Rome although she was not theirs to sell, and they must have thought also that they themselves were superior to those insolent troops whom everybody seemed to fear. The Praetorians had been spoiled by Emperors and had grown soft in the city. The Illyrians were not afraid of them.

Severus said that the wrongs of Rome must be righted. With him at their head, the Illyrian legions could restore honor to Rome. They let out a great shout, proclaiming him Emperor.

He set off for Rome almost at once, putting his legions through some of the longest days of marching that they had ever experienced. He did not stop unless absolutely necessary; the object was to act quickly, to reach Rome before people had recovered from the auction of the Empire, to overthrow Didius Julianus immediately, and then turn his attention to Pescennius Niger. Fortunately for him, Severus had a much shorter route to cover than Niger did. Besides, in addition to the loyal Illyrians at his back, he could depend on other legions to support him—those in Rhaetia and Noricum, a couple in Dacia, several in Moesia, and several in Germany. But Niger had many loyal legions too. As for Julianus, he was the least of Severus' worries; he could be disposed of quite easily.

Severus had never been a man to luxuriate, and on these long, tortuous marches he realized that he could best retain the devotion of his men by sharing their hardships. His tent was like theirs; his food was as plain as theirs; what they could endure, he could endure.

It had been over a century since Italy had seen an invading army, or even since a protecting army had been stationed in Italy. But the Italians were not really disturbed at the advent of Severus' legions. They did not think of resisting; on the whole, they were pleased. They saw in Severus the avenger of Pertinax, on his way to punish the senator who had purchased the Empire. Sometimes, when Severus passed near a sizable city, the inhabitants rushed out rejoicing, wreaths of flowers in their hair. Already the march was beginning to look like a triumph.

Meanwhile in Rome poor Julianus did not know what to do. He could, he hoped, rely on the Praetorians, but they looked as if they would not be very useful. Unaccustomed to warfare, they showed little inclination to die for the Emperor they had created; unaccustomed to strict military discipline, they performed their exercises in a dilatory fashion. Julianus sent for the soldiers of the fleet at Misenum, but naturally they were not used to fighting on land. He sent for the gladiators at Capua, but these strong men owed him nothing and promised to be of little help. He thought of the elephants which had been transported to Rome to amuse the people at the spectacles; the size and smell of these tremendous beasts might strike terror into Severus' cavalry. The elephants were therefore armed for battle, but they threw off the towers that had been put on their backs, and the drivers too. The people laughed.

He had ditches dug; he betrayed a certain lack of confidence by having the palace barricaded. As Severus' army marched ever closer, he lost whatever dignity he might have possessed in a frenzy of fear. He resorted to magic; it is said that he sacrificed children. He suggested that the Senate send out the Vestal Virgins to ask Severus' troops to withdraw, but the Senate did not believe the Illyrian legions would be deterred by these ladies. An augur told him bluntly that if he could not fight he did not deserve to be Emperor.

Without striking a blow, he retreated behind the barricades of his palace, a foolish, frightened man, and waited for what he knew was to come. The Senate declared that he was no longer Emperor, condemned him to death, ratified the Illyrians' choice of Severus, and announced that Pertinax was to receive divine honors.

Neither the Praetorians nor anybody else helped Julianus. Early in June some soldiers headed by a tribune were sent to the palace to carry out the senatorial decree. They found the forsaken Emperor hiding in his bed.

"What have I done wrong?" he asked them. "What have I done wrong?"

He had bought a reign of sixty-six days. His body was presented to his ambitious wife and daughter for burial in the family tomb.

Before entering the city, Severus summoned the Praetorian Guards in order to address them. They came in peace, unarmed except for the short sword which they customarily carried; they had left their fighting equipment in camp. They wore branches of laurel, as they usually did when assisting at a public ceremony. While they stood before the imperial tribunal, facing their new sovereign, the Illyrian legions surrounded them.

Severus began to speak. He said that the Praetorians were responsible for Pertinax' death, since they had not bothered to protect him; reproached them savagely for auctioning off the Empire; and called them cowards for abandoning the buyer. They deserved to die, he told them, but he would be merciful. They were to be Praetorians no more; they were disbanded in disgrace. From now on, if any man of them was found within a hundred miles of Rome, he would be put to death as a matter of course.

They laid down their short swords and their military belts. The Illyrians stripped them of their badges and of their armor. Hooted and jeered at by the Illyrians and the Romans, they slunk away.

Septimius Severus was now Emperor in actuality. His son Bassianus was five.

# ❧ II ❧

# The Wars of Septimius Severus

There were important things to be done before Severus could consider his rule consolidated. A new Praetorian Guard had to be created, Pertinax had to be given a proper funeral, the citizens of Rome had to be made happy, and Pescennius Niger had to be conquered.

The new Praetorian Guard, increased from ten thousand to fifteen thousand men, was composed of Severus' own Illyrian veterans. This was a change that shocked many Romans. Until now, the men allowed in the Praetorian Guard had been principally legionaries from Italy or from highly Romanized areas such as Spain, Noricum, and Macedonia. For a long time, in fact, only Italians had been admitted to the Guard. To admit Spaniards, Noricans, and Macedonians had constituted enough of a relaxation of standards in the eyes of conservative Romans; but to admit a horde of Illyrians was outrageous. The Illyrians were barbarians, scarcely preferable to those dwelling beyond the borders of the Empire. Ancient senators whispered indignantly to one another, but Severus was determined to rule with a strong hand. Even late in his reign, the Praetorian Guard continued to be made up largely of Illyrians and Pannonians; the Italians were not brought back into favor. Actually, however, Rome had spread so far by the end of the second century that many Illyrians were almost as Romanized as inhabitants of older portions of the Empire.

Being politically astute, Severus had the Senate decree that it would be unlawful for him to put any senator to death without the consent of the Senate itself. Even more politic was his pose as the avenger of Pertinax, whose name he had assumed as one of his own.

He announced that a chariot drawn by elephants would carry a golden statue of Pertinax to the Circus Maximus, and that a throne would be set out for Pertinax at public shows. And he staged a magnificent funeral—one of the finest funerals that Romans had ever witnessed.

An ornamental platform was constructed in the Forum—a platform looking like stone but really made of wood. On it, in a shrine with columns of marble and gold, was a couch draped in gold and purple, and on the couch lay the wax replica of Pertinax in his triumphal robes. He seemed to be sleeping. A handsome slave, plying a fan from the tail of a peacock, kept flies away from his realistic but motionless countenance. The object was to make him look as alive as possible, since this was his funeral. The senators and their ladies, in robes of mourning for the murdered divinity, seated themselves around the structure, the ladies under porticoes. Severus was very much in evidence.

After a period of solemnity, the funeral procession began. Images of heroic Romans from the past were carried by; then came men and boys singing a funeral hymn; then, bronze figures representing the many peoples that Rome had conquered and ruled, identifiable by their native costumes; then, further to illustrate the greatness of Rome, the bronze busts of men who had performed noble exploits, the standards of societies, infantry and cavalry units, and choice horses from the Circus Maximus. Last came a gilt altar decorated with ivory and jewels.

The Emperor Septimius Severus mounted the Rostra and read a speech to the assembly. He praised Pertinax highly, in a formal manner. From time to time, the listening senators shouted acclamations; they also moaned and wept. Magistrates and priests picked up the couch draped in purple and gold, with the wax Pertinax still lying on it, and put it in the care of members of the knightly order, who would bear it to the Campus Martius.

The senators walked in front of the couch, wailing and striking their chests, or chanting a funeral song, while flutes played. At the end of the procession was Severus himself.

In the Campus Martius, a three-story tower had been built. It was richly ornamented with gold, ivory, and statues, and on top of it had been placed a gilded chariot which Pertinax had driven. The couch was now placed on the tower. Severus and the kin of Pertinax filed past and kissed the lips of the waxen image. In front of the tower, the magistrates, knights, cavalry, and infantry executed a military maneuver. The two consuls, chief magistrates of the state, set the tower on fire.

Up from the flames flew an eagle which had been imprisoned in the tower. Probably frantic, the bird soared into the sky, carrying the soul of Pertinax to its home with the other divine Emperors.

Severus spent only a few weeks in Rome. But in addition to reforming the Praetorian Guard, satisfying the Senate, and staging the funeral, he managed to please the populace by increasing the corn supply, distributing money to the citizens (as was expected of a new Emperor), and providing expensive games in which both men and beasts died for the enjoyment of the spectators. Then he went off to fight Pescennius Niger.

Niger, like Severus, had been born into a family of equestrian rather than senatorial rank. His early life had been largely a military one; his military prowess had been praised by Marcus Aurelius. Under Commodus he had fought the Dacians, and he is said to have been sent to Gaul at the time Severus was there in order to help quell a revolt. Commodus had raised him to senatorial status and later had made him a suffect consul (a title of high if empty honor). As governor of Syria he held one of the most important administrative posts in the Empire. His career had been successful and distinguished. He certainly possessed as good a right to be Emperor as Severus.

He was a military disciplinarian of the antique Roman mold. When, on a campaign against barbarians, he discovered some Roman soldiers drinking from a silver cup, he commanded that no silver be used in the camp; he said he did not want to give the barbarians a chance to boast that they had seized Roman silver, as they might do if the baggage happened to fall into their hands. He also forbade his troops to drink wine; vinegar had been good enough for the soldiers of the Republic. Perhaps, he occasionally stretched discipline too far. There is a story that when one of his men was brought before him for stealing a chicken, he decided that not only this man but the nine others who had eaten the chicken should be beheaded. But the army grew angry at so stern a pronouncement against fellow Romans, and he had to compromise. Each of the ten men, he declared, would restore ten chickens to the owner. In addition, none of them would be allowed to use fire for the rest of the campaign. They would eat their food raw.

The troops might have been more discontented if he had not been severe with himself as well. His food was simple; his table was set outside his tent, where the men could see what frugal meals he was eating, and where the sun or the rain would discommode him.

On the whole, he elicited the same heartfelt respect from his legions that Severus elicited from his. When he addressed his troops near Antioch after the news had come that Didius Julianus had bought the Empire, he was certain that they would proclaim him Emperor; otherwise he would not have addressed them. In addition to the nine legions in the Roman East, most of the citizens of this part of the Empire were enthusiastically behind him. Not only Syria but the provinces of Asia Minor declared for him, and potentates of the Middle East sent embassies to him promising their assistance. He soon heard that Severus also planned to be Emperor, but he probably felt confident. He idled at Antioch, providing his loyal subjects with the games and spectacles they loved, when he should have been marching toward Europe— although he could not have reached Rome before Severus in any case.

When he did set off, he marched all the way through Asia Minor, crossed over to Europe, and occupied Byzantium, which welcomed him. Meanwhile Severus had sent soldiers to eastern Africa in case Niger tried to add this to his part of the Empire, and had sent a legion to Thrace (Byzantium was on the coast of Thrace). Taken aback, Niger suggested that Severus and he could rule jointly. Severus declined.

The resulting war was not a great one, but it was the first civil war that the Roman world had seen in more than a century, and it was a disturbing omen of possible things to come. The glory of the Antonine age now seemed over. In that age, one could depend on the legions to drive the barbarians from the borders of the Empire. Now, within the Empire, legions were fighting legions.

Not only that, but cities were ranged against cities. The Roman East was to a great extent Greek, and its Hellenized communities had inherited a spirit of fierce civic pride. This spirit had some point in the ancient days when independent city-states looted one another in order to increase their income; but in the Greek Asiatic cities under Roman rule the spirit served no purpose and had degenerated into mere animosity. In Bithynia, Nicomedia supported Severus because its neighbor Nicaea supported Niger. In Syria, Laodicaea eventually favored Severus because Antioch was loyal to Niger. In Phoenicia, Berytus liked Niger whereas Tyre liked Severus.

After crossing into Thrace, Aemilianus, proconsul of Asia and military commander for Niger, recrossed into Asia Minor. Severus apparently left some of his troops to lay siege to Byzantium but, considering the defeat of Niger himself more important than the capture of the city, sent most of his soldiers across to establish themselves on the Asiatic side. Aemilianus did not succeed in driving them back to Europe; there were apparently small fights around the city of Cyzicus, in one of which he was killed. The first battle of importance occurred near Nicaea. When it was over, Niger's army retreated eastward through Asia Minor, with Severus' army following across the mountains. The last battle was fought near Issus, where Alexander the Great had inflicted a momentous defeat on the Persians five centuries before. This time it was the partisans of Niger who were defeated, and the carnage was much less.

Severus, although he had been trained as a warrior and would continue to be one, had not taken part in any of the fights against Niger. He had probably not even taken part in the siege of Byzantium, which now demanded his attention if not his presence. Niger was conquered, but Byzantium was still loyal to him. Niger fled to Antioch and from there toward the kingdom of Parthia, whose ruler had expressed friendship for him. Severus sent horsemen after him; they caught up with him and cut off his head. The head was brought back to Severus, who dispatched it to his army at Byzantium and commanded that it be stuck on the point of a spear in order to demonstrate to the citizens that they did not need to hold out any longer. But they disregarded it.

This Greek city had been thriving for many hundreds of years; its situation between the Propontis and the Black Sea was extremely advantageous to trade. Nobody then living could foresee that, under the Emperor Constantine, it would be converted into the capital of the Roman world and have its name changed to Constantinople. As Constantinople, it would enjoy an eleven-century-long career during which it would be known as the golden city, the New Rome, and regarded as the center of civilization. Although the pre-Constantinian Byzantium was much less glorious, it was still an important port, and it could not be permitted to resist the Emperor.

As Greek cities went, it was neither large nor small. Severus directed both his army and his navy against it.

The most valuable inhabitant of Byzantium at the time was an engineer named Priscus, who excelled at devising machines of war. These machines helped greatly in keeping Severus' land forces out of the city. Some hurled heavy boulders over the massive, turreted walls at the attackers, or sent weighty beams crashing down on the enemy. If the Roman legionaries stayed at a distance from the walls, the machines would batter them with smaller stones and shower them with spears. More than once the Romans were forced to retreat.

Severus also had problems elsewhere. Beyond the boundaries of the Empire, between the Tigris and the Euphrates rivers, stood the fortress-city of Nisibis, a vassal of Rome, very useful as a Roman base. Three trading peoples, the Adiabeni, the Osrhoëni, and the Scenite Arabs, had decided to take advantage of the troubles within the Empire by seizing more territory for themselves, probably with the encouragement of Parthia, historically the most potent enemy of Rome. The Adiabeni and the Osrhoëni besieged Nisibis, and Severus, even during the war against Niger, had sent troops to quell them. When the Adiabeni and the Osrhoëni heard that Niger was dead, they adopted a somewhat naïve plan. They sent an embassy to tell Severus that they had attacked Nisibis, not for any acquisitive reasons, but because it had shown signs of siding with Niger and needed to be punished. Now that peace had returned, they would be glad if the Emperor removed his troops from Nisibis. Of course he saw through the device and renewed war.

Byzantium continued to be obstinate and embarrassing. In order to keep Severus' navy at a distance, a great chain had been stretched across the harbor. At the ends of the piers extending into the harbor, the Byzantines erected towers from which to toss missiles at enemy ships that sailed too near. In addition, Byzantium possessed about five hundred of its own ships. Their iron prows had sharp points for digging into the flanks of enemy vessels, and some of the ships had a rudder at each end so that they could reverse direction without bothering to turn around—a very useful device.

Sometimes Roman vessels were captured without a fight at all.

Young Byzantines would dive off their own ship and swim, mostly under water, to where the Roman fleet rode at anchor. Still under water, they pounded nails into the side of a Roman trireme and cut its anchor cable. Attached to the nails were strong ropes; the other end of the ropes lay on the Byzantine shore. When powerful men pulled on the ropes, the proud Roman craft would come sailing into port.

The third Mesopotamian nation, the Scenite Arabs, also sent a deputation to the Emperor, making outrageous demands for concessions. Severus was infuriated. The chiefs dispatched another embassy; the terms were now less offensive to Roman dignity, but the haughty chiefs themselves refused to come. Severus declared war on the Scenite Arabs too.

He did not participate actively in the Mesopotamian battles but trusted his finest generals to take care of the situation. Nisibis in particular must not be allowed to fall into the hands of the tribesmen. It was the bulwark of defense for the province of Syria against the kingdom of Parthia.

Severus' generals did take care of the situation, and the Mesopotamian tribesmen proved to be less annoying than Byzantium. They were fairly easily conquered, whereas Byzantium was almost impregnable and extraordinarily stubborn. The inhabitants knew that if they were to yield, the fate of their city would be extremely unpleasant. Severus had already punished other disloyal cities, taking away much of their territory, subjecting them to neighboring cities, and degrading them to the status of villages. Besides, there was the strong likelihood of plunder, rape, and destruction of property if a Roman army and navy incensed by two years of resistance were allowed to enter. In the battles in the harbor many Byzantine ships were sunk; the citizens were by this time in a paroxysm of patriotism. They donated the wood of their houses for the construction of new vessels. They tore down their theatres and put the stones into engines of war to be flung at the besiegers. They even took their statues of gods and famous men and threw them at the besiegers, bronze gods and heroes zooming through the air to help crush the enemies of Byzantium. Many of the women had lost husbands, lovers, and sons; forsaking female vanity, a luxury of peace, they cut off their hair so that it could be twisted into ropes for the ships.

But the citizens had to eat. Their provisions had seemed ample, but after two years they were running out. People soaked leather thongs in water to make them soft, and sucked at them. It was said that they began eating their own dead. Many citizens, realizing that the place could not hold out much longer, tried to sail away under cover of a storm. Their boats, however, were loaded down with whatever possessions could be taken along; heavy and sluggish, they were easy prey for the Romans. The Roman vessels rammed into them, capsized them, grabbed at them with boat hooks, and split them wide open with beaklike prows. On shore, the Byzantines watched their women, their children, and their remaining sailors drown—and sent up cries to the gods, but the gods favored Rome. The next day the wrecked ships drifted into shore, and some of the corpses floated in too. At that point, the city gave up.

When Severus received the news, he summoned his soldiers and announced that Byzantium had fallen at last. There was great cheering. The Emperor confiscated the property of the Byzantines; he had the magistrates and soldiers executed; he reduced the city to the status of a village, without privileges, and put it under the control of its jealous neighbor Perinthus, which soon became abusive; he pulled down its buildings and demolished its fortifications. Before the end of his reign he was to build it up again, but for the moment it lay exhausted and disheveled beside its quiet harbor. Under the water, Byzantines and Roman sailors lay in their ships.

Severus had another would-be Emperor to deal with. This was Decimus Clodius Albinus, governor of Britain, who was called Albinus, people said, because he had been a very white baby.

In his youth Albinus had not shown a great deal of interest in intellectual matters; he had been born to be a soldier, and he entered upon a military career as soon as he could. Under Marcus Aurelius he is thought to have commanded the Fourth Flavian Legion during the war against the barbaric Marcomanni, then later commanded the First. He commanded in Bithynia in 175, and kept the area loyal to Marcus Aurelius during the revolt of Avidius Crassus. Under Commodus he was made a consul and led troops against barbarians both on the Danube and on the Rhine. He was then sent to Britain, which the wild Caledonians were invading, and still held the office of military governor when Severus assumed the imperium.

Recognizing in this able general a possible successor but also a potential rival, Severus decided to keep him content by offering him the title Caesar. The term had come to designate an associate in the imperial power—subordinate, of course, to the Emperor (one of whose titles was Augustus), but still carrying a great deal of authority. Severus probably thought that by getting the governor of Britain on his side, he would prevent him from causing trouble; otherwise Albinus could easily march to Rome while Severus was busy in the East. The plan worked for a while, but after the defeat of Niger it ceased to be effective. Severus may have begun to regret that he had given another man so much authority. He soon received information that important senators had written Albinus to the effect that he deserved the imperium and that he should march on Rome. The governor of Britain had himself declared Augustus and Emperor by his army, probably late in 195. That meant war.

A significant number of the senators, very likely a majority, preferred Albinus to Severus. Albinus was by birth of senatorial rank like themselves, whereas Severus had originally belonged to the knightly order and was also of Punic blood. In addition, the Emperor had apparently angered the Senate earlier in 195, while he was still in the Orient, by declaring himself the adoptive son of the deified Marcus Aurelius and the adoptive brother of Commodus, and by having his army deify Commodus. His motives were largely political; to ally himself with the beloved imperial house of the Antonines would, he surmised, improve his image throughout the Empire. Probably some senators, however, viewed the move as a piece of gross impudence, an insult to the name of the good Marcus. But what annoyed many of them even more was the association with Commodus, who had treated the Senate with supreme contempt and whose memory was as despised by the patricians as much as it was revered by the soldiers. In making himself the brother of the infamous Commodus, and in having Commodus deified after the Senate had condemned his memory, Severus had affronted outrageously the leading nobles of Rome.

The Emperor left the East as quickly as possible. At the capital of Upper Moesia, Viminacium on the Danube, he addressed his soldiers. They were very willing to fight for their leader, who seemed to be favored by the goddess Victory. In order to sustain their willingness, Severus distributed a munificent amount of money.

Many Romans had no clear notion of an afterlife, but they felt strongly that if they were remembered after death they possessed immortality of a sort. Rituals in reverence of ancestors and, under the Empire, the proliferation of memorial inscriptions, statues, and buildings named in honor of their donors all testified to such a feeling. By this point in his career Severus, covetous of immortality, wished passionately to be remembered as the founder of a dynasty. His descendants would venerate him as the man who had given them the world to rule, and in a sense he would continue to rule through them. It was the year 196; his son Bassianus was about eight years old, his son Geta a little younger. He had the army confer on Bassianus the title Caesar. Bassianus was too young to exercise the authority that went with the title; Caesar meant in his case, as it had during the previous two centuries of Emperors, that he was heir presumptive. Having Bassianus named Caesar was, from Severus' point of view, an announcement that he wanted to clear the way to establishing a dynasty immediately.

Severus also changed Bassianus' name to Marcus Aurelius Antoninus. The new name connoted the late age of Roman glory, suggested a connection between the Severan house and the Antonines who had recently become the Emperor's dead relatives, and was therefore highly desirable from a political standpoint. The subjects of Marcus Aurelius Antoninus, however, were eventually to call him Caracalla. Since people of future centuries were also to call him that, he will be Caracalla from now on.

Albinus crossed the Channel into Gaul with his legions. Severus advanced with his legions through Pannonia westward. He evidently left behind at Carnuntum, as safe a spot as anywhere, the new young Caesar, Caracalla.

Sending most of his army on ahead, he swung south to Rome, where he intimidated the Senate into declaring Albinus a public enemy and wooed the populace with games. These political maneuvers finished, he rejoined his army, already marching through Gaul.

The morale of the Roman populace was low. One could never tell where a civil war would lead—it might even lead to Rome herself. Even chariot races would not cheer the people. An enormous crowd gathered in the Circus for the races, but there was no enthusiasm. At a spectacle that normally provided the citizens of Rome with one of their greatest emotional outlets, the mob sat listless. The war against Niger and the war against the Oriental barbarians had been enough; it was more than three years since Severus had made himself Emperor and there was no sign of peace. The chariots swept past, the horses strained, the favorite drivers exhibited the skills that usually won them wild applause, and there were spills which should have been exciting. After the sixth race members of the crowd began to murmur, "How long are the civil wars to last?" People shouted: "Rome, what will become of you? What will become of us Romans?" Raising their hands to the sky, they cried: "Gods, let us have peace!" That was their emotional outlet; they quieted down and watched the rest of the races.

Severus was not extremely worried; although news came that Albinus had won battles, the goddess Victory was still with the Emperor. A clever tactician, he stationed garrisons in the western passes of the Alps in order to block Albinus from entering Italy—assuming that Albinus got that far—and his legions were descending on Albinus' headquarters at Lyons from the north in order to cut off the usurper from his strongholds in Britain and northern Gaul. He had even received help from an unlikely quarter: a schoolmaster named Numerianus took it upon himself to champion the Severan cause. Without authorization from anyone, Numerianus hurried to Gaul, raised an army of loyal men, beat Albinus in a cavalry engagement, and collected for the Emperor a sum which today would amount to many millions of dollars.

There was only one great battle in this war, but it was the costliest battle that Romans had fought in a long while. The historian Cassius Dio, a contemporary, says that each of the armies contained about 150,000 men; and although his figures may be exaggerated, the armies were certainly large, including a great many barbarian auxiliaries as well as the legionaries. The two forces came together on a plain north of Lyons, one of the greatest cities in the western part of the Empire since the time of Augustus. Severus himself was very much in this fight, leading his men like the excellent general he was. The war horses snorted, the armor gleamed, the shields reflected the sun; the swords of Romans rang against each other and found soft flesh below the bronze, and barbarians stuck spears into barbarians. The men mixed and tangled and slaughtered until there were many dead, bloody bodies on the plain.

It was not a battle like Thermopylae or Salamis, Hastings or

Manzikert, Iwo Jima or Gettysburg or Waterloo. It did not check an invasion, it did not subdue a nation, it did not overthrow a tyrant, it did not promote a religion, it did not further a cause. It was not an historic occasion. The men who fought in it were not fighting for any ideal; nothing of value inspired them, except their pay. There was neither right nor wrong; Albinus, if he had won, might have ruled the Empire as capably as Severus. It was a great battle that served no great purpose.

After Severus had won, Albinus fled to Lyons with many of his supporters. He knew that along with the battle he had, in effect, lost his life, since he could expect no mercy from Severus, just as Severus could not have expected any mercy from him. So, in a house near the Rhone, he committed suicide; or at least he tried. Some say that he was found by a troop of Severus' soldiers and carried, mostly dead, to the Emperor, and that the Emperor ordered him to be decapitated. Some say also that Severus kept the headless corpse lying outside his tent so that he could trample on it with his great horse and make the blood run, and so that in the succeeding days he could gloat over the mutilated body that had recently been a would-be Emperor. When the putrefaction got too offensive, he had the whole mess thrown into the Rhone.

So far in his wars Severus had shown considerable leniency, but he could not afford to continue this course. If he was really to be Emperor, he had to demonstrate that he could be rigorous and unfeeling. The wife and children of Albinus consequently were killed, and their bodies also tossed into the Rhone. Niger's family, in exile since his defeat, was also put to death. Many eminent provincials who had helped Albinus were executed.

One of these provincials seems to have pleaded with the Emperor for his life. He argued quite reasonably, "Try to put yourself in my place. What crime have I committed? You might have lost the battle, and if you had, and if you were in my position now, how would you feel?"

The Emperor replied, "I would feel resigned to the death which you are about to experience."

The Senate had to be dealt with too, and back in Rome, he dealt with it directly. His spies and informers told him which senators had been adherents of Albinus, until he had collected sixty-four names—

probably a very incomplete list. Each of the men, however, was allowed a trial, and he declared thirty-five of them innocent. The other twenty-nine went the way of the argumentative provincial. The Emperor was just but stern. He made it plain that he did not respect the Senate any more than his new posthumous brother Commodus had respected it; his strength was the army, not the patricians. If all sixty-four of the accused had been proved guilty, all would have been executed. Some of those who died were among the most influential citizens of Rome, former consuls, men of high prominence; but they had chosen the wrong side.

Severus also divided Britain into two provinces; after the defeat of Niger he had done the same thing with Syria. If governors were given less territory to govern, if they were given less power, they would be less likely to attempt to become Emperors. Severus now felt relatively secure.

The Emperor, however, could not rest long from his wars. The Parthians had attacked Nisibis.

Of all the peoples outside the Roman world, the Parthians had for a long time been the strongest and most dangerous. Barbarians could usually be subdued without too much trouble, but the Parthians were a civilized, intelligent nation. Their kingdom had arisen in what is now Iran when the Seleucids, the Syrian Greeks who ruled a large portion of the area conquered by Alexander the Great, were growing weak. It had spread over a vast territory, a great feudal monarchy of a million square miles with pretensions to Hellenic culture. Its nobles were rich, its soldiers were brave. In 53 B.C. it had given Rome one of the most overwhelming defeats which she had ever experienced. The head of the Roman general Crassus, associate of Caesar and Pompey, was brought to the Parthian court while the king and his nobles were watching selections from a Greek play, the *Bacchae* of Euripides. The head was fit cleverly into the performance, and the king watched with heightened interest, knowing that he had humbled the Romans.

That had been a long time ago. The Parthia of A.D. 197 or 198 was an enervated kingdom, given to luxury and demoralized by murders within the royal family. Perhaps wisely, it had abandoned most of its Greek pretensions and had gone back to Oriental ways. Although Parthian power was fading, the kingdom still constituted a very serious threat to Roman security, and the name of Parthia ranked among the few names that Romans respected. To conquer the Parthians would mean indisputable greatness for Severus. The war that Severus now set out on was partly a war for the defense of the Empire and the settlement of conditions on the eastern border, but it was also a war for glory.

He took with him his Illyrian Praetorians, his cavalry, and other seasoned troops that he had brought from the campaign in Gaul. Advancing into the territory of his old enemies the Osrhoëni, he executed a valuable political move by recognizing the independence of their king, Abgar, whose dominions he had made a Roman province a couple of years before, and granted him the title King of Kings in return for his allegiance.

Severus proceeded toward Nisibis. On receiving word of his approach, Vologases IV, king of Parthia, gave up without a fight and crossed to the east bank of the Tigris. Severus continued to advance. He was guided by a certain Antiochus, a Graeco-Syrian philosopher-adventurer of the Cynic persuasion who knew the region well. The Cynic displayed his contempt for material things by rolling around in the snow. He shamed the Roman troops into physical exertions that they might not otherwise have attempted. Severus, grateful for his usefulness, rewarded him amply. Years later he gathered up his money and went over to the Parthians.

Severus proceeded south down the Euphrates. The city of Babylon, which had been great for many centuries, was great no longer. The Parthians did not consider it worth defending; it fell without resistance to the Romans, who then advanced eastward to the Tigris. The much newer city of Seleucia had also been abandoned and was an easy prey to the Emperor. Ctesiphon, the Parthian capital, did not prove much harder to take, and plundering it gave joy as well as riches to the soldiers. Only Hatra, a short distance north of Ctesiphon, caused the Romans serious trouble.

A center for the caravan trade, Hatra was located in the Sendjah Desert. Populous, rich, and unwilling to be Romanized, it was surrounded by a double wall and provided with a plentiful water supply. The Romans gathered under its outer wall, but the war machines of Hatra sent projectiles plummeting down on them. The Romans brought up their siege engines; from over the walls came burning naphtha, which set the engines on fire. The Romans made attempts to scale the outer wall, but the ingenious citizens had collected venomous winged insects in pots, and the pots, shot over the walls, broke on the heads of the legionaries. Besides, there was the intolerable heat of the desert. And in addition, the Romans were embarrassed by dysentery. In some disgust, Severus abandoned the siege.

A while later he was back. Byzantium had yielded to him, and so would Hatra. Despite the fiery naphtha, despite the insects, the Romans managed to make a hole in the outer wall. But then Severus made an unwise move; he ordered his troops to withdraw. Apparently, he knew that a great treasure lay in the Temple of Baal and did not want his soldiers to find it, as they would do if they rushed into the city and began the same kind of full-scale looting which they had indulged in at Ctesiphon. If Hatra, her wall breached, offered to surrender, the Romans could enter the city in an orderly manner and he himself could seize the treasure.

The next day he waited impatiently, but Hatra made no overtures of surrender. During the night she built up the wall. On the following morning Severus commanded his European troops to attack, but, with some justification, they declined. Since the Europeans were fractious, he ordered his Syrian soldiers to scale the walls; they obeyed, but they were demoralized, and the citizens drove back those whom they did not kill.

An eager officer said to Severus: "Give me five hundred and fifty European troops and I'll take Hatra for you."

But Severus asked sarcastically, "Where am I going to find that many soldiers?"

He never got Hatra, but he got Mesopotamia. The land between the rivers became another province of the Empire, which it had not been since the reign of Marcus Aurelius. The Senate, moreover, bestowed on Severus the title Parthicus Maximus. He now had glory.

# ❦ III ❦

## *The Family Circle*

Julia Domna, wife of the Emperor and mother of his two sons, had been a lady of high distinction even before she married. A Syrian quite a few years younger than Severus—he married her after the death of his first wife, Marciana—she was descended from a long line of priests of the Sun at Emesa (a city about a hundred miles from Antioch). Her ancestors, in fact, had been priest-kings. In Emesa they had constituted the great family, the possessors of enviable wealth as well as prestige. At the time of the marriage Julia Domna was probably the more eminent of the two partners. It was apparently her father's oracle that had declared that the man she married would be a monarch, but Severus must have felt that even if the oracle proved wrong, she was a very desirable match.

She also happened to be beautiful, and although she possibly bestowed her favors on various men after her marriage, she was not egregiously unfaithful, if unfaithful at all. An Empress, besides, could in large measure do as she pleased, especially if she stood in no danger of divorce, and Julia Domna knew that Severus would not divorce the wife who had provided him with a dynasty. Mundane laws were for lower ladies, for women in general; they did not apply to her. She was not only Empress; in some places she was a goddess. Many Greeks identified her with either Demeter, goddess of growing grain, or Hera, queen of the gods; at Aphrodisias in Asia Minor, there was a temple to her as Demeter. She moved with the grace and dignity that befitted an Empress-goddess.

We know very little about her manner of educating the young

Caracalla and Geta aside from the story that Caracalla was given a Christian nurse—a story which is very likely untrue, but, if it was true, would not be completely surprising in view of his mother's great curiosity about religions in the part of the Empire which she regarded as home.

We do know that in addition to being well-born and beautiful, she was remarkably intelligent. She could not rest content with womanly things, or even with the manifold diversions of the court; she became attracted to the complex matter of running an Empire and took an enthusiastic interest in her husband's affairs. She accompanied him on more than one campaign, and consequently received from the Senate the title Mother of the Camps, a most respectful title implying that the soldiers adored her. Severus must have consulted her on many decisions and on many matters of policy, since he recognized the sharpness of her mind, the shrewdness, the hard practicality that lay at the bases of her intellect. She was in this respect too an excellent wife for him, a valuable partner in the difficult jobs of managing most of the civilized world and establishing a dynasty.

But her intelligence had another side as well. Humanistic and spiritual concerns—the artistic, the literary, the philosophical, the beautiful, the ethical, the mystical—drew her as they were drawing many Syrians. Her part of the Empire, where Greeks, Hebrews, Phoenicians, and many other peoples came together, where the interest in old creeds and new faiths was intense, comprised one of the most intellectually active regions of the Roman world. Ragged Cynics on street corners lashed at life, perfumed rhetoricians performed fantastic feats of word manipulation, Christians prayed fervently to the God of mercy and loving-kindness, and worshippers at Emesa danced elaborately in honor of the Sun. Julia Domna had been influenced by the Syrian atmosphere and carried her interests to Rome. Because of her, the court patronized literature and philosophy. Especially in the years when the wars were over and her family was growing up, she gathered around her a circle of intellectuals.

With regard to literary figures, this did not mean a great deal. Rome's literary might had shrunk. No one in the Empire was capable of creating the literature that had been produced during the late Republic, during the principate of Augustus, or even during the reign of

Trajan only a century before. The taste of the period was for an extremely artificial, contrived, ornamented, precious style. Rhetoricians were enormously popular, as they had been for some time, and these men were dextrous performers with words, but no more. In the lecture halls of Rome and other Italian cities they delivered cunningly devised talks. They did not really believe anything (except that money was valuable), and they often demonstrated their skill by speaking on some outrageous topic thrown out by a member of the audience. Somebody would suggest: "Give us a lecture on the flea," or, "Prove to us that cowardice in battle is preferable to bravery," and the sophist would construct a soaring (if flimsy) showpiece of verbal architecture, putting in as many tricks and arabesques and rhetorical devices as he could, to the delight of an audience which admired and appreciated such entertainment and paid generously for it. The literary figures of Julia Domna's circle conformed with the tone of the age. Aelian wrote sweetly phrased anecdotes and books on natural history; Serenus Sammonicus wrote recondite antiquarian works; Oppian's style in his long poem about fishing was charming but not vigorous.

The conversations must have been superior to the literature, since the members of the circle were, if not powerfully creative, at least erudite. Serenus Sammonicus had a library of sixty-two thousand volumes. Diogenes Laertius was the author of a book on the lives of the philosophers—a book that he considered dedicating to a feminine member of the group, a learned lady named Arria. Antipater, who came from Phrygia in Asia Minor and who in part conducted Caracalla's education, was Greek Secretary to Severus. Rhetoricians and philosophers visiting Rome were welcomed in the group; one of them, Alexander of Aphrodisias, was head of the Aristotelian School at Athens. Stoicism, Epicureanism, Platonism, and Cynicism were talked about, and so were the old gods and the mystic religions flooding Rome from the East. These intellectuals estimated the worth of the material world and speculated about the destiny of the soul. They also reviewed the Greek and Roman masters of poetry and prose of former times, and pointed out the devices these writers had used for achieving striking literary effects. They discussed Aesculapius, the healer-god, whose temples were reported to work wonderful cures (sick people crawled from great distances to be made well by Aesculapius). They probably deliberated about Christianity; the Empress' niece Julia Mamaea, who sometimes joined the group, was especially attracted to that subject.

And they marveled over the miracles said to have been performed by Apollonius of Tyana, who had lived a century and a half before, and who was thought to have been divine or to have attained divinity. The Empress was so much interested in this particular god-man that she commissioned one of the most accomplished members of the circle, Philostratus, to write the history of Apollonius' life. Philostratus, a famous professor of rhetoric and author of a book *The Lives of the Sophists* as well as of poems, naturally wanted to oblige his patroness; and the *Life of Apollonius of Tyana,* which he eventually produced, was by far the finest work of literature to come out of the coterie—a sensitive, appreciative biography of an extraordinary man who was, perhaps, part mystic and part charlatan, preacher and parable-maker, moral reformer and wanderer over the world in search of wisdom.

The venerable Galen may, during the last years of his life, have contributed to some of the discussions in the circle. He came from Pergamum, one of the great Greek cities of Asia Minor, where he had been official doctor to the gladiatorial school, and under Marcus Aurelius he had distinguished himself not only as the finest physician of the age but probably as the finest of the ancient world since Hippocrates. As a young man Severus had known him well and respected him highly. An insatiable desire for truth impelled him to investigate unflaggingly and to write at length about his findings or surmises. He speculated on anatomy and the functions of the body (in particular the nervous system), on education, the fine arts, athletics, mental health, the soul, and immortality, questioning the concept of an afterlife for the soul and then questioning his questions. The ascertainment of truth meant more to him than it did to many of the Empress' intellectually facile friends.

Because Julia Domna came to Rome, her relatives came too. Most prominent among them during the reign of Septimius Severus was her older sister Julia Maesa, who moved to Rome about the year 193. Her husband, Julius Avitus, was rich and prominent, especially after the elevation of his sister-in-law to an imperial position. He governed Asia,

Mesopotamia, and Cyprus, and in the year 209 was a consul. We do not know much about him or about the relationship between him and his wife, but the likeliest assumption is that Julia Maesa went her own way in large degree. Like her sister, Maesa was a woman of great intelligence; she had all Domna's shrewdness without the wide intellectual interests that made Domna a much more admirable woman. Later, as a widow, she was to become the grandmother of two Emperors and to play a very important role in politics.

Julia Maesa's older daughter, the voluptuous Julia Soaemias, had inherited the good looks of the family. In 204 or earlier she married Sextus Varius Marcellus, an eminent man from Syria who held high government posts, many of which took him far away from Rome. Soaemias probably did not miss him. She enjoyed life at court, and a considerable number of men enjoyed her. She was the most lascivious member of a family not famous for its sexual restraint. We can only guess at whether the Emperor was embarrassed by his niece's promiscuous activities. At any rate, she added her own splash of color to the court.

Her sister, Julia Mamaea, wife of a Syrian named Gessius Marcianus, was her opposite in character. It is not known whether the marriage was happy, but presumably she was faithful. Perhaps her unexceptionable conduct was intended as a comment on Soaemias, of whom she was not fond, or perhaps she was simply not very much interested in sex.

These Syrians—Julia Domna, her sister Julia Maesa, and her sister's daughters, Julia Soaemias and Julia Mamaea—contributed their share to the Orientalization of the Roman Empire. The Empire was never Orientalized in a great many respects, but the East was influencing the Romans as it had influenced the post-Alexandrine Greeks. The Eastern provinces, with their Graeco-Asiatic culture and their long heritage of civilization, sometimes aroused feelings of inferiority in the sturdy, efficient, unsubtle young conquerors of the world; and the Romans, not at all above being imitative, borrowed much from those areas. A Syrian Empress, Syrian ladies at court and their Syrian husbands, Asiatic intellectuals figuring prominently in the Empress' own private circle, and a half-Syrian youth heir presumptive to the Empire —in a way, these were factors in a steady process. Not very many years in the future, another Emperor would try to overturn the traditional gods of Rome and to set up instead his Syrian Sun God as the sole great divinity; even during the reign of Severus, belief in the old gods was being challenged by deities imported from the East, such as Serapis and Isis of Egypt, the Great Mother for whom Phrygian priests castrated themselves, and Mithra, Persian god of light, whose worship was spreading fast among the soldiers. Another religion from the Eastern provinces, Christianity, was competing with Mithraism and would, of course, in time overtake the aged Latin gods and become the faith of the Empire. Meanwhile government as well as religion would be Orientalized; in less than a century, Diocletian, abandoning even the pretense of ruling as the first citizen of a republic, would turn the administration, sweepingly and undisguisedly, into a despotism more suggestive of the absolute Eastern monarchies than of old Rome so careful of her liberties. As figures in the pattern of things to come, Julia Domna and her relatives had a significance of which they themselves were probably unaware.

The imperial brothers were both good-looking, like their mother. Julia Domna evidently preferred her younger son, Geta, since he seemed to be more mild-mannered, somewhat more tractable, a little less spoiled than Caracalla. His feelings seemed more humane, at least when he was a boy of eight.

According to one story, Geta heard his father announce that all Albinus' partisans in the Senate would be put to death. He asked why.

Severus explained, "Because they are our enemies, and if I do not kill them they may harm you later on."

"How many of them are there?"

Severus made it clear that there were quite a few.

"Do they have any mothers and fathers or other relations?"

Severus said that they had many close relatives.

"Then our victory won't do us any good. More people will be sad than happy."

But little Caracalla, who had been listening, snapped, "Kill all our enemies! Kill all their children too!"

And Geta, shocked, exclaimed, "You're so bloodthirsty I think you would even kill me."

Caracalla's reaction was, of course, the more practical one; if the sons of the executed senators were allowed to grow up, they might very well cause trouble. But Geta's final point in this conversation, which may or may not have actually happened, was justified. Even in boyhood, Caracalla would probably not have felt very sorry about killing Geta. It may also be true that Geta, if sufficiently provoked, would not have minded killing Caracalla. Less than two years younger than his brother, he returned Caracalla's hatred with a childish enthusiasm which was to mature into sheer savagery. Even at play they were serious rivals; if they got a cockfight going, or a fight between two quails, or if they arranged a match between two wrestlers, each of them would cheer his champion with great enthusiasm, avid for victory. Once, several years later, they had a private chariot race; each youth whipped his team of fast horses on in a spirit of brotherly rivalry, forgetting everything except the desire to beat the other, until Caracalla in the strain and fury fell off his seat and broke his leg.

Perhaps not at the beginning, but soon enough, the question of what was to happen at the death of their father sharpened the edge of their hatred. When the army gave Caracalla the title Caesar in 196 and the Senate confirmed the title in 197, it seemed relatively certain that he was to inherit the Empire; to make this even more certain, the Senate proclaimed him *Imperator Destinatus,* or future Emperor. But titles meant little; both boys knew that the best guarantee of power either could have was the death of the other. Besides, Severus was too fond a father to let only one son enjoy what the other perhaps equally deserved. About the year 198, in celebration of the capture of Ctesiphon, the title Caesar was conferred on Geta. At the same time Caracalla received the title Augustus, which meant that from then on he could share the imperial authority with his father. Geta, it is true, was not declared Augustus until at least ten years later, but even so, the assumption now was that the sons would rule the Empire together after Severus' death. This expectation must have teased and tickled their enmity.

As they grew older their parents, very much concerned, tried various devices to check the fraternal hatred—talked to them, cajoled them, reasoned with them. Severus urged the senators and other courtiers to remind the two boys as often as possible that brothers should be helpful and affectionate toward one another. Coins were struck showing the brothers about to shake hands. Every year the

Festival of Brotherly Love was celebrated in Greece and Asia Minor. But all these artifices were an irony, if not a downright travesty. Each youth had his own associates—his own flatterers, sworn defenders, panderers to his pleasure: gladiators, chariot drivers, pimps, ignoble sons of patricians, and lovely, loose ladies. Each had his own faction to support him at the chariot races in the Circus—Caracalla the Blues, Geta the Greens—and each supported his faction with an ardor that reflected the cockfights of childhood.

Although Geta remained the more amenable of the two, neither youth was exemplary. The glowing vices of Rome strongly attracted the boys. For this reason, as well as because the great city was not much to his taste, Severus preferred to take his family south of the capital to Campania. No matter where they happened to be, however, Caracalla and Geta succeeded in succumbing to temptation. As sons of the Emperor they had a free rein, and they were good-looking besides. They could indulge in whatever pleasures appealed to them; they could choose their courtesans from all over the Roman world, although the court would probably have provided an adequate supply.

All this license went to Caracalla's head more than to Geta's. When it was combined with the knowledge that he was the older son of an Emperor and that he was expected to rule Rome some day, his arrogance burgeoned into a monstrous thing, and he forgot to be grateful to his father. Severus kept hoping; but the Emperor, strong with his subordinates, was weak with his sons. In this respect, primarily, he was a poor man to launch a dynasty.

Severus also was unwise in choosing as his principal lieutenant a man completely unworthy of the honor.

Plautian, like Severus, had been born in Africa. He is said to have got into trouble there and was reportedly banished, but he found a friend in Severus. What Severus liked about him is difficult to determine. They were both apparently of Punic extraction, but their common racial ancestry need not have provided a very strong bond between them, as it was not a thing of great rarity. Some people thought that they were kin, yet even if this was true it does not offer much of an answer, since Severus accorded much less honor to his own brother than to Plautian. Perhaps Severus saw in Plautian a man who was clever enough to carry out the most devious duties and unscrupulous enough not to boggle at the bloody trifles that had to be accomplished if the Emperor was to retain his authority. And perhaps Severus felt that Plautian's humble birth would prevent him from ever aspiring to the Empire himself. In other words, as long as he was paid enough, he could be trusted to give excellent service.

After Severus became Emperor he made Plautian his Praetorian Prefect. Although there had usually been two Praetorian Prefects, Plautian held the office alone most of the time. It was an office carrying an enormous amount of power. Because one of the Praetorian Prefect's duties was that of guarding the life of the Emperor, most of the troops in Italy were under his command. In addition, he inspected arms and arsenals and superintended military provisioning. He had civil as well as military authority, and his civil authority was augmented by Severus. He was the Emperor's representative, presiding at the council when the Emperor himself could not be there and hearing cases which the Emperor for one reason or another was unable or unwilling to hear, cases originating both in the provinces and in Italy (with the exception of Rome and the area one hundred miles around it, which were under the jurisdiction of the City Prefect). He could order the arrest of persons who might be guilty of some crime, or who were not considered necessary to the health of the government, or who possessed an important amount of money. His powers were, in the last analysis, ill-defined and consequently unrestricted; an ambitious man, or an avaricious one, could have used them for almost any purpose.

Plautian soon became incalculably rich. He confiscated wealth, extorted it, grabbed it. It was simple to invent an accusation, if he needed that justification. Those with the greatest fortunes wondered when his greedy hand was to descend on them. His cupidity did not stop with private persons. He plundered cities on a variety of pretexts, including failure to send him magnificent presents. A glutton even in his eating habits, he stuffed his belly with food and drink, then made himself vomit so that he could start all over. Only his riches he did not vomit. For many years he sat gathering wealth, gulping it down, incurring the hatred of the aristocracy, enjoying the whole business.

His insolence outraged people as much as his avarice. The story may not be true that he took a hundred well-born Romans, some of them the sons of noble families, others the fathers of noble families, castrated them, and made them serve his daughter. But even if the story is false, or exaggerated, it illustrates the tenor of opinion concerning him. He kept his wife secluded in their home, where she could grace only his eyes, and did not permit even Severus or Julia Domna to see her. On travels with the Emperor, he appropriated the better lodgings and the finer food: if Severus, departing from his usual simple tastes, wanted a dish that was out of the ordinary, he sent to Plautian for it. The favorite had statues erected to himself all over the Empire —larger statues than the ones honoring Severus, Caracalla, Geta, and Julia Domna. During his long tenure of the Praetorian prefecture, people wondered whether he or the Emperor held supremacy in Rome.

Julia Domna resented his intrusion into her family circle, a circle which may not have provided a good example of a perfect whole but which, she felt, should at least be confined to the family. And as he became bloated with insolence he even started treating her in a contemptuous manner. She hated him, and she did not keep her hatred secret. He was proud enough to proclaim openly that he considered himself at war with her. In an effort to influence Severus against her, he invented a scandal involving her. According to one story, he insinuated that she was in love with her older son; according to another story, he arrested several distinguished ladies who were her close friends and subjected them to torture so that they would reveal interesting details of her private life.

He was once in disgrace, but it was only temporary. The Emperor became alarmed at the size of the statues that were being erected in honor of Plautian, and even more alarmed at their quantity. What really angered him, however, was Plautian's inclination to put his own statue among those of the imperial family. Severus punished this presumption by ordering the statues of Plautian to be destroyed. Provincial magistrates gladly obeyed, and ordinary inhabitants of the provincial cities gladly helped them. The bronze statues were melted down. People in Rome began laughing at the Praetorian Prefect, first in private and then in public; some said openly that he was an enemy of the state. But Plautian must have been busy flattering the Emperor; and when Severus restored him to favor, he had his revenge on those who had been prematurely happy.

He was now more secure in power than ever. The Emperor made him a consul, and his ambitions were most fully realized when in 202 he became Caracalla's father-in-law.

It must have been a time of great strain for Severus. He knew that Caracalla did not want to marry Plautian's daughter Plautilla—that Caracalla, in fact, detested Plautian and did not think much better of the girl. On the other hand, he wished to do all he could for the friend whom he had recently injured—and Plautian kept urging the matter. Besides, it would probably be to Caracalla's advantage to have a wife as rich and high-placed as Plautilla; the fact that she disgusted him was not important. Julia Domna naturally opposed the marriage—the very mention of it stirred up in her an agony of hatred and frustration—but she was so unreasonably prejudiced that her objections were not given serious consideration. Therefore, the girl who had apparently been waited upon by one hundred new-made eunuchs because she was so desirable became the bride of the *Imperator Destinatus* (who did not desire her at all), amid much rejoicing at court and through the city. The sullen husband was in his middle teens at the time.

The wedding proved to be magnificent. Severus entertained the whole Senate at a banquet, and each guest, after gorging, was presented with unprepared food and live animals to take home with him. Meanwhile the populace could enjoy a view of the fantastic dowry provided by Plautian for the young couple; the ornaments, the jewels, the carriages, the whole glittering mass, in quantities that only a man of Plautian's abundance could afford, was put on public display and then carried across the Forum to the palace in a procession worth the revenues of kingdoms.

From the beginning, the marriage was unhappy. If Plautilla had been self-effacing it might not have gone too badly, but she was as proud as her princely husband. She gave him orders, she disparaged him, she vexed him; and he had all the patience of a month-old baby. His mother might seek consolation in philosophy, but not he; his mother might escape to her coterie of learned men and ease her anger in erudite discussions of Plato or Pythagoras, but he could not. Since the wedding, furthermore, the father-in-law was almost unbearable, proceeding through the streets in insolent pomp, with slaves going before him in order to stop all vehicles that might obstruct his passage and to tell passers-by to keep their eyes on the ground so that they would not commit the insult of looking the Praetorian Prefect in the face. Caracalla could easily see from whom Plautilla had acquired her haughtiness. He resolved to have nothing at all to do with her; in fact, he did not even eat with her. To anyone who would listen he said: "If I'm ever Emperor, the first thing I'll do will be to have Plautian and Plautilla killed."

Fortunately for Caracalla, the Emperor's brother happened to die and with his last words blasted Plautian, whom he needed to fear no longer. Severus, who respected his brother's opinions, was shaken, and Caracalla was quick to take advantage of the situation. In January of 205 he had his tutor persuade a centurion named Saturninus to tell the Emperor, in substance: "Plautian has ordered me to murder both you and your older son." There were a few more centurions in on the plot, but the number was kept safely small. Caracalla, young and impetuous though he was, probably would not have tried such a bold plan unless he had been reasonably sure of its success; Severus' faith in the Prefect must really have been tottering at the time. As the Prince had hoped, the Emperor accepted Saturninus' story as true. A written fabrication, which purported to be Plautian's instructions to Saturninus concerning the killing, was read before the Emperor, and apparently he believed that it was genuine. Or if his belief was not absolute, at least he doubted the Prefect's loyalty enough to send for him immediately.

Plautian came in something of a hurry, and his mules stumbled in a courtyard of the palace. This was a bad omen. His attendants were ordered to wait outside the palace. This looked even worse than the fall of the mules, but Plautian had proceeded too far to go back home now. An admission of fear would do him no good, would not prevent whatever was in store for him, and besides, it would be demeaning.

It was the old story of the man who rises to power in the favor of a monarch, exercises that power selfishly and nefariously, aggrandizes himself outrageously, taking his security and authority for granted, and falls from grace.

Caracalla was in the room, and so were some soldiers. The Emperor asked Plautian mildly: "When I have been so kind to you, why do you want to take my life, and that of my son the Augustus?"

Plautian, of course, denied the charge with all the rhetoric of which he was capable, and with much more truth than was often the case. As he glanced at Caracalla leering in the background, he probably suspected that the prince was at the bottom of the matter.

The Emperor, however, had had a dream the night before in

which Albinus had tried to murder him. The meaning of the dream was now clear: Albinus stood for Plautian.

He mentioned the story which he had just been told by the centurion Saturninus—that Plautian had ordered Saturninus to assassinate both him and his son.

Maligned for perhaps the first time in his life, Plautian pleaded his case with a mixture of outrage and desperation. The notion of killing his Emperor had never occurred to him in all his years of service. Why should he wish to kill the finest Emperor that Rome had ever had? Saturninus' story was a lie; some malefactor had obviously bribed him to repeat it.

Caracalla may have been worried that his father would believe Plautian, and even that his own role in the whole matter would be revealed. Either in the desire to silence this dangerous man or else in a sudden, uncontrollable upsurge of loathing he rushed at Plautian, grabbed the Prefect's sword, and hit him in the face with his fist. Plautian staggered back, saying, "I might have killed you, but you have anticipated me."

Caracalla drew his own sword.

"No!" Severus shouted. "Don't you kill him!"

Caracalla glared at a guard and ordered him to kill the Prefect.

The Augustus had to be obeyed unless Severus countermanded the order, and Severus said nothing. Therefore the guard stabbed Plautian to death.

A soldier yanked a few hairs from Plautian's head, brought them to where Julia Domna and Plautilla were sitting together in mutual hypocrisy, and identified them, causing one lady anguish and the other ineffable relief. Plautilla, who knew that she had fallen along with her father, was not killed; but she was banished to the island of Lipari to reflect on meretricious pride, and remained in fear for her life. With both of the Plautians out of the way, Julia Domna could try to pick up the pieces of her family circle.

In his speech to the Senate on the day after the killing, Severus reflected vaguely on the weakness of human nature and blamed himself for giving Plautian too much honor and power. But the Senate treated Plautian as it customarily treated the high who died disgraced: it condemned his memory. In spite of the temporary drop from favor a few years before, many statues of Plautian still existed; they were ordered destroyed. His name was to be effaced from all inscriptions. Throughout the Empire the order was carried out, and very soon one could no longer see what Plautian had looked like or read his name. It was almost as if he had never existed.

# ❧ IV ❧

# *Managing an Empire*

Even when Severus was not at war his daily routine had organization and purpose. He rose early, conferred with his ministers while pacing back and forth, and spent the remainder of the morning hearing and judging the lawsuits of private citizens. At noon he rode a horse for exercise, then bathed and ate, sometimes in solitude, sometimes with his bickering sons whom he was trying to train to succeed him. After a short nap he attended to whatever business had not been disposed of in the morning, and if there was time left, he perhaps conversed with learned men. He went to the baths again before supper. He kept his suppers as small as possible, because he disliked crowds. It was the life one might expect of a military man not on campaign, and it was the life of a conscientious Emperor.

Severus possessed intelligence but not great learning. He never thoroughly mastered Greek or Latin, although he wrote the languages well enough; he was said to speak his native Punic better. His intellectual curiosity, however, was strong. Even as a young man, it will be recalled, he had known and admired the great physician Galen. On a visit to Egypt about the year 200 he investigated the Pyramids at Ghizeh, incredibly ancient even to Romans, and more impressive than they are today because their stone facing was still intact. He saw the great Temple of Serapis at Memphis; he assessed the temper of the citizens of Alexandria, subtle and volatile and fond of a joke; he made the Egyptians show him the sacred books kept in their temples, and then, it seems, took the books along so that nobody after his imperial self could read their secrets. He even explored the Nile, apparently with the object of discovering its source, but could not proceed to the borders of the Sudan because of an outbreak of a plague.

Since he was a military man and since he never forgot that the Empire depended on his armies, he kept the Praetorian Guard at its full strength of fifteen thousand men and also quartered a regular legion less than twenty miles from Rome. This legion was one of three which he had created for the Parthian war; the other two stayed in Mesopotamia after the war, but he brought the Second Parthian Legion back to Italy in a precedent-breaking move. No legion had ever been permanently stationed on Italian soil before. Traditionalists—especially members of the Senate—felt that to put the Second Parthian there was to treat Italy as just another province, and to turn the reign into a military despotism.

There may have been some foundation for this feeling. Showing favoritism to the army was a consistent part of Severus' policy. He gave his troops medals of silver (or of silver set in gold), allowed the junior officers to wear a gold ring, which became part of their uniform, let recruits serve in their homelands rather than sending them to unfamiliar and uncongenial parts of the world, raised the soldiers' pay, improved their rations, and bestowed liberal gifts on them. He opened positions in the civil service to men who had risen through the ranks in the army and encouraged the formation of small military clubs at the bases—a club of trumpeters, perhaps, or a club of buglers. The clubhouses, which were decorated with statues of Severus and other Emperors in order to promote loyalty to the government, were used for assemblies and for recreation. These military societies, like many funerary societies of the lower classes during the period, also functioned as mutual insurance companies; the members, in return for money contributed, received financial benefits if they retired or were promoted, and their families received financial compensation if they died.

Being a soldier under Severus, then, had advantages. It had been true that if a married man became a legionary he had to either live away from his wife for the twenty-five years of his service or else divorce her. In case he was single or divorced, however, he had long been able to contract an extralegal marriage with his native concubine, if she appealed to him that much. Severus gave such marriages legal recognition. Under Severus, apparently, it also became possible at

some camps for a man to live with his native wife in a civilian settlement near the post.

Another group that the Emperor favored was the equites, the
knightly order. He enabled the knights to occupy administrative and
military offices that had previously been open only to senators, or posts
which had been the rewards of highly capable freedmen (former
slaves). He gave more power, especially judicial power, to the Praetorian Prefects, who came from the equestrian order; Plautian is a case
in point. One of his motives in all this was to make the Senate suffer.

Perhaps he had sworn never to let the senators forget that many
of them had been actively or passively disloyal to him during the
Albinus crisis. Quite possibly he resented the senators as members of a
class that was superior to the one into which he had been born—the
knights. Most important, probably, he saw in the knightly order as well
as in the soldiers his own surest adherents, whereas he saw in the
senators potential traitors who had to be cowed from the beginning. At
any rate, he encouraged the admission of non-Italians into the Senate,
particularly Orientals—even an Egyptian sat in the body for the first
time during his reign—since this infiltration of men from the provinces
could provide a valuable minority. And he tried to create around himself an aura of tyranny, so that the Senate would quake and obey. The
Senate, which had not shown much courageous republicanism for over
two centuries (or, in fact, much collective courage of any kind),
quaked and obeyed without question.

It even anticipated the will of the Emperor, as in the matter concerning Apronianus, governor of Asia. A charge of high treason was
brought against Apronianus because the nurse who had suckled him
had dreamed that the child to whom she gave milk would be an
Emperor one day, and because, when this dream was reported to him,
Apronianus had sought confirmation of the prophecy from fortune-
tellers and had indulged in magical sacrifices. He was in Asia, unable
to defend himself before the Senate, but he was still condemned to
death, since his guilt seemed obvious. That would please Severus.

During the Senate's consideration of the case, testimony was read
that a bald-headed senator had been present when the dream was related to Apronianus. His presence of course implicated him too, but his
name was not known. The Senate was demoralized by the uncertainty;
rumors circulated among the people. Those gentlemen whose heads

were shiny sat in dread that they might be accused, that they might suddenly die; and men with retreating hair involuntarily felt the tops of their heads to ascertain how much they had left.

It finally became evident that the bald senator had been clothed in the *toga praetexta*, the toga with a purple stripe worn by curule magistrates. That reduced the number of possibilities. But the chill had not lifted from one Marcellinus, who had been curule aedile at the time stated in the evidence, and who was bald. The eyes of everyone were turned toward him; silence fell over the assembly.

Marcellinus rose slowly. "If I am the man whom the witness saw, he will surely recognize me. Let him be brought in."

The witness was summoned, and he surveyed the assembly for a long while. He did not know one senator from another. They sat in silence again, each man waiting for the gaze of the witness to fix on himself.

One gentleman nodded slightly toward Marcellinus.

"That's the one," said the witness. "I recognize him."

In their relief, in their new-found sense of freedom, the senators condemned Marcellinus and led him toward the Forum for execution, in this way trying to demonstrate their loyalty. On the way to the Forum Marcellinus met his four children. He embraced them. "I am sorry," he said, "that you have to keep on living. I am sorry you were not born in a better time." When he got to the Forum his head was cut off.

Severus was not a tyrant; he did not know anything about the Marcellinus affair until afterwards. On moral or philosophical grounds he might not even have approved of the business. But he had to keep the Senate in his power, and he was glad to know that that was exactly where it was. He did not reproach the senators for their patriotic action.

Catering to the citizens was another important aspect of Severus' policy. There was nothing original in it, of course; many Emperors before him had buttressed their despotism by giving the people full stomachs and glorious shows. But it worked, and its practicality was all that mattered to him. From time to time he distributed money to the people, as an Emperor was expected to do. He saw to it that the city's supply of grain was sufficient for seven years, and the oil supply for five. In 202 he celebrated the victory over Parthia, his return to Rome, and the tenth anniversary of his reign by putting on magnificent shows and by giving each citizen and each member of the Praetorian Guard ten aurei (gold coins that had a value equal to approximately fifty dollars). The people enjoyed seeing novelties; one of the novelties of the anniversary games was a group of sixty bears that had been taught to engage one another much as human wrestlers might have done. Another unusual touch was a great vessel built like a warship with sides that collapsed to let out lions, tigers, panthers, bears, ostriches, wild asses, buffaloes, and various domestic animals—seven hundred beasts in all—that were hunted and slain at the rate of one hundred a day while the delighted spectators bet on the huntsmen.

In 204 occurred the Secular Games. No living Roman had ever witnessed Secular Games before, since they were supposed to be held at intervals of 110 years, when, according to ancient Etruscan belief, the old age was buried and a new age was born. They had last taken place under Domitian in A.D. 88. Why Severus celebrated them six years late is not known; very likely he felt that the Parthian campaign, the visit to Egypt, and the spectacles of 202 were good enough reasons for the delay. The people of Rome, in any case, must have considered them worth waiting for; they were sufficiently sensational to mark the birth of a new era.

Severus also beautified Rome, and honored himself, by having erected in a corner of the Forum the great Arch of Septimius Severus, commemorating his defeat of the Parthians in reliefs which probably represent the finest occasional sculpture of the period. Like other triumphal arches, it was designed to serve no practical purpose; steps prevented carts from passing underneath it. Its purpose was simply to glorify the Emperor and his Empire, to act as a magnificent symbol. It still stands, an encomium in stone, contributing as much as anything else to make Severus' name immortal.

His kindness extended to the provinces. The time had not quite come when depopulation would be noticeable in the provinces, when agriculture would dwindle and cities decay, and when starving people would put all their hopes for happiness in an afterlife. The Orient and North Africa flourished especially. Roman colonists settled at Nisibis, and Mesopotamia became a bulwark of the Empire. Roman roads stretched across the desert; Roman towns sprang up in remote desert places. Cities on the edge of Roman territory, such as Baalbek and Petra, enjoyed an era of new luxury as a result of trade; grandiloquent Roman temples were built there. In Africa, which had first known real growth under Trajan and Hadrian, Roman civilization reached to the Sahara. The residents of the populous North African cities shopped under white Roman colonnades and had floors of tiny colored glass tiles laid in their houses, and the merchants of the coastal cities shipped grain to Rome and grew rich. At Leptis Magna, the Emperor's home town, a grandiose new Forum was built, surrounded by columns whose leafy capitals blossomed into arches. A triumphal arch in honor of Severus embellished this city too, as was fitting; at the time of the Emperor's death the triple-aisled basilica adjacent to the Forum was still incomplete. In its finished form it had pillars of red granite from Egypt and green marble from Greece, and on the white marble pilasters were carved the exploits of Bacchus and Hercules, whom Severus considered the protectors of his dynasty.

Severus helped the increasingly Romanized provinces not only by the construction of roads (which of course had a military function as well as a civil one), the erection of buildings, and the encouragement of trade, but through legislation. He granted higher civic status to many provincial towns, prohibited Roman officials from inheriting anything from rich provincial wives (whom they might otherwise have married for money), prevented soldiers from buying up provincial land, and adjured governors not to allow soldiers or other Romans officially quartered in the provinces to take expensive advantage of the natives. He exercised extreme care, besides, in nominating men for governmental posts. Except for the brigandage which was rife in the provinces and which the unsettled conditions in the early years of his reign had to some extent occasioned, there was peace and there was plenty—and few people were wretched except the poor.

Technically, it had been the Senate rather than the Emperor that possessed the power to enact legislation, but Severus' jurists now recognized that the Emperor's interpretations of law, or rescripts, had legal force. Severus' rescripts were numerous and generally wise, equitable, even beneficent; some of them were probably influenced by the outstanding jurisconsults, such as Ulpian, Papinian, and Paulus, who added distinction to his reign, and on whom he frequently relied for advice. For instance, during Severus' reign guardians were directed not to alienate the property of their wards without permission from the proper authority; formerly there had been many cases of guardians taking advantage of those whom they were supposed to protect. Jews could now become candidates for municipal offices without first having to renounce their religion. Granting freedom to slaves had long been common throughout the Empire, but the custom was complicated when a slave had several owners, as quite a few slaves did, particularly in the army. Under Severus, if one master decided to enfranchise a slave, his other owners had to offer him his freedom also, on condition that he pay each of them a sum set by the praetor. A slave owned in common could previously be subjected to torture if one of his masters was being prosecuted; Severus changed that too. In the eyes of the senators the Emperor might have been a tyrant, but from the popular viewpoint his tyranny was benevolent.

Early in his reign Severus was not unfavorably disposed toward Christianity. Having been cured of a disease by a Christian called Proculus, he kept the man around and acquired considerable respect for the religion. The idea of persecuting the Christians did not seriously occur to him. The Roman government was traditionally tolerant of religions anyway. In large degree, it permitted the peoples of the Empire to follow whatever religious roads they chose—to bow down before a whole conglomeration of gods or to worship one, to make sacrifices to some wild divinity of the Celtic forests, to attain the state of mystic ecstasy that some Asiatics sought, to identify strange Eastern gods with the dignified old state gods of Rome such as Jupiter and Minerva, to perform rites honoring animal-headed deities of the Nile, to celebrate fertility in orgies, to translate God into a philosophic concept, to adore the shining Olympians of ancient Greece, or to be purified in the blood of a bull. The Roman Empire was inhabited by such a multitude of religions that toleration was necessary to its well-being; persecution would have been very impractical.

Gradually, however, Severus had to admit that Christianity constituted a particular threat to the government. It denied the existence of all the old gods, even the state gods of Rome, whom adherents of other religions were willing to recognize. This unflinching monotheism was unpatriotic and could be treasonable. Jupiter, Juno, Minerva, Mars, and the other Latin divinities to whom the Romans erected great temples were the protectors, the guardians, the patrons of the Empire.

Besides, the rulers of Rome for many generations had done much to encourage Emperor worship, especially in the Eastern provinces, where it met with a better reception than it did in the West. Eastern provincials liked to put up temples in honor of deified Emperors, and in worshipping these Emperors they were in a sense worshipping the genius of Rome herself; their loyalty was therefore stimulated and reinforced. According to the Christians, of course, Emperor worship was sacrilegious.

Then there was the matter of exclusiveness. Many Christians refused on religious grounds to serve in the army, which would have obliged them to kill their brothers; or to occupy civil posts, which would have obliged them to support the measures of a government founded on institutions and beliefs of which they disapproved; or to engage in commercial activities or lend money for interest. The more moderate ones did not have all these scruples, but so many Christians were immoderate that the religion acquired a reputation for intransigent aloofness which in itself constituted a tacit condemnation of ordinary Roman life. The Christians were not participating in the Empire; they were not like everybody else; they sometimes said that the only true Empire was in heaven, and such pronouncements bordered on subversiveness.

And they were spreading. Although they had not yet attained anything like the power which they were to enjoy in the fourth and fifth centuries—although they had not yet begun to dominate—they were well organized and they attracted proselytes. Already the government had relaxed its tolerance in order to persecute them several times, the first time under Nero, but they seemed to flourish under persecution. Tertullian the North African, the most outspoken Christian in the reign of Severus, a fighter of tremendous rhetorical power who attacked the established order savagely and sardonically, boasted that the Christians now occupied the pagans' cities, Senate, and armies, leaving the unbelievers only the temples and the theatres (the Christians did not want the latter because of their lewdness). The boast was, of course, a gross exaggeration, but under Commodus, who had a Christian mistress, members of the faith had multiplied among the poor and even to some extent among the rich. Christianity was still largely a religion for the downtrodden, the starving, the enslaved, and the leprous, but certain prosperous people, men of cultivated minds and great intelligence, were also beginning to be attracted to it. Severus thought something had to be done.

Trajan's rescript against the Christians had called the public demonstration of Christianity a crime against the state but had instructed magistrates not to go looking for Christians: believers were to be punished if they made themselves obvious but were not to be sought out like thieves. In 202 Severus issued a rescript which, in effect, prohibited the Christians from propagandizing and which made the act of becoming a convert a punishable offense. It was this evangelism, he felt—this strenuous campaign of conversion—that must be checked if Christianity itself was to be checked; without new members, the religion would shrink and die. Already existing Christian communities could continue undisturbed; the priests could teach those who were already Christian, and when a propagandist or a new proselyte was arrested, his brethren could come to him in prison and give him counsel before he went to the lions. Tertullian could keep writing his antipagan, antigovernment polemics, and bishops could carry out their usual ecclesiastical duties.

The persecution was therefore not extremely harsh; the severe persecutions were to come toward the middle and end of the century, under Decius and Diocletian. A number of provincial magistrates were reluctant to send men and women into the amphitheatre just for trying to make others believe as they did, or for suddenly renouncing the great old gods. Some of these magistrates might not have felt certain about these gods themselves, or they might have been gentle by nature. They tried to show the Christians Roman mercy; not all of them were inflexible, even about requiring sacrifices to the divine wardens of the state and to the Emperor, although there was nothing more unpatriotic than refusal to comply with this requirement.

But even so there were horrors. A girl named Potamioena, for example, was thrown into a pot of boiling pitch with her mother. And at Carthage occurred the martyrdom of Perpetua and her associates.

Perpetua was a lady of noble birth who lived south of Carthage. She was in her early twenties, well educated, married, and the mother of a baby boy. (Her story testifies to the fact that Christianity was beginning to attract the upper classes.) Her mother had probably turned Christian, and so had her two brothers, one of whom, however, was not yet baptized. Her youngest brother contracted a facial ulcer and died a pagan at the age of seven. Her father was a pagan. Around the time when Severus issued his rescript, Perpetua decided that she would become a convert. Before she had gone so far as to be baptized, she was arrested and kept under guard in a country house with several people who were, like her, still catechumens, or persons receiving the instruction requisite to their admission into the ranks of the faithful. One of her companions was a pregnant slave called Felicitas, another was a male slave called Revocatus, and the other two were young men named Saturninus and Secundulus. They were soon joined by a baptized Christian, Saturus, who had given himself up; a religious teacher, he had probably been responsible for their conversion and wanted to be with them now.

Perpetua's father came to plead with her to renounce what he considered her foolishness; she was his favorite child, and she ran the risk of being killed, perhaps torn to pieces in public. She said: "I can call myself only what I am—a Christian." In ungovernable grief and rage, he fell on her as if to pummel her, but she stayed steady in her faith. Amazed, he went away.

She had peace for a while after that, and she and the other catechumens were baptized. A few days later they were taken to Carthage and locked in a prison—a dark, dirty, putrid-smelling place, the kind of environment that the delicately bred Perpetua had not often experienced; and at first she found it difficult to endure. She was also worried about her baby. He had not yet been weaned; who would give him milk? When would she see him again? Two deacons visited the prisoners and, by slipping money to the jailer, made it possible for them to spend a few hours in a less rank part of the prison. Perpetua's baby was brought to her, and she gave him suck. When her mother and brothers visited her, she put the child in her mother's care.

One of her brothers suggested that she ask God to reveal whether she was to be a martyr. The result was a vision in which she saw a golden ladder extending from earth to heaven. It was a very narrow ladder, and to each side were attached cruel instruments of metal—knives, swords, hooks, and lances—so that a person ascending was likely to be gashed and cut open. A great and terrible dragon sprawled at the foot of the ladder to frighten away whoever wanted to climb. But her teacher and fellow prisoner Saturus was already part-way up, and when he reached the top he called to her, "Perpetua, I'm waiting for you, but be careful that the dragon doesn't bite you." She answered, "In the name of Jesus Christ, he won't do me any harm." In fact, he helped her, gently raising his head so that she could put her foot on it. She climbed.

At the top she saw a garden stretching wide, and in it a white-haired man who wore the clothes of a shepherd. The man sat milking his sheep while thousands of people in white garments stood watching. He welcomed her and offered her some curds made from the milk of the ewes. Cupping her hands, she took them and ate them; and the thousands of people in white garments cried: "Amen." She awoke with a sweet taste in her mouth.

When she related the vision to her brother, they agreed that she was to be a martyr.

The prisoners learned that they would be examined soon. Her father learned it too, and came to Carthage in order to make another attempt on her Christianity. He begged her not to ruin her family, because of course all its members would be in danger if she confessed her faith—he begged her to remember how he loved her, to take pity on him, to relieve his suffering, to live as his daughter again. He was a pathetic old figure, unable to understand. Sobbing spasmodically, he clutched her hands and kissed her fingers as she stood there.

"Whatever happens," she told him, "will happen because God wants it to. We can't do anything about it."

She felt sad, however, because of all the members of her family, only her father would not enjoy her martyrdom.

A day or so later the prisoners were summoned to the market and placed on a kind of platform facing Hilarian, procurator of the province. Hilarian was substituting for the governor, who had recently died, and he wanted to do as good a job as possible. He knew not only that the Emperor was disenchanted with the Christians but that the Carthaginians as a whole hated them. A large crowd of onlookers had collected in the market and they wanted Christian blood.

Those questioned before Perpetua—that is, all except Secundulus, who had died in prison—professed the Christian faith without hesitancy. When Perpetua's turn came her father stepped forward from the crowd, with her baby in his arms. Once more he pleaded. Hilarian urged her to take pity on the old man. Would she sacrifice to the gods for the health of the Emperor? No.

Was she a Christian?

She affirmed that she was.

Her father, importunate, frantic, kept interrupting, kept doing anything to prevent what was going to happen. When he tried to take her off the platform, they had to beat him down with a stick.

In a few days there were to be games in celebration of Geta's birthday. Perpetua and her associates were condemned to be exposed to the beasts in the amphitheatre during the games. They gave thanks to God.

Back in prison, Perpetua dreamed of her youngest brother, the one who had died at the age of seven, still a pagan. He was in trouble—dirty, suffering from the ulcer, tortured by thirst, tortured also by a font of water too high for him to reach. She prayed for him. When she dreamed of him again, the ulcer was healed and he was clean, well clothed, and happy. The font stood no higher than his waist.

Before their execution they were transferred to a prison in the military camp; the games were to be military games. The jailer Pudens, eventually to become a convert, allowed Christian friends and relatives to visit them. Perpetua's father came too, in order to make one last effort. In his distress he tore at his beard, fell to the ground, cursed, and cried. Perpetua and the others felt very sorry for him, but essentially he was not wanted. They longed for the end, which would be the beginning; they longed to die for the faith—to turn their beautiful visions into reality. They were ravenous for immortality; nothing else made much difference.

Perpetua had another vision, in which she stood in the amphitheatre facing a gigantic, grotesque Egyptian. A man taller than the top of the amphitheatre told her that she had to fight this monster. The man carried a green branch from which hung golden apples; if she won the fight, the bough would be hers. She became male. Like an athlete she was stripped and rubbed with oil by a group of handsome youths. Like an athlete she fought the ugly Egyptian, hitting him with her fists as he hit her, avoiding him when he tried to grab her feet. Lifted off the ground by an invisible force, she kept ramming her heels into his face. Then she threw him down and stamped on the back of his head. The spectators cheered, the handsome youths sang psalms, and the tall man gave her the branch with the golden apples, saying: "Peace, daughter." She realized that in the arena she would be fighting not wild beasts but Satan.

The female slave Felicitas, eight months pregnant, yearned for immediate martyrdom with the others, but she would not be exposed to the animals as long as she was with child. She prayed fervently to be delivered of her baby so that she might die, and two days before the games she bore a girl. The birth was painful, making her shriek terribly. One of the guards laughed at her and sneered, "If you're suffering so much now, what are you going to be like when you're fed to the animals?" Felicitas retorted, "I'm suffering now by myself; but in the amphitheatre someone else will be inside me and will suffer for me— and I for him."

On March 7, 203, the games for Geta's birthday took place. Inside the gate of the amphitheatre the jailers tried to make the Christians dress in articles of clothing similar to ones worn at pagan ceremonies; the men were to put on red cloaks like the mantles of the priests of Saturn, and the women were to display on their heads fillets of the priestesses of Ceres. But Perpetua launched into a fine fury. With her eyes flashing she raved at the riffraff. She and her friends were sacrificing their lives in protest against pagan ceremonies; surely the idolaters should respect their wishes on this occasion if on no other. She won her point.

The Christians provided a brave sight as they entered the arena. Saturus and the other men warned the spectators against the wrath of God; as they passed under the balcony where Hilarian sat, they shouted up, "You may judge us now, but God will judge you later." Felicitas, whose baby girl had been adopted by a Christian and who consequently had nothing to worry about, smiled in sweet happiness because she was with her companions in this moment of triumph, because she was going from the blood of childbirth to the blood of martyrdom. Perpetua, aristocratic even now, strode straight and noble, singing.

The outraged mob screamed, "Scourge them!" and the request was granted. In single file they walked past the *venatores* or hunters, and each man lashed out at them with his whip. They felt glad, remembering that Christ had been scourged.

Young Saturninus hoped to win a crown of great glory by being exposed to more than one animal. A leopard came first, swift and wiry —springing, clawing—but not quite killing. A bear then mauled him and chewed out life. In the stands the people seemed pleased with the way things were going. But the wild red-eyed boar to which the teacher Saturus was now tied just trampled Saturus and dragged him around, then turned on his keeper and gored him (the man died a few days later). Saturus was tied close to where a bear waited, but the bear declined to come out of its den, and Saturus was removed from the arena alive.

He told the sympathetic jailer Pudens that a leopard would end the affair in one bite. He was put back in the arena. The graceful beast lunged and bit deep, so that Saturus was suddenly covered with blood. Delighted, the crowd roared, "You've really been washed this time." But not yet dead, he returned to Pudens. "Remember me," he said, "and remember the faith. Don't let these things dismay you; they should make you stronger. Give me the ring you have on your finger." Pudens took off the ring; Saturus graciously dipped it in his own blood and handed it back. That done, he died.

As a novelty, the clothes were taken off the women, and they were exposed naked in a net to the public view—the two young mothers, the lady and the slave girl, their breasts swollen with milk, their soft bodies soon to be ripped and bloody. But the crowd did not react well to the joke, and Perpetua and Felicitas had to be taken out, clothed in tunics, and brought in again.

They were pitted against a wild cow. Ungainly even in rage, she charged with head lowered. She knocked them down, hoofs flailing, and trampled them and tried to gash them. Weak and bruised, but modest, Perpetua pulled her torn tunic over her thighs. Then she asked for a pin and calmly arranged her hair; disheveled hair was for mourners, whereas she was going to glory. She did not notice that the heifer was loping off. Nearby, Felicitas was still on the ground. Holding her tunic together, Perpetua walked over to the girl and helped her get up.

They left through the gate of the living, to be killed after the show. Perpetua, who seemed dazed or in ecstasy, asked when she was to encounter the cow. She was told that she had fought the cow already, and when she saw her bruises and her bloody clothing she returned to reality. Her brother was summoned. "Stand steadfast in our faith," she urged him, a catechumen. "Love your fellows, and do not let our sufferings disturb you."

The crowd was crying for the immediate deaths of the Christian survivors. Killing these Christians after the show would not please the people; the crowd wanted to see them die now, stabbed by gladiators in full view. So they gave one another gravely the kiss of peace and walked back into the arena where Saturus had preceded them to heaven.

Felicitas died quietly and splendidly.

But the young gladiator assigned to Perpetua was not an expert executioner; he muffed the job and struck the bone, so that she suffered screaming agony. Remembering glory, she guided his hand until the point of his sword was at her throat. Now he could drive it in.

About the year 207, the anti-Christian campaign having subsided, Severus felt obliged to take care of another matter. A thief named Bulla Felix was making the imperial government look ridiculous. For two years Bulla, at the head of a band of six hundred men, had been robbing travelers in the vicinity of Rome, having resisted all attempts of the government to stop him. His six hundred followers were poor people—most of them escaped slaves—and under his leadership they were able to find a little happiness. It was a free life and a merry one, with the chance of much money and the chance of a night with a girl who liked beautiful trinkets. Bulla organized his loyal adherents so well that they knew what persons were leaving Rome or arriving at the port of Brundisium, how many were traveling in a group, what valuables they had with them, what social stations they occupied. If a man was rich, the band did not relieve him of quite everything; it kept most of his money and baggage, however, and sent him chastened on his way. If an artisan happened to be captured—someone whom the band needed for making arms or utensils—he was retained until he had manufactured what was wanted, then dismissed with thanks and a present. And the troops of the Emperor could do nothing.

Bulla enjoyed tempting fate. When the imperial soldiers finally managed to apprehend two members of his band, for example, he entered the town where they were imprisoned and visited the keeper of the jail, pretending to be an important magistrate. He announced that he needed condemned criminals for some specific purpose. His two followers had already been condemned to meet the beasts in the arena, but the keeper of the jail obligingly released them to the magistrate.

A centurion who had been sent with a party of soldiers to capture him was another of his dupes. Disguised, Bulla walked up to the centurion, introduced himself as somebody else, began talking against Bulla in a most enthusiastic manner, and offered to disclose his hiding place to the centurion. More gullible than many Roman military officers, the centurion allowed himself to be led into a narrow valley full of thickets where members of Bulla's band suddenly leaped out and seized him. He was taken to the thieves' camp, where Bulla, having put on a magistrate's robe, ascended the tribunal and judged him.

The robber ordered some of his men to shave the centurion's head. After this indignity he set the officer free with the words, "Go back to your employers and tell them this: if they feed their slaves better, the slaves will not become outlaws."

The offended Emperor, before whom millions trembled, whose wishes were anticipated by the quaking Senate, whose name the Parthians pronounced with awe, sent a tribune from his own bodyguard to dispose of this pack of runaway slaves and their impudent chief. The tribune was accompanied by a body of horse and carried inside him the threat of terrible punishment if he did not succeed in his assignment; Severus had not been subtle at all about that matter.

He decided to meet trickery with trickery. Having learned that Bulla's mistress was a married woman, he approached her through her husband, made her aware of the precariousness of her position (neglecting to mention the precariousness of his own), and promised her a full pardon if she betrayed Bulla. She betrayed him. Bulla awoke in his cave to find the tribune glowering over him.

He was conducted to Rome and brought before Papinian, who held the office of Praetorian Prefect now that Plautian was dead. The greatest jurisconsult of the age, friend and advisor to Emperors, full of dignity and integrity, looked at the greatest robber of the age, who returned his look.

Papinian said, "I wish you would tell me—why did you choose to be a thief?"

Bulla rather jauntily replied, "What made you a Prefect?" That was all that Papinian could get out of him.

Many people came to watch so famous an outlaw be torn to pieces by wild beasts. Some of the members of his band may have mingled with the spectators, in silence and appreciation. The band disintegrated afterward; without Bulla, it had no leader. The Emperor could rest assured that law and order prevailed once more on the roads from Rome.

## V

# *The War in Britain*

By the early third century Britain had already been part of the Empire for over a century and a half. Roman civilization had succeeded to some extent in pacifying its wild, remote parts. There were Roman roads and forts and fortress-towns and coins, an occasional Forum or bath or amphitheatre, and in the countryside an occasional great villa with amenities imported from the more luxuriant southern climes. The soldiers introduced the worship of the Emperor; the gods of the state were worshipped too, or were amalgamated with the gods, goddesses, and godlings of the British tribes. The more docile of the Britons were becoming Romanized, insofar as they could be. Londinium on the Thames, with its basilica five hundred feet long, its vast fort, and its recently constructed walls ten feet thick, constituted one of the greatest centers of Roman culture beyond the Alps—a busy tangle of trade and administration. But the country was still largely a place of vast deep forests, dismal swamps, and chill mists; the weather was too cold to allow for civilization.

Barbaric hill tribes—Caledonians and Maeatae, the people who were later to be called Picts—lived north of the Wall, the strong stone rampart which had been completed under Hadrian about the year 127. Bristling with forts, fortlets, and turrets, it extended for more than seventy miles across a narrow part of what is now northern England, from Solway Firth to the mouth of the river Tyne. But in spite of it and other measures for containment or defense, the wildmen sometimes made inroads into Roman Britain, and had to be subdued, or at least frightened.

When Clodius Albinus left Britain to fight Severus for the Empire he had taken his legions with him, so that the fortifications were manned by skeleton forces, if they were manned at all. The barbarians took advantage of this situation to wreak havoc. In the years following the defeat of Albinus, the Wall had to be rebuilt from ruins in many places, and the frontier forts had to be reconstructed. Although the job of refortification proceeded steadily, the barbarians proved difficult to quiet. They were especially obstreperous, it appears, from the year 205 on; a real show of Roman war power was needed in order to quell them. In particular, the Emperor was needed in order to put fear into them.

Therefore Severus, well along in middle age now and suffering from acute pains in the legs, set off for war again early in 208. Julia Domna, Mother of the Camps, accompanied him, as she had accompanied him on those earlier expeditions when he and she still had worlds to win. Caracalla and Geta went to Britain too; in fact, Severus very likely sent Caracalla on ahead. Removal from the luxuries of Rome and southern Italy would do both his sons good; the marches, the battles, the strenuous life of soldiering would harden them, would give them some training in the imperial responsibilities that were soon to be theirs, would recommend them to the populace as worthy successors to himself in the dynasty he had established, and might possibly draw them closer together. The wish to oversee them on a campaign may have been Severus' main reason for venturing on the expedition in person.

As for Caracalla, he was not really sorry to leave Italy. He had inherited from his father, from many previous Emperors—in fact, from Roman tradition itself—the strong sense that an Emperor was the commander-in-chief of the armies of Rome, a military leader, a great warrior. He welcomed the military experience that he would obtain in Britain. Perhaps he would even be able to win distinction at the head of his men. In any case, the British campaign would be valuable.

Severus felt certain that he himself would not return from Britain. In an age when comets and earthquakes were seriously regarded as signs that great events were about to occur, when augurs were considered highly important to the state, and when even conscientious historians recited portents of a famous man's fall, it was not surprising that the Emperor, probably not more superstitious than most men, believed in such omens. With regard to the British expedition, his horoscope was not favorable. Not only that, but lightning had struck a statue of himself which stood near the gate through which he was to march out of Rome. The lightning had erased three letters from his name inscribed at the base of the statue. His seers had no difficulty in interpreting this sign; within three years, he would be dead.

The tribes north of the Wall, the Caledonians and the Maeatae, occupied just about the lowest level of barbaric living that a Roman could imagine. They lived in the mountains and in murky fens, unable to construct cities, unable to practice agriculture, unable even to fish. They knew enough to be herdsmen, however, and flocks provided part of their food supply; the rest came from the fruits of the forest and the wild animals that they hunted when they were not hunting human beings. Their homes were tents; their clothes were skins when they wore any at all; the hard soles of their feet did not need shoes. Marriage was a conception too complex for their culture; the men had the women in common and the women the men; children were reared in common, not certain who their parents were and not caring to know.

Their life was oriented around warfare; the main object of their existence was to plunder other barbarians, to plunder the Romans, to kill, to show courage, and to lead their friends to victory. Their chosen chieftains, therefore, were the boldest men, and the tribal talents were directed toward successful battle and preservation of life. The men bred war ponies, devised war chariots, and kept their bodies physically fit so that they could run long distances without tiring, endure cold and hunger without incommoding themselves greatly, and hide under swamp water, with only their heads sticking out, for many days. Artisans concentrated on making shields, spears, and daggers, and to the spear-shafts they attached bronze bells that would rattle when the spears were shaken. The idea was that the clangor would frighten the enemy, and it probably did if it arose from the spear-shafts of thousands of battle-mad savages rushing down a hill.

Against the Romans they used canny tactics, letting sheep and cattle graze where the Roman soldiers would be sure to see them. The soldiers would chase the animals, dispersing into small bands, wear themselves out, and get lost in the swamps. Then the barbarians would attack.

For a long time there was little battle except for these guerrilla actions, since Severus was still occupied mainly with preparations for a great campaign. Early in these preparations the Caledonians and the Maeatae, already apprehensive of the imperial legionaries, had asked for peace, but Severus would not give it to them; he knew better than to trust them, and besides, he wanted to hand them a defeat that they would remember long after he was dead. When he was ready he directed his troops against the Caledonians, probably proceeding to the northern part of the island by means of the sea. He led his legions from a covered litter, as his legs were paining him terribly. Having left Geta in Roman Britain to keep affairs in order there, he let Caracalla participate with him in the Caledonian campaign north of the Wall; and Caracalla, who took naturally to war, did well. The Romans defeated the Caledonians on their own ground, far beyond the Wall, and the barbarians had to sue for peace again. Their surrender was unconditional: they relinquished their arms and agreed to pay tribute.

They had been humiliated, but one of their women succeeded in humiliating the Empress. After the treaty, when Julia Domna was joking with her about how promiscuous the Caledonian women were, lying with any man who happened to like them, the barbarian female retorted, "We follow our natural impulses better than you women of Rome do. We have sex openly with the strongest and bravest men of the tribe, but you give your bodies in secret to the worst men."

Although the Caledonians were defeated, the war was not yet over; it was to limp on for many more months. In the winter of 209/210 the Maeatae, not sufficiently impressed by what had happened to the Caledonians, took to arms and had to be shown that the Romans were their superiors. In the winter of 210/211 the Maeatae and the Caledonians both broke the treaty, and the fighting was on again. It must have seemed to some of the Praetorians and other soldiers used to more hospitable regions that they would never get out of this desolate part of the world—that slicing at savages and being sliced at by savages was to be a perpetual state of affairs. The legionaries regularly posted along the Wall or elsewhere in Britain were accustomed to the cold mists, bleak landscapes, and abominable winters, but some of the other soldiers grew discontented and, in private, blamed the Emperor.

We know few details about the campaigns of Severus in Britain, or about the life of his family there. The aging Emperor, expecting to die soon, was doing all he could to hand on the Empire intact and at peace to his sons; that much we do know. Both young men were co-Augustuses with him now; Caracalla had been Augustus in name for a long time, and Geta was given the same honor in 209, so that Julia Domna became the first woman in Rome's history to be simultaneously the wife of one Emperor and the mother of two. But the dream of reconciling the brothers through warfare had been crushed; we know that too. As the time came closer when they were jointly to assume control, their rivalry, military and otherwise, intensified. Each of them tried to ingratiate himself with the soldiers so that if the situation degenerated into an open clash he would have adherents. And one of them, so greedy for power that he could hardly bear to wait any longer, appears to have intrigued against the life of his father.

At least, that is what ancient historians say, although it is doubtful if the stories that came back to them from the far-off lands were strictly true; it is also doubtful that they resisted the chance to abuse a man whom they detested. According to them Caracalla made more than one attempt against the Emperor's life. The most credible stories are these:

First, he bribed a large number of soldiers to support him if he created a disturbance. Then he ran out of his tent shouting that he had been abused by Castor, a freedman who was a favorite of Severus and was actually a man of great integrity. The bribed soldiers clustered around Caracalla, who hoped to foment enough of a riot so that his father would be killed. But Severus appeared on the scene and restored order quickly, and Caracalla went back to his tent to think of something else.

Second, he tried to murder the Emperor on the march. It happened to be a time when Severus felt well enough to sit on horseback. Behind him rode Caracalla, and behind Caracalla came the legions. In the distance an army of barbarians could be discerned. In this inappropriate setting, with many Romans looking on and with the barbarians massed nearby, Caracalla drew his sword in order to stab his father in the back. Officers cried out, and Severus turned around, saw the sword, and said nothing. The sword went back in its sheath. Severus continued to say nothing, at least to Caracalla, until later in the day, when the Emperor was in his tent. Then he had his son summoned. Castor the freedman was there too, and so was Papinian the Praetorian Prefect. The scolding was a severe one. Severus reproached

Caracalla not only for trying to murder him but for being such an idiot as to make the attempt in public, with both Romans and savages watching. He nodded to a sword which had been set out for Caracalla's benefit. "If you really want to kill me," he said, "do it now, with that. It wouldn't be difficult. You're young and strong—I'm old, sick, sometimes scarcely able to move." He made the further suggestion that if Caracalla was afraid to commit the murder himself he should order Papinian to do it; the Praetorian Prefect would have to obey the Augustus.

These stories do not ring true, although there may be elements of truth in them. But certainly the young man was eager.

As it turned out, he did not have to chafe much longer. At the garrison city of Eboracum (York), in the cold of early February 211, the Emperor lay on his deathbed. He had managed the Roman world for eighteen years, and he thought about it as he prepared to die. His reign had been, on the whole, good. Perhaps he had killed many men in the process of making himself Emperor, but he had been what Rome needed—a strong man, a military man, a man with ideas, an intelligent and ruthless leader. When he won the Empire it had been in a state of chaos; today there was quiet within its borders. No new difficulties loomed beyond the frontiers; the Parthians were conquered, a strong settlement had been imposed on the Eastern boundary, in Britain the war was almost over. His sons, however, troubled him in those hours of contemplation before leaving life. He is reported to have said, "I turn over to my sons a mighty Empire. If they are good men, it will endure. But it will weaken and decay if they are bad men."

He asked for the urn of purple stone in which his ashes would be placed; and when it was brought to him he ran his fingers over the smooth surface and smiled. "Soon," he told it, "you will hold a man for whom the whole earth was too small."

Caracalla and Geta stood at his bedside, possibly a little ashamed of their impatience now that he was actually dying, for he had been an indulgent father and was giving them Rome. He had a few final instructions for them: "Please live in harmony with each other; cater to the soldiers; don't bother about anybody else."

His last words are said to have been: "Let's get to work."

# ❧ VI ☙

## *The Joint Reign*

For generations it had been the custom for the Roman Emperor to keep in his bedroom a gold statue of the goddess Fortune. This image accompanied him wherever he traveled; if his bedroom was a military tent, Fortune stood in the tent. The statue meant a great deal: it was believed that it helped an Emperor be victorious over his enemies at home and abroad. Immediately upon his death, it was transferred to his successor.

Severus had wanted a duplicate made so that Caracalla and Geta would each have one of his own when they were Emperors together. But since there was not time to complete a duplicate, Severus had ordered that his sons should share the one existing statue: every day it was to be carried first to one young man's bedchamber and then to the other's. When Severus died, however, Caracalla hurried to confiscate it. This golden bringer of victory, this representation of the great goddess Fortune herself, was too valuable to be allowed to pass into Geta's hands for even a few minutes of the day.

In spite of that initial strain, however, things were not quite as bad as they might have been. Julia Domna pleaded with her sons to be reasonable toward each other, to put the peace of the Empire above their personal animosity even if they could not become true brothers in spirit; Severus' advisors, particularly Papinian, pleaded with them too, and as a result there was a reconciliation. It may not have been sincere, but it was better than an open feud.

Caracalla was by far the more forceful of the two young Emperors. In his early twenties, he wanted to do great things, to win fame, and to guard the territory that his father had left to him and (lamentably) to his brother. He ended the war against the barbarians, made them promise to stop plundering the tribes within the Empire, and equipped the outpost forts with special military units to keep the peace; he ushered in an era of security which was to last a long time. This, he felt, was only the beginning.

With his mother, his brother, and the ashes of his father, he returned to Rome. It was a long trip and an unpleasant one: the apparent reconciliation had already broken down, and despite all the efforts of Julia Domna, the two Emperors would not tolerate lodging together, would not eat together, and took very obvious precautions against being poisoned by each other. The Roman Empire stretched from Britain to the Sahara, from the Rock of Gibraltar to Mesopotamia. Most of Europe lay within it, and northern Africa and nearer Asia. It contained old civilizations such as those of Egypt, Lydia, Crete, Greece, and Judea; it contained the savages of the forests along the Danube and the Rhine. But it was not big enough for both Caracalla and Geta.

When they reached Rome, each appropriated a particular part of the palace and barred it against the other; each had his own servants, his own soldiers, his own friends, his own flatterers and hangers-on, and each kept campaigning for more adherents. The barriers were up; the Emperors were seen together only in the presence of their mother on public occasions. Julia Domna still had recourse to philosophy, but her apprehensions made her life unquiet. In this manner the business of the Empire was conducted. The historian Herodian says that the brothers even considered dividing up the Empire, Geta to receive Asia and eastern Africa, Caracalla to receive western Africa and Europe, but that Julia Domna killed the plan by suggesting that they might cut her in half too. Although Herodian probably invented this whole story, the fact that he could expect it to be believed by his contemporaries testifies to the condition of the government at the time.

Almost the only official act participated in by both Caracalla and Geta was the apotheosis of Severus. Like Pertinax, Severus was given a magnificent funeral, in the course of which he assumed his divine status. Like Pertinax also, he was represented by a realistic wax replica. It was exposed to public view for a week, while the state physicians consulted over it, discussed what was to be done, agreed that Severus' condition was growing steadily worse, and finally decided that he could not live. The funeral pyre was several stories high, each story smaller than the one beneath it. The elaborate bed was put on the second story, with the wax body lying on it. The highest story held the eagle which, on being released, flew up to heaven with Severus' soul.

Members of the Senate and other courtiers were uncomfortably caught up in the middle of the intrigues and counterintrigues in which the Emperors were continuously indulging. On the whole, people probably preferred Geta, since he showed a taste for intellectual things and since he was generally friendly. Caracalla, who had certainly been given as intellectual an education as his younger brother, forgot what he had learned, or seemed to forget it—pretended to despise it, in fact —and threw himself into strenuous physical exercise. He also played up the life of a soldier, depicting himself as the vigorous military man, which he in some degree was and which remained his ideal. Much less approachable than Geta, he tended to be curt and sharp with people, sometimes even brutal. But even so he had many followers. After all, he was the stronger Emperor; there seemed to be more of a future with him. People were attracted to Geta because Geta was relatively likable, but that was an imprudent reason.

Almost as worried as Julia Domna, the Senate decided to offer a sacrifice to the goddess Concord; it might help. This idea, however, turned out to be an unfortunate one. The consul who was to preside over the sacrifice was unable to locate the attendants deputed to perform the slaughtering, and the attendants were equally unable to locate the consul; the beast was left standing at the altar. This seemed a very bad omen.

Meanwhile Caracalla enjoyed playing the tyrant. He hastened to have Plautilla executed, as well as her brother, whose family relationship must have constituted his principal offense. Around this time he apparently also had a famous old charioteer executed, because the man had raced for the faction which Caracalla did not like. The freedman Castor, his father's favorite, was naturally put out of the way, and Papinian was removed from his office of Praetorian Prefect.

The brotherly hatred waxed through the months: Caracalla eyeing Geta with malign intent whenever he eyed him at all; Geta trying to rally all the support he could so that he would be ready for the crisis which now seemed inevitable and which he almost welcomed. Then, about a year after the death of Severus, the scarcely credible happened. Caracalla told his distraught mother that he would like to be reconciled with Geta. After all, the enmity between them was doing neither themselves nor the Empire any good. Perhaps Geta and he could meet in her apartment and talk things over, and perhaps she could help them reach an agreement, because she was a wise lady. She came close to hoping now; it really looked as if the long enmity might soon be over.

In their mother's apartment, they did not have time to do more than exchange a few distant courtesies before several centurions rushed in and started stabbing Geta. He ran to where his mother was seated, the centurions following and stabbing. Caracalla looked on, or gave them instructions, and possibly rendered them a little assistance with his own sword. "Help, Mother!" Geta screamed. "Mother, save me!" She held him to her breast, the young son whom she loved, and his blood spilled over her robe. One of the centurions, striking carelessly, wounded her in the hand, but she hardly noticed. "Help, Mother, help!"—but the mother was helpless. Geta lay dead across her knee.

Caracalla hurried through the palace crying out that his life had been in danger, that he had barely managed to save it. He ordered his guards to escort him to the camp of the Praetorians. In a kind of sanctuary full of military ensigns, statues of the gods, and statues of the deified Emperors, he offered thanks that he had not been killed and performed sacrifices. Evening was coming on; the soldiers were at ease, some already in their quarters, some bathing, some chatting desultorily; but Caracalla's sudden appearance and strange behavior made them curious, and they flocked around. When the Emperor had completed his religious observances he addressed them.

He glossed over the details but made it clear that Geta was dead. To judge by his nervousness, he might actually have had a narrow escape from death at the hands of a homicidal brother, but he was not too nervous to forget his father's dying injunction: "Cater to the soldiers; don't bother about anybody else." So he promised that each Praetorian would receive a great deal of money. "Rejoice, fellow soldiers," he exhorted them, "since I'm now in a position to be of service to you." He would give them riches because he loved them and because they deserved riches. His strong admiration for the military enabled him to partly believe what he said; as his father had declared, soldiers were the only people that mattered. He told them that he wanted to be one of them—to live with them or, if that was not possible, at least to die with them. He was not afraid of death, he said, and he believed that death in warfare was far preferable to any other kind. A man, he thought, does best to die in battle.

After hearing these brave words the Praetorians recognized him as their Emperor.

Caracalla passed the night among his loyal Praetorians. The next day, with his guards close beside him and with a coat of mail underneath his robe, he spoke to the Senate, for which he did not feel any more respect than his father had felt. He explained that the killing had been performed in self-defense—that if he had not killed Geta, Geta would have killed him. That seemed to satisfy the senators. He also uttered a proclamation in celebration of this happy day: all persons exiled from Rome were free to return. Some of these persons had, of course, been exiled unjustly, but others had not, and Caracalla's generosity filled the city with criminals. The young Emperor still had much to learn about government. He did not possess Severus' political sense.

Geta's name was effaced from inscriptions just as Plautian's had been. All over the Empire people were busy chiseling out his name and titles, replacing them sometimes with grandiloquent titles and flattering adjectives applied to Caracalla. The very mention of the word "Geta" was treated as if it were a crime. The name had often been used for slaves in comedies, but it could not be used any more. Furthermore, if a rich Roman had a servant called Geta, he was not allowed to leave him a legacy in his will: should the name occur in a will, the whole fortune would be confiscated. Geta was dead—Geta was to be forgotten. The Emperor wished it.

As for the mother, she was not permitted to weep. Caracalla commanded her to smile, to laugh, to be joyful, as if she was glad to get rid of her treacherous younger son. In secret she may have cried her heart out, but she had to take care not to be discovered. At night in solitude she may have remembered the warm blood of her son on her robe, his shivering wounded body, his terrified screams of "Help, Mother, help," and her own womanly weakness. She may have remembered the frantic arms tight around her, then the poor corpse across her knee, and Caracalla looking at Geta with real pleasure for perhaps the first time in his life. But in public she had to be joyful. The Emperor demanded it.

# ❧ VII ❧

# *The Model Tyrant*

It had been a long time since Rome had seen so many executions, assassinations, and enforced suicides as occurred after the death of Geta. Caracalla, whose mind was becoming more and more twisted, possibly succeeded in rationalizing the murder; he perhaps felt that the act really was one of self-defense, since if he had not killed Geta, Geta might have killed him some day. It may have been in further justification of the murder that Caracalla decided to have Geta's partisans killed too: if Geta had been dangerous, so were they, and the need to kill them proved how great a menace to the public safety their leader had been. This may have been the reason for the executions, or perhaps Caracalla just wanted more money in order to pay his supporters, especially the soldiers. The property of those executed on the charge of treason was confiscated.

Palace servants, soldiers, prostitutes, freedmen, actors, wrestlers, musicians, singers, slaves—all those who had conspicuously liked Geta, even those who had been so incautious as to let themselves be seen in his part of the palace, were taken away to be put to death. According to the historian Cassius Dio, as reliable a contemporary as anybody, twenty thousand were executed; his figure is probably extreme, but it is indicative of the extent of the bloodshed. The Romans saw the carts containing the bodies pass through the streets; some of the bodies were unceremoniously burned, and others were just thrown out to be eaten by birds of prey and stray dogs.

These victims, not eminent, were defenseless, but the rich suffered too, partly because Caracalla coveted their estates and partly because he wanted to be feared by everybody, servants and senators alike. If we can believe the historian Spartian, several people were executed merely for urinating near statues of Caracalla.

He alone was Emperor, and an Emperor did not need to be loved. In sculpture and on coins he had himself portrayed as fierce and brutal. When a high-ranking man told him that he always looked angry, he took the remark as a compliment and sent the man a million sesterces. It was a revival of the old-fashioned tyranny that had terrorized Rome under such rulers as Caligula, Nero, and Domitian. Caracalla may have thought that he was following the example of his deified father, but the deaths of senators after the defeat of Albinus had been much more excusable on political grounds than the slaughter of the friends of Caracalla's brother.

Some men died as a result of being notoriously good. He reasoned about them in this way: good men asked him for no favors; this meant that they lacked confidence in him, which meant that they thought he might harm them; this meant that they hated him, which meant that he had better contrive their deaths before they contrived his.

Caracalla sent his first cousin some rare food as a mark of high regard. The next day, evidently, he sent some of his soldiers to his cousin's house to stab him. Having learned of the Emperor's intention, the cousin jumped out of a window, breaking his leg in the fall, and crawled in pain to the room where his wife was. The soldiers found him there, laughed at his plight, and stabbed him.

Pompeianus, grandson of Marcus Aurelius, was one of the most distinguished men in the Empire. He was also a man of great integrity, and his virtues were criminal enough in the eyes of Caracalla. Pompeianus was apparently assassinated, but the story released to an incredulous world was that he had been killed by robbers on a highway.

Papinian had been a friend of the Emperor Severus since youth, when they were law students together. Already under Marcus Aurelius he had served as advocate for the imperial treasury. Severus had put him in charge of resolving the uncertainties of judges, answering legal inquiries submitted by provincial governors, and attending to the petitions of private citizens. Later, Severus had made him a Praetorian Prefect, responsible principally for the increasingly important judicial aspects of the post; another Prefect was responsible for the military aspects. A man of lucid intellect, penetrating insight, and incorruptible integrity, Papinian had perhaps no equal among the jurisconsults of the age and few among the jurisconsults throughout Rome's history; two centuries later the Theodosian Code would rank him above all the others. Caracalla did not like him but, respecting his intelligence, asked him to provide plausible justifications for the killing of Geta and to write a persuasive, reasonable speech explaining the murder; for such a man this would be easy. Papinian, however, is said to have replied that it is more difficult to justify a fratricide than to commit one and that to blacken the name of an innocent man is to kill him again. Not long after this the Praetorians, probably at Caracalla's covert instigation, demanded that Papinian be executed. His head was cut off with an axe. The Emperor, however, was displeased; so great a man should have been killed with a sword.

Fabius Cilo, who had been a consul twice, was more fortunate. For a while he had supervised the education of Caracalla and Geta, and, with little foresight, he had tried to resolve their disputes and had censured their animosity as bad for the future of Rome. Caracalla therefore despised him as a critic and a sympathizer with Geta, yet he pretended to be very fond of the old man and even called him "my father." Ordering Cilo's execution would have been inadvisable in the light of all this hypocrisy; instead he had some soldiers, in charge of a tribune, seize him as if of their own will, on the pretense that he had done something treasonable which the Emperor should know about. But as they dragged him through the streets toward the palace, tearing off his clothes and beating him in the face, the crowd grew rebellious. The soldiers of the city cohorts, which he had once commanded, recognized him and shouted in protest. Caracalla rushed from the palace, having decided that Cilo was less dangerous alive than dead. "Stop hitting my father. This man is my old tutor; he guided me through childhood." In a dramatic gesture he offered his own robe to cover Cilo's nakedness. As for the tribune and the soldiers, they might have mismanaged the whole affair but at least they proved useful as scapegoats; they were executed for mistreating old Cilo.

Women died too. The most noble of them was Cornificia, granddaughter of Antoninus Pius and daughter of Marcus Aurelius—an ancient lady from another age, when justice and mildness reigned. She had wept over the murder of Geta. Because she was very eminent,

Caracalla let her select her manner of dying. She did not want to die, but she thought of her grandfather and her upright, self-sacrificing, Stoic father. She would show this latter-day tyrant and his myrmidons that a true member of the Antonine house was not afraid to bring life to an end. "Go, my miserable soul," she said, "my wretched soul locked in a wretched body. Show them all how it's done." She calmly laid aside her jewels, settled herself gracefully, and opened her veins.

One of Caracalla's occasional poses was that of moral reformer, although his own private life was a rather lurid example of licentiousness. He imposed the death penalty on those convicted of adultery, and he condemned four Vestal Virgins to death for violating the vow of chastity. One, Lanutia, avoided being killed officially by killing herself: she hurled herself from the top of a building onto the pavement. The other three were buried alive. Ironically, the Emperor himself had tried to rape one of these three and, according to the girl, had not succeeded. On her way to her own burial she shouted, "Caesar doesn't need to be told that I am still a virgin."

Tyrants are often depicted as bleeding the people whom they rule, and Caracalla conformed to this picture. He did not favor moderate taxation. After he had been Emperor for a couple of years he set out on a series of wars, and these wars had to be paid for. The soldiers, the only people that mattered and the only people that loved him, needed much money. He devised new taxes and increased existing ones. He obliged the provinces through which he marched to volunteer provisions for the maintenance of his armies, and he extorted "presents" from cities and from affluent subjects. He apparently required these affluent subjects to build magnificent residences on the roads along which he might march, so that if he happened to pass that way he could be accommodated in imperial style. Cities in which he intended to settle for the winter had to erect amphitheatres and circuses for his entertainment. He was Emperor: the Empire endured for him.

Julia Domna, concerned over his lavish expenditures, ventured to tell him that there were no more sources of revenue left, either fair or unfair.

"Don't worry, Mother," he answered, pulling his sword from the scabbard, "as long as we have this, we won't be poor."

Actually, however, it was not only by his sword but by a clever idea that he augmented his revenues. As early in his reign as the year 212, he granted Roman citizenship to all inhabitants of the Empire except slaves and, apparently, certain freedmen. This was a final step in the process that had been going on for two hundred years. Under Augustus the Romans had still been chary about bestowing the privileges of citizenship on people in the provinces—decadent Greeks, perhaps, or undependable Asiatics, or barbaric Gallic folk. But in succeeding years Rome gradually spread herself thinner and thinner; more and more people, all around the Mediterranean and beyond, were gathered in as citizens. Some of the Emperors came from the provinces—Trajan from Spain, for example, or Severus from Africa. There were still millions of free people within the Empire, however, who were not citizens. Caracalla welcomed them. On the surface this looked generous, but as Roman citizens they were subject to inheritance taxes which they would not otherwise have had to pay.

Caracalla may not have been aware that his reform contributed to the de-Romanization of the Empire. He may not even have been aware that the Empire was being de-Romanized. The granting of citizenship to more and more people outside the city was part of this larger process; so was the Oriental influence that was beginning to color the lives of ordinary Romans; so was the philhellenism which had held the upper classes for many generations, inducing them to scorn the ancient Latin ways and admire only that which was Greek; so was the extent to which barbarians, some of them only very superficially civilized, were occupying important posts. The conservative, sturdy little city on the Tiber was turning into an amorphous monster that sprawled all over the Mediterranean world and no longer knew its own identity.

Like most people who realize that they are hated, Caracalla went to extreme lengths to protect himself, both while he was at Rome and later, on his campaigns. Not entirely confident of his own soldiers, he used wild Germans and wilder Scythians as bodyguards, calling them his lions. He bought enormous quantities of poison—rare varieties, many of them extremely costly; it is doubtful whether even during the Renaissance anybody had as fine a collection as his. A whole army of informers and gossip-mongers was in his employ, and they kept him aware of what was going on at court and in the city, what people were whispering about, what people thought of him. If he concluded that a courtier or a sycophant was becoming subversive, the connoisseur of poisons would choose a subtle, swift, and certain silencer.

Although he carried his hatred for the dead Geta with him wherever he went, it was a strange thing—at times he seemed to see Geta before him, and at times he seemed to feel sorry about the murder. Something troubled him very much, and it would not let him alone; it may not have been a conscience, but whatever it was, it would not relent. He tried to assuage it by putting to death several of the people who had been concerned in Geta's murder, most prominent among them the Praetorian Prefect Laetus, whom he commanded to drink poison. But this did not work; there were periods when he cried for Geta. Even as a tyrant he was weak; even as a killer of aristocrats he was not the man that bull-necked Domitian had been, or crazy Caligula. Something kept bothering him, making his life unhappy.

He tried to lose himself by attending chariot races and gladiatorial combats, watching these with the hope of escape. At the races he cheered on the Blue faction (Geta had championed the Greens). Senators and rich freedmen found themselves obliged to furnish wild beasts for the arena. The Emperor furnished other beasts at his own expense—tigers, elephants, rhinoceroses—the fiercer and more exotic the better. What he particularly enjoyed was to see a man ripped apart by one of them, or to look on while two skillful gladiators tried to kill each other, and to feel vicarious victory surging through him when one succeeded. Then he was truly happy; the excitement of the moment enabled him to forget about the brother who tormented his spirit. The gladiator Bato was remarkable; he could watch Bato all day. So he made Bato fight three times the same day, and in the third fight the opponent unfortunately proved more expert. Or perhaps the opponent was just fresher physically. Caracalla did not blame Bato for losing; he showed his high regard for the man by giving him a splendid funeral.

The Emperor was not always content to be merely a spectator. He prided himself on his ability to drive a chariot and would sometimes drive for the Blues. The excitement of those races—the thrill of competing, the thrill of speed, the feel of power, the dust and the wind and the straining horses and the whip tight in his hand—gave him more pleasure than he got from almost anything else. The Sun God drove a chariot across the sky every day, governing the great unruly horses that Phaëthon could not manage: driving a chariot was a godlike thing to do. After an especially fine race Caracalla would salute the cheering crowd gallantly with his whip and ask for pieces of gold.

He also slew beasts on the sands of the arena—a hundred wild bears in one day, other animals on other days. He was a hero to himself when he saw them die by his own hand; the spectators yelled around him, and even the knights and the senators applauded. He probably had some notion of what these knights and senators secretly thought about his performances, but he did not care. He knew that he was putting himself on a level with the slaves, the criminals, the strong scum who customarily killed wild beasts in the arena. As for chariot drivers, he knew that they too were recruited from the ranks of the slaves. If one of them became famous some admirer would buy his freedom, but even so, his social station was scarcely an exalted one. Caracalla, however, was Emperor: nothing could diminish his dignity. When a great tusked boar gushed blood or when the crowd cheered his mastery over four horses, he was almost a living god.

Another of his passions was astrology, for which he had probably inherited a taste from Severus. He consulted the horoscopes of the chief figures in the Empire in an effort to determine which of them would defend him in a crisis and which would gladly turn against him, and he bestowed favors on those whose horoscopes pictured them as most friendly to himself and planned punishments for those whose secret dislike the stars betrayed. His belief in the supernatural went far deeper than mere superstition; it was involved with Geta, with the regret, or conscience, or guilt that tormented his mind. He needed the supernatural in order to free himself. He needed to make magic sacrifices, since they afforded relief—or, at any rate, they sometimes did.

One of the divinities he often relied upon was Apollonius of Tyana, the man who was a god and whose biography Julia Domna had asked Philostratus to write—the wonder-worker to whom many temples had been raised; the magician who drove out demons, who could read the future and never lost an argument; the brave philosopher who had defied Domitian and who possessed the wisdom of India. But there were occasions when even Apollonius was not of great assistance. The Emperor had recourse to other divinities too, but they were not always helpful either.

He even tried to summon the ghosts of his father and Commodus. He could explain to his father, who would warn him if some dire punishment was in store for him. However, his father was accompanied by Geta. As for Commodus, his adoptive uncle ever since Severus had had himself made a legal member of the Antonine house, he was a man whom Caracalla could respect—a bloody and much-feared ruler, a warrior, and most important, a gladiator. Commodus had patterned himself after Hercules to the extent of wearing a lion's mane and carrying a club; Commodus had killed men and beasts in the arena, with the staid old senators watching because they were afraid not to watch. Commodus would understand. But Commodus did not. He told Caracalla that the gods demanded judgment.

Sometimes the torment became so acute that Caracalla would dash around the palace or through the city in agonized pursuit of whatever pleasures lay open to an Emperor, but these also did not give him the peace that he sought.

He did not like to administer justice, to decide right and wrong for his contentious subjects; he would much rather race a chariot or toughen his body by swimming rough waters or by riding on horseback a hundred miles without stopping to rest. Determining right from wrong better fitted a shrewd man than an active one, and besides, it was too easy and it bored him. He possessed a real sense of responsibility, he knew that governing an Empire was a tremendously important and difficult job, his father had taught him that; but he could not bring himself to spend every morning on legal problems and a swarm of other details. Sometimes he would call his senators together in the morning, giving notice that they were to assist him in judging cases or in otherwise taking care of public affairs, and then keep them waiting all day while he practiced swordsmanship with gladiators, got drunk with his friends, or served wine for the refreshment of his guards. That at least was pleasant; it showed the senators that he never for a moment contemplated abandoning his father's policy of contempt toward them. His sense of responsibility was primarily a military one. An Emperor's foremost duty, in his opinion, was to lead the armies of Rome. He was willing enough to carry out that duty.

It is doubtful, however, that the most famous single undertaking of his reign was military any more than it was administrative. Many people who know nothing about him have heard about the Baths of Caracalla.

Called the Antonine Baths in their early years, they stood in a lovely garden setting, a vast colonnaded enclosure with beds of flowers, rows of trees, and grassy spaces for lounging in the sunny weather. The main building—apparently the only part finished at the time he died —was 750 feet in length and more than half that in width. Three thousand people could be accommodated in the hot pool at one time, and the cold bath was also enormous. There were in addition a tepid bath and rooms for disrobing and sweating. The wings and the rear portion of the building contained a theatre, libraries, museums, study halls, lecture halls, and colonnaded courts, all full of mosaic work, paintings, and statuary; at the back was a stadium for watching those who wished to indulge in vigorous athletic exercise. Like former Roman baths, this one fulfilled many functions; people could come here for cleanliness, for health, for art, for serious thought, for erudite discourse, for gossip, for a stroll, for news, for sex, for beauty, or simply for something to do.

At Rome the only structures of comparable size built after it were the Baths of Diocletian and the Basilica of Constantine, and not many of comparable size had been built before. It ranked with the Circus Maximus and the Flavian Amphitheatre (the Coliseum) as one of the huge public glories of the city. It was a case of Romans trying to outdo their former selves. A man excluded from the residences of the rich could come here when he wished—could bathe at his pleasure, buy food and drink from vendors, wrestle with his friends, and read the poets of the Golden Age; and he could show the Baths proudly to visitors as part of his own heritage, a tremendous and beautiful thing made for him by his countrymen under the auspices of his Emperors. The Baths would continue to be used in the fourth century and in the fifth, when the city, Christian now, sat there afraid of barbarians. The savages who invaded helpless Rome must have wondered at this solid splurge of magnificence, this great heavy jewel in the civilization they had conquered. Vigorous and uninhibited, they probably cavorted under its veined green marble and wallowed in its water.

# ❧ VIII ☙

# The Wars of Caracalla

Alexander the Great was Caracalla's idol. The Macedonian king, whose huge conquests had occurred almost five hundred years before Caracalla's own military exploits, had been the greatest of soldiers, the greatest of tacticians, the greatest of monarchs—young and unafraid and godlike (descended, in fact, from Zeus)—a hero throughout his life, defeating the Great King, defeating everybody who came up against him, until his territory extended from Egypt on the west to India on the east and included the major part of the known world. Men served him devotedly, fought for him courageously, gladly gave up their lives for him—the Greeks had never been as great since Alexander's death. He had changed the history of man, destroying the Persian despotism, bringing Greeks into central Asia and northern India, founding Greek cities wherever he passed, spreading Hellenic culture among the barbarians, and establishing an empire out of whose ruins new nations arose. Here was a being to pattern one's life after, to imitate in so far as one could; here was a model of excellence fit for a military man and an Emperor.

There was nothing very original in Caracalla's intense admiration for Alexander, since for centuries he had been idealized and adored as a god by many people; his cult was probably the most unbridled manifestation of hero worship in ancient times. Caracalla was by no means the first ruler to adopt Alexander as a model. The trouble was that Caracalla had no real conception of what he was doing.

He organized a military body called Alexander's Phalanx whose members were Macedonians, sixteen thousand of them, and equipped them in the style in which he believed Alexander's soldiers to have been equipped—with long pikes, short spears, bronze shields, thick linen breastplates, ox-hide helmets, high boots, and swords. He drank wine from a goblet which Alexander was reported to have used. He collected weapons and all other objects that had reputedly belonged to Alexander. He had statues of Alexander put up in cities throughout the Empire, and particularly in the camps so that the troops would be inspired. Once he happened to sit in judgement on a man whose name was Alexander; the man was not a Macedonian, and there was no association with Alexander the Great except for the nominal one, but his accuser kept referring to him as "the god-forsaken Alexander," "the bloodthirsty Alexander," and these terms annoyed the Emperor so much that he dismissed the case. Another time, noticing that a tribune had mounted his horse with remarkable agility, he asked the man where he came from. "Macedonia," was the reply. He asked the man his name. It was Antigonus, the name of one of Alexander's generals. He asked the man his father's name. It was Philip, the name of Alexander's father. He promoted the tribune immediately and soon procured him a seat in the Senate.

Because of an untrue story that Aristotle had contributed to Alexander's death by feeding him poison, Caracalla detested the memory of the philosopher. Aristotle's books were to be burned, he said, and scholars at the Museum at Alexandria who adhered to Aristotle's teachings were to be deprived of their pensions. He even attempted to convince himself and others that he was a reincarnation of the soul of the great hero. In front of a mirror he practiced a gesture which was said to have been characteristic of Alexander. Some of the statues which he commissioned had faces which looked like Alexander on one side and Caracalla on the other. Just as the Macedonian king had spent very little of his reign in Macedonia, the Roman Emperor spent most of his reign away from Rome, pursuing a military career in imitation of his other self.

Like Alexander also, but in a very different way, Caracalla demonstrated his high esteem for the soldiers. For example, he raised their pay by half, to the distress of influential citizens. He also permitted those he had with him on his campaign in the East to pass the winters in cities, rather than making them live in military camps during the off season as Roman troops had done previously. This relaxation of winter quarters was, of course, very much to the soldiers' liking, and although they might have felt less respect for their commander than Alexander's soldiers felt for theirs, at least they thought that life had never been so good as under the indulgent Caracalla. In the cities they could drink and have women and pillage and see races all through the mild Asiatic winters.

Perhaps the most striking proof of his affection for his troops was that Caracalla tried to live like an ordinary soldier. He made long marches on foot instead of riding at ease on a great horse, practiced the same military exercises as his men, and swung up on his own shoulders the heavy legionary standards which were borne before the troops on the march. The men's meals were his meals, unpleasing though they must often have been to the palate of a person reared in a palace; according to the historian Herodian, he carried his military simplicity so far as to grind grain with his imperial hands, knead the dough, bake it into bread, and eat it. He refrained from taking baths because the common soldiers were often unable to bathe on campaign.

Alexander had been an excellent soldier too, but Alexander had been first of all a general. Critics said that Caracalla failed to follow his paragon in this respect, although his military record was by no means a disgraceful one. Others whispered that his practice of military simplicity was obviously all pretense. They affirmed that he found armor too heavy—that instead of wearing the burdensome clothing that his soldiers wore, he had some special armor made. It looked like a real cuirass and consequently would deter hopeful assassins, but it was light enough not to be uncomfortable. Fortunately, few of his men were aware of this false protection.

In 213 he evidently turned Narbonnese Gaul upside down, ordering the death of the governor and committing outrages against the magistrates and the citizens with the help of his soldiers. Gaul, nevertheless, soon palled. This area was almost as Romanized as Italy itself, and Caracalla wanted to see new things, to learn new ways of life, to observe new customs, to try new beliefs, to do anything different, anything that might constitute a change.

It was probably among the Gallic tribes, however, that he found one new thing which attracted him immediately—a red, fitted cloak or coat called a *caracallus* or *caracalla*. He apparently had garments of this kind, but longer than the Gallic ones, made for his soldiers, and later had them distributed to the Roman poor. Since nobody addressed him as Caracalla, he probably never knew that he had acquired a nickname.

North of the Alps he inspected the *limes,* the fortifications extending in a continuous line for a great distance along the northern border of the Empire, separating territory subject to Rome from territory where the Germanic tribes raided and quarreled. The *limes* were enormous ramparts of earth, with a ditch in front for Germans to fall into and a wooden palisade for Germans not to climb, and with wooden watchtowers so placed as to command a sweeping view. Men in these isolated towers, on the alert against the enemies of civilization, could communicate with one another by means of smoke signals or, at night, fire signals or blasts on the trumpet. The *limes* were an essential aspect of Rome's ability to endure, and they excited Caracalla's interest. Here was something remarkable, something to take his mind off himself. He repaired forts and had a stone wall completed on the border of Rhaetia.

The Alemanni were a union of several Germanic tribes; the name is supposed to have signified "all men." They were unheard of by Romans until about 213, when they made savage inroads into the Roman Empire. The provinces that the tribes invaded were Rhaetia and Noricum, thickly forested, partly mountainous regions south of the Danube. The Alemanni came in great numbers; this was a large-scale invasion. Rome was not seriously disturbed, however; a large-scale invasion meant simply that the barbarians had to be fought in force, warded off, sent back to the green depths out of which they had come. Very few Romans, if any, anticipated a time more than two centuries away when the barbarians would overrun the Empire. Caracalla set off to conquer these Germans, at the head of a diverse army containing even some Osrhoënian bowmen from the environs of Parthia. He was accompanied by the Empress Julia Domna, who had decided to go with her son on his wars just as she had gone with her husband.

Caracalla apparently defeated the Germans gloriously enough, although we do not know much more about his activities in Rhaetia and Noricum than we know about his activities in Britain. In the spirit of a real hero, he evidently sent challenges to the German chiefs, inviting them to single combat, but these invitations do not seem to have been accepted.

The campaign ended with his buying the Germans off. Although this move may not have been in the finest military tradition, it was highly expedient and, on the whole, wise. It avoided a great deal of discontent on the part of the barbarians and consequently a great deal of senseless warfare. There was nothing dishonorable about it. Romans had occasionally followed the same course in the past, and their successors the Byzantines were to follow it in the future. It was not a policy that one could readily associate with an Alexander the Great or a hero-Emperor, but no man could always exist on an ideal plane.

In his search for what was new and strange, for distractions, Caracalla found much to absorb his attention in the Germans. They were truly brave people, these barbarians—worthy of the admiration of an Emperor. Wounded by the arrows of the Osrhoënians, they pulled the arrows out with their teeth so that they could keep their hands free for fighting. Even the women were fearless. When Caracalla asked some female captives whether they preferred being sold as slaves to being killed, they told him they preferred to be killed. He had them sold anyway, and they committed suicide. Some of them killed their children too, so that the children would not grow up without freedom.

In his enthusiasm for these people Caracalla decided to make their boldest and sturdiest young men his personal bodyguard; he could rely on them to protect him against his countless enemies. He adopted their barbaric clothes too, sometimes even for public appearances, and wore a light-colored wig in imitation of the Germans' blond hair.

When he was sufficiently Germanized he proceeded by long marches into Thrace, where he battled perhaps against the Dacians, perhaps against the Goths. His mother still accompanied him, as did a numerous court.

From Thrace he crossed the Hellespont in a fierce storm and landed in Asia Minor, in need of new distractions. Close to the ruins of Troy he thought intensely about the Greek heroes of the *Iliad*. The fact that the Greek heroes had nearly exterminated the Trojans, who were supposed to be the ancestors of the Romans, did not deter him any more than it deterred his philhellenic countrymen. In particular he admired Achilles, the greatest of the Greek warriors and perhaps the cruelest enemy of Troy. It was Achilles who, after sulking in his tent for a long time because Agamemnon had confiscated his mistress, rushed back into battle when his devoted young friend Patroclus was killed by the Trojan Hector. It was the grief-stricken Achilles who killed Hector in revenge for the death of Patroclus and dragged Hector's body at the rear of a chariot around the tomb of his friend to the distress of the dead man's mother and father. Caracalla had a bronze statue set up to Achilles, poured libations on what was reputed to be the legendary hero's sepulcher, placed wreaths of flowers on it, and ordered his troops to perform military games in honor of the great Greek.

Encamped near the ruins of Troy with an army that was not composed of Homeric Greeks but of Italians and Osrhoënians and German mercenaries, Caracalla did not find it difficult to imagine that he was Achilles. One element, however, was lacking: he required a Patroclus. There were few people whom he liked well enough or who liked him well enough to fit the part, but he managed to find a Patroclus in a freedman named Festus, one of his two or three favorites. To be chosen was a high honor and Festus must have felt gratified, except that Patroclus had died.

For several days Caracalla treated his favorite with the warmest affection—Festus his faithful friend, his courageous follower, for whom he would gladly give his life. Then Festus was dead—poisoned, according to the rumor that circulated through the camp. And Caracalla, Achilles-like, mourned. Nothing would console him except the plans for his friend's funeral—because Festus was to have a stupendous funeral, just like Patroclus. An elaborate pyre was erected; the young corpse was laid on it and sprinkled with the blood of many animals; Caracalla poured libations and uttered prayers and even cut off some of his own sparse hair to throw into the flames. Since he was prematurely bald, this last piece of ritual was the most difficult of all; he had to expend considerable effort before he could locate enough hairs to represent a respectable offering. No sacrifice, however, was too extreme for his Patroclus.

Caracalla lingered in Asia Minor in quest of relief from his mental and physical ills. We are not sure what his physical ailments were; sexual impotence may possibly have been one of them, but he was also in real physical pain. Not long after the burning of Patroclus he turned to the being who he thought could probably do most for his physical condition and perhaps something for his mental condition too—Aesculapius, god of health. At a temple of this divinity in Pergamum he begged for alleviation of his sufferings.

The god of hygiene, Aesculapius, was the son of Apollo by a Thessalian princess and had been brought up by the knowledgeable centaur Chiron. He was said to have restored dead people to life; and snakes, signifying rejuvenescence, were kept in his sanctuaries. When he appeared to human beings he frequently assumed the form of a snake. Although he had been worshipped for many hundreds of years, he had acquired new importance during the great pestilence that occurred in the reign of Marcus Aurelius. The more people were preoccupied with sickness and death, the more they resorted to him—and sickness and death obsessed people during the second and third centuries. Many temples went up to Aesculapius, especially in the eastern half of the Empire. They were often situated in a place overlooking the quiet countryside and near a spring of medicinal water.

The crippled, the deaf, the blind, the emaciated, the swollen— people with running sores and people with pains in their bellies—came in hordes to these temples, some of which could accommodate several hundred patients at a time. During the waking hours the patients would adhere to a careful diet, take herbs administered by the priest-physicians, bathe in the medicinal waters, enjoy the salubrious rural air, submit their tormented bodies to the care of male or female nurses, and worship the god. At night they would sleep in dormitories through which blew soft southern breezes, and perhaps they would have dreams in which Aesculapius prescribed cures for their diseases; or else they would lie awake waiting for visions.

Sometimes it seemed that a concealed panel in the wall would slide open, and in the near-dark and the perfect silence a vague form would approach the bed of a sick man and in a low voice offer solace. But not all the patients' visions were manufactured. Many elements in the atmosphere of the place combined to create real ones—the peacefulness, the beauty, the aura of holiness, the unfamiliar rituals to the great god, the clear waters of the spring, the kindliness of the priest-attendants, the throng of hopeful believers who had limped or crawled or been carried here for help, the prayers which the patients had listened to just before retiring. Besides, the patients had already heard stories of miraculous cures performed by Aesculapius—stories that had attracted them to the temple in the first place and which led them to expect something supernatural.

Recourse to Aesculapius, however, did not help Caracalla. The Emperor dreamed too, but the god did not send the dreams to cure him. Caracalla went to the oracle of Aesculapius' father, Apollo, since Apollo was the god of medicine; even earlier, on the German campaign, he had sought help from Apollo Grannus, the Gallic god who healed. But there was still no respite from his physical ills and mental agonies. Neither war nor religion could give him peace.

# 𝕏 IX 𝕏

# Antioch and Alexandria

After traversing Asia Minor, Caracalla entered Syria with his army and held court at Antioch, a city whose luscious diversions might do more than anything else to alleviate his pains.

Antioch was already over five hundred years old, having been founded in the year 300 B.C. by Seleucus, who had commanded the Macedonian heavy infantry under Alexander the Great. Like many other Greek cities away from Greece, it did not start off as a small town: it was impressive from the beginning. In fact, Seleucus had intended it as one of the four principal cities of the kingdom he established for himself in and around Syria. It was systematically planned and was ornamented with stately buildings in the Greek manner. On one side Mount Silpius overlooked it. The river Orontes ran past it to the sea. Along the river extended the agora, or market place. At Daphne, a suburb to the south, gardens spread out for the esthetic or sexual gratification of the citizens.

At Daphne too, Apollo was worshipped in a most magnificent temple. People believed that on the site of Daphne, the nymph had been metamorphosed into a laurel tree in order to escape Apollo, who was chasing her with rape in his divine mind. It was said that before the founding of the suburb, Seleucus while on a hunt paused at this very laurel, already ancient, and that from the ground emerged a golden arrowhead, and that a snake reared its head to hiss at him and then passed on. Seleucus knew by these signs that he should consecrate a temple to Apollo at Daphne.

In it stood a great statue of the god holding a lyre in one hand and a golden vessel in the other. Bryaxis the Athenian had created the statue, and if a man in trouble went to it he lost his fear, or his sorrow, or his sickness. The Apollo of Daphne, however, did not help Caracalla.

Under the successors of Seleucus, Antioch became the capital of the Seleucid dominions. More temples were built, and so was a large public library, since some of the Antiochenes, like their cousins of Alexandria, valued the cultivation of the intellect. Macedonians, Athenians, Cretans, and Ionians came to the city; native Syrians came also, and occupied their own quarter. The Seleucid kings held a sumptuous and sensual court, which colored the customs of the capital. These monarchs, who were usually named Antiochus or Seleucus, could not preserve intact the kingdom fashioned by their strong ancestor. There were heroic days under Antiochus III, but the over-all pattern was one of degeneration. Most of the energy of the Seleucids was exhausted in family battles, sometimes cases of brother against brother. The citizens of Antioch, however—Orientalized Greeks and luxury-loving Orientals —had created a place of wide renown out of all this decadence, or perhaps because of it. They produced by their own soft living a city famous for voluptuousness. It may not have had moral force, but it had beauty and it gave delight.

Pompey's entrance into Antioch in 64 B.C. ended what was left of the Seleucid kingdom, but Antioch flourished as the capital of Roman Syria. Roman and Jewish merchants prospered there. The metropolis was a military base for operations against the Parthians (one reason Caracalla came to the city was that he had designs on Parthia), but its military character, though adding excitement, was always superficial. Underneath, Antioch was the same center of soft luxury, even lovelier now with the efflorescence of riches. The Romans were munificent toward it: they enlarged the theatre, where whores and pimps enacted the loves of the deities; they constructed temples to the gods of the Empire, basilicas, lavish baths, and ornamental gates. Under Augustus and Tiberius—and partly, it seems, through the generosity of King Herod—a grand avenue two miles long was built. Bordered with roofed colonnades for its entire length so that shoppers would not have to walk in the hot sun or the rain, and adorned at frequent intervals with statues of bronze or marble, it rivaled or surpassed the thoroughfares of Rome.

The Olympics were celebrated at the city every few years; first competitions lasted for a month, later for a month and a half; the athletic events, plays, musical programs, and races in the hippodrome drew enormous holiday crowds to Antioch from all over the East and beyond. The unimaginable wealth of the upper classes led to the erection of private dwellings on a more and more splendid scale— residences containing ivory furniture, iridescent glass vases, walls covered with cool landscapes by clever Greek painters, beautiful nude statues, and mosaic floors depicting in luminous colors the deeds of heroes and the affairs of gods.

This Graeco–Roman–Oriental metropolis had blossomed into the third most important city of the Roman world, surpassed only by Alexandria and Rome herself. A sick and worm-eaten rose, perhaps, but a flower of overpowering gorgeousness.

Caracalla enjoyed its delights and fascinations, at times almost forgetting the troubles of his mind and body. In addition to its beauties and the pleasures it offered, Antioch had a special appeal for him because he himself was half Syrian. As for his Syrian mother, she knew it and loved it. Not much more than a hundred miles away from Antioch was her own city, Emesa, where she had passed her girlhood, where her father had been high priest of the Sun God, and where her ancestors had ruled as priest-kings. Rome excelled all other cities and she liked Rome very much, but now she could luxuriate in her own country.

She could also be more imperial than she had been in a long time. Although Caracalla (despite the distractions of the city) paid some attention to public affairs, dispatched some important business, and performed political maneuvers, he delegated considerable authority to his mother, allowing her to act very much as his secretary of state. She had begun to fulfill this role for him earlier—even at Rome she had taken a hand in governmental matters, and in Asia Minor she had participated still more in running the Empire—but it was at Antioch that she displayed her political talents and powers at full strength, perhaps because Caracalla's mental and physical ills were incapacitating him more and more for an active administrative life. She had her own Praetorian guards; she received all communications and documents except those of the most extreme importance, which were presented to the Emperor; she sent dispatches in both Latin and Geek to all parts of the Roman world. Men in high posts competed for her favor. She enjoyed the eminence, and she enjoyed the daily routine itself. It helped her to forget about Geta, but escape was not her main motive. Basically, she loved to rule.

She was now on intimate terms with her son, conferring with him, supporting him, advising him. The greatest decisions were still his, of course; and if he thought that a certain policy was wise, nothing she could say would change his mind. But their relationship was relatively smooth. Perhaps she felt flattered by the extent to which he trusted her to take care of imperial business, and she certainly was grateful to him for handing her so much authority. She may even have been able to forget at times that this was the son who had killed his brother in her lap.

Much of the political activity of Caracalla and the Empress concerned Parthia. After the death of the Parthian king Vologases IV, his two sons started to battle for the throne, with Caracalla's enthusiastic approval. The public display of fraternal dissension amused him so much that he even claimed to have fomented it. He apparently did not perceive any similarity between the Parthian troubles and the quarrels between himself and Geta after the death of Severus. Or if any parallels did occur to him, he did not mention them. He merely laughed at these Parthian barbarians who could not get along with each other and whose discords were doing their kingdom great harm.

The civil conflict in Parthia delighted Caracalla not only because it was good to have enervated neighbors, but also because he contemplated attacking the kingdom. At Antioch he was making serious preparations for another war. Parthia occupied what used to be Persia, and Alexander the Great had won his most brilliant victories against the Persians; Caracalla would treat the Parthians in the same way and gain glory. The Senate would give him the title *Parthicus*, "Conqueror of the Parthians," which it had once given his father.

His pretext for war was that the young king Vologases V was shielding two enemies of Rome. One of them was an Armenian prince named Tiridates; we know scarcely anything about him except that he had apparently plotted against Rome and then fled to Parthia for protection. The other was Antiochus, the Cynic philosopher and adventurer who had accompanied Severus in his expedition against Parthia and had since defected to Parthia, perhaps in order to conspire against

Rome along with Tiridates. Caracalla threatened war unless these two *personae non gratae* were delivered up to him.

Vologases V, however, was not eager for a war with Rome; fighting his brother was enough of an occupation for him. He quelled the imperial indignation by giving up the fugitives before Caracalla had so much as marched out of Antioch.

Cheated of his excuse for making war on Parthia, Caracalla turned in the opposite direction and led his troops toward Egypt. He would vent his indignation on Alexandria, which had insulted both him and his mother.

One might suppose that Caracalla would have been favorably inclined toward the most prominent of the many cities named after Alexander the Great, but the Alexandrians, a sophisticated, sharp-tongued, humorous people, had made jokes about the Emperor and his mother. They had been partly responsible for supplying Julia Domna with the nickname "Jocasta" and for referring to Caracalla as "the Emperor Oedipus." It occurred to them that Julia Domna could be called "Jocasta" because of the widespread and readily believed rumor that she and Caracalla were living in incestuous love. In addition, Julia Domna and the Theban queen had both been the mothers of inimical sons. Jocasta's sons Eteocles and Polyneices had slain each other for possession of Thebes, and the half-parallel with Caracalla and Geta amused the Alexandrians. They thought Caracalla was rather comical in any case, with his posturings and pretensions, trying to imitate Achilles, trying to imitate Alexander himself, whom he no more resembled than a goose resembles an eagle. Since they did not keep their thoughts secret, perhaps even indulging in demonstrations against their Emperor—whose sense of humor was not generous—he determined that they should feel his anger as soon as possible.

Alexandria had been founded by Alexander himself in 331 B.C. as a Greek capital for newly conquered Egypt, and although Alexander had certainly foreseen that its situation on the Mediterranean near one of the mouths of the Nile would turn it into a prosperous trading center, even he could not have foreseen that its commerce would one day be unsurpassed. Having given directions, he hurried on to more immediate glories: he returned to the place only once again—in a gold coffin. Against the will of Alexander's other generals, his corpse had been taken to Egypt by an adherent of the great general Ptolemy, soon to be the first Macedonian king of Egypt. Ptolemy thought it would enhance the prestige of Egypt if she rather than some other country possessed the body of the conqueror. At Alexandria the preserved Alexander lay in a splendid tomb.

Like Antioch and many other cities of the Hellenistic world, Ptolemy's capital had been carefully planned. The streets were regular; a long mole extended from shore to the island of Pharos, creating an eastern and a western harbor; a vast area at the end of the eastern harbor was reserved for the palace; temples were raised to the gods and an eastern and a western cemetery were laid out. Under the rule of Ptolemy I and his successors, Ptolemy II and III—as Greeks, Egyptians, Jews, and Syrians flocked to it—the city became a shining splendor of white marble, a glory at which even Athenians could gape. The Greeks, the Jews, and the native Egyptians each had their own quarter; later the Greeks shared theirs with the Romans.

Alexandria's most lavish structure was probably the Royal Palace overlooking the eastern harbor—a complex of gleaming buildings whose magnificence the earlier Greeks would have considered suitable only for gods. (But the Ptolemies were gods in a sense, worshipped by their subjects as divine beings; like their divine predecessors, the Pharaohs, they sometimes married their sisters.) The palace had its own harbor within the eastern harbor, and from the buildings extending along the busy shore one could look across the water to the Lighthouse on the island of Pharos.

The Lighthouse, completed during the reign of Ptolemy II, was a more sensational architectural accomplishment than the Royal Palace, and took its place as one of the seven wonders of the world. Standing approximately four hundred feet high and surmounted by a statue of Poseidon, the god of the sea, it threw its beacon to ships far out at sea and protected both harbors against attack. To Greek sailors, Levantine sailors, and Roman sailors watching it from their ships, it represented the fascinating city which drew them in.

After a while there were a stadium, a gymnasium, an amphitheatre, and other buildings for public recreation. The Caesarium, where the cult of the deified Emperors was carried on under the Romans, contained libraries, pillared porches, courts and galleries, rich in paintings and statuary, glutted with the gold and silver gifts donated by

Emperor-worshippers. Two antique obelisks, now termed "Cleopatra's needles," stood outside it. Not far away was a park dedicated to a god who had died but who had never been a man—the goat-god Pan, who liked to run after nymphs. In this park, apparently, was a hill with its summit carved to represent a pine cone, a phallic symbol suitable for Pan.

In spite of their sarcastic frame of mind, Alexandrians were among the most fiercely religious people of the ancient world. During the late imperial period, Alexandria would become a center for Christianity and the site of violent sectarian riots. In Hellenistic times the principal god of the Alexandrians was probably Serapis, whom the first Ptolemy had introduced. His temple occupied a hill in the Egyptian quarter. Set in the midst of a cloister, to which it was joined by colonnades, it was another triumph of Greek architecture in this city, where the Greeks were a minority but, until the Romans came, the ruling race. The central portion of the temple evidently consisted of a spacious hall and an inner shrine where the enthroned, dark blue image of the god himself, holding a scepter, overawed his devotees. The temple also contained an immense library which eventually included the collection of two hundred thousand volumes belonging to the Greek kings of Pergamum that Mark Antony gave to Cleopatra.

Ptolemy I had introduced Serapis to the Alexandrians for political reasons. In the third century it was relatively easy to combine gods (the process became even easier in succeeding centuries as religious syncretism spread throughout the Mediterranean area), and Serapis was a combination calculated to please both Greeks and Egyptians. One ingredient in him was Osiris, an Egyptian deity of long standing, ruler of the underworld, lord of the afterlife, provider of immortality—a god who had been killed and torn to pieces but who, reassembled, lived as king of the dead and could not be killed again. Another ingredient was Apis, the bull-god of Memphis, who had come to be thought of as Osiris incarnate. In form, however, Serapis was not an animal god of old Egypt but an anthropomorphic deity of Greek aspect, his bearded face majestic yet benign—a version of Hades, Greek god of the underworld. He grew to be even more powerful than Hades; in the minds of many citizens of Alexandria, he subsumed the earlier gods. As syncretism developed into a hunger for monotheism, he began to be regarded as the one god, the god that satisfied everybody. In Roman times his cult attained enormous popularity in parts of the Empire far from Egypt. His inclusiveness was probably one reason why he greatly impressed Severus, who paid particular attention to this divinity on his visit to Egypt and apparently transmitted his enthusiasm to his family. Caracalla consecrated temples to Serapis, even at Rome itself. A hope to gain through the universal deity the respite which other gods had denied him may have been one reason for his eagerness to make the trip to Alexandria.

Ptolemy I had wanted his capital to be superior to other cities in as many ways as possible, and being a Greek, he did not overlook the importance of intellectual activity. In order to stimulate it in Alexandria he founded the Museum, technically a place for the worship of the Muses, but actually a center for learning. Under the lavish patronage of the Ptolemies it could afford to attract and keep erudite men; and scientists, mathematicians, textual scholars, philologists, and poets came here to think and write, perhaps to teach. A library of about half a million volumes was furnished for the use of these men. If a large portion of it had not been burned in a war that Alexandria carried on against Caesar, many works of ancient literature would not be irredeemably lost.

The scientists and mathematicians at the Museum during the third century worked in a spirit of pure investigation and systematic inquiry. They were seldom interfered with by the Ptolemies, who were content if the findings of those scholars redounded to the credit of their patrons. Euclid and the later Apollonius of Perga devoted their lives to geometry; Sostratus designed the Lighthouse; the astronomer Conon named a constellation for a lock of hair which Queen Berenice, wife of Ptolemy III, had dedicated to ensure her husband's well-being; the geographer Eratosthenes came up with almost the exact measurements of the earth's circumference and diameter.

Literature, like scientific thought, reached its height in Alexandria under the early Ptolemies. At best, it was not a profound literature and did not have the force of the old masters; it was the literature of a silver age, the Hellenistic Age; but it was sensitive, sensuous, refreshing, and beautiful—beauty was, in fact, its god. Theocritus, father of the pastoral, dreamed of the Sicilian hillsides from which he had come, with their sunshine and their sheep and their herdsmen; and although he may have idealized his rural homeland after reaching Alexandria, his pastorals were not as artificial as many of those written by later poets. Callimachus wrote urbane verse, learned yet graceful, sometimes revolving around the pleasures or perplexities of love. His pupil Apollonius Rhodius rebelled against him by producing an epic. In Callimachus' opinion, epic poetry was much too monumental a literary form for the delicate, epigrammatic taste of Alexandria; and it was true that people did not write epics there but instead performed literary scholarship on Homer, dividing each of his lengthy poems into twenty-four books and making textual emendations. But Apollonius' epic turned out not to be monumental at all. Dealing with the expedition of Jason and the Argonauts to obtain the Golden Fleece, it too was Alexandrian rather than Homeric—a highly polished work, lovely and lyrical in many places, decorated with rustic similes, regarding the gods with an amused smile (especially notorious Aphrodite and her son Cupid), and probing deep into love psychology in the treatment of passionate Medea. Notwithstanding the forebodings of Callimachus, it pleased the Alexandrian temper.

The decline in the influence of the Museum under Roman rule did not mean a decline in the intellectual activity of Alexandria. As early as the middle of the third century, long before the Romans came, work on the Septuagint was started by Jewish scholars for the benefit of their fellow Jews who, having been brought up to speak Greek, needed a Greek translation of the Hebrew Scriptures. Under the Romans the city's intellectuals expended their efforts primarily on theology.

In the first century after Christ lived Philo Judaeus, the most distinguished member of the large Jewish community at Alexandria and an excellent representative of the fusion of cultures which characterized the metropolis. Attracted to the teachings of Plato, the Pythagoreans, and the Stoics, but yet believing that the Mosaic books were divinely inspired and therefore true, he tended to find Greek philosophical concepts in the Pentateuch. God, he said, is without qualities, incomprehensible to man, existing in perfect abstraction, out of contact with the world; but He works in the world through forces which proceed from Him, which Philo seems to have viewed sometimes as Platonic ideas, sometimes as angels. All these forces, he affirmed, are comprehended in the Logos or Reason, the prime mediator between the world and God, which he also viewed as the Son who formed the world from inert matter and through whom God expresses himself.

Reason makes possible all communication between the concrete and
the abstract, the impure and the pure, the worldly and the unimaginable. In addition, Philo held that human souls, struggling to reach God,
can occasionally succeed through ecstasy, but that unless a man has re-
nounced the pleasures of the senses his soul will not be released to God
after his death but will be destroyed. Both ecstasy and the conquest of
the flesh were to continue to be extremely important in Alexandrian
religious thought, and to religious thought in general when Christianity
was taking form.

According to tradition, St. Mark brought Christianity to Alexandria some time around A.D. 45. The city was receptive to the young religion. With its promise of immortality and its belief in Jesus who died
and then resumed life, Christianity seemed to resemble the creed of
Serapis. The Virgin reminded Alexandrians of Isis, wife of Serapis, who
was often depicted nursing the child Horus in a Madonna-like posture;
Christ reminded Alexandrian Jews of the Logos described by Philo, except that he was not just a principle but God incarnate. For these reasons and for many others, quite a few Alexandrians found Christianity
easy to accept; it did not shock them, it was not viewed as an entirely
new thing. Most Alexandrians, of course, remained pagan during the
first two centuries, but enough were converted so that by the reign of
Severus, if not before, the Bishop of Alexandria had acquired extraordinary influence in the clandestine church, rivaling in power the Bishop
of Antioch and the Bishop of Rome, who was not yet supreme.

Among the more orthodox Christians in Alexandria the most famous about the time of Caracalla's visit to the city was Clement, a
benevolent and very intelligent man who had been educated in Greek
poetry and philosophy. He evidently realized that despite the superficial resemblances of Christianity to the cult of Serapis and other religions, many Alexandrians, particularly those who were intellectually
inclined Greeks like himself, would be unwilling to receive the new
religion if it wholly rejected the philosophies which were part of their
own culture. Perhaps partly for proselyting purposes, therefore, but
certainly from personal conviction as well, Clement taught that the
ideas of the classical Greeks had not been basically wrong, that they
represented approximations of the absolute truth which Christianity
possessed, and that God had assigned to them and to Judaic doctrines
the function of helping to prepare the way for Christianity.

Like Philo Judaeus, Clement conceived of Christ as the Logos of an ineffable God, and although he added that this Reason had been made flesh in order to lead man to the divine, the human Christ was not vivid for him. Like Philo Judaeus also, he emphasized the renunciation of sensual pleasures as a necessary element in approaching God. To him and to his audience, sensual pleasures probably meant above all else the pleasures of Alexandria.

For this capital of many races and many creeds, where men could go wild over a new concept or a new song, where the ceremonies in honor of Serapis (with their fanatic priests and their weird music of flute and harp and cymbal) could excite people to religious ardor and a close race in the hippodrome could excite them to a frenzy, where clear Hellenic reason and wild emotion tangled, where Isis and the Virgin Mary sometimes coincided, where strong believers could despise their bodies, and where the populace could relax from fury by laughing at ridiculous Emperors, Caracalla planned tremendous vengeance.

He announced that his main reason for visiting the city was to worship at the Temple of Serapis, and in spite of their scorn for him, the Alexandrians were flattered that he was attracted to their most magnificent sanctuary. Flowers garlanded the streets, the air was perfumed. Crowds went out to the outlying part of the city to greet him. The richest citizens went out too, and Caracalla gave them a splendid banquet. It seems that after they had eaten he had them killed.

Having instructed the Alexandrians to stay in their houses, he marched into the city at the head of his loyal army. His soldiers occupied streets, squares, rooftops. Then they began the massacre. Systematically they went all over the city, kicking in the doors of houses and running their swords through men, women, and children. The terror continued for several days; Caracalla did not wish to stop it, and as for the soldiers, the longer it went on, the more booty they could collect. They did not care whether a man was old; if he had gold and silver, he died. They paid some attention to whether a woman was beautiful; then they would rape her before robbing her. Visitors to the city —prosperous merchants who had come to sell their wares and perhaps pick up bargains, sailors from Italy or Ionia who had been enjoying themselves ashore—were murdered along with the rest, because the soldiers did not stop to ask each his identity. The helpless poor died in throngs. It was like a plague, only more devastating. The bodies lay decomposing in the hot sun and in the houses, or they were slung into ditches, corpse onto corpse, so that the number of the dead could not be counted.

From the roof of the Temple of Serapis, Caracalla watched the proceedings for a while. Inside the temple he made sacrifices and also offered up the sword with which, according to himself, he had killed Geta. This was probably his greatest piece of bravado. Whether he had actually used the sword on Geta is unimportant: what he was trying to do was to call the murder a heroic act by suggesting that the god would be pleased to receive the sword.

At the tomb of Alexander he made more offerings. He pulled off his purple robe and his jeweled belt, removed the rings from his fingers, and laid these personal treasures on the coffin, thereby paying his respects to his idol.

The massacre went on.

When the white marble vistas were sufficiently stained with blood, Caracalla decided that Alexandria had been punished. The screams of the dying could be heard as he withdrew from the city. He wrote a letter to the Senate describing what he had done.

# ❧ X ❧

## *Caracalla's Last Wars*

While Caracalla was at Alexandria a war was fought in his name against the Armenians. The general he relied on to conquer them was a man named Theocritus, formerly a dancer. Born a slave and the son of a slave, Theocritus took up dancing as a youth because he had been raised in the theatre and danced better than he did anything else. His talent was, however, not great enough to please the eclectic Romans, who drove him out. At Lyons, the Gallic city near which Severus had defeated Albinus, he was a success: the Gallic provincials did not have the highly cultivated Roman taste. In time, having won some degree of fame, he was appointed young Caracalla's dancing teacher. He also received his freedom. In fact, he became, like Festus, one of Caracalla's half-handful of favorites; and, more fortunate than Festus, he did not have to play Patroclus at Troy. Caracalla gave him an army to command, made him a Prefect. He traveled through the Empire on official business, mainly the obtaining of provisions; and because he traveled with authority, he could put people to death. For example, there was Flavius Titianus, procurator of Alexandria. When this man offended him somehow, Theocritus jumped up, drawing his sword. Flavius said, "Even when you did that, you looked like a dancer." He had just pronounced his own death sentence.

Theocritus apparently conducted the Armenian war like a dancer too. The Armenians slaughtered his troops.

Back at Antioch in 216, Caracalla turned his eyes on Parthia again. Alexander had had an Oriental bride, Roxana, the Bactrian princess. Caracalla would therefore and for other reasons have a Parthian bride.

He demanded the daughter of King Artabanus, Vologases' now-victorious brother, one of several monarchs who wished that the Emperor had stayed in Egypt. Caracalla wanted to attach Parthia to the Roman Empire so that he might increase his own glory and especially so that he, like Alexander, might be said to rule over central Asia.

Artabanus was weak, but not weak enough to accede at once to Caracalla's wishes. His refusal gave the Emperor a pretext; the disappointed suitor hurled his troops against Parthia.

Artabanus was caught with his defenses down; whatever soldiers he had were not in readiness. The Roman army marched unopposed through Parthia, plundering, raping, burning, and ravaging—conducting more an orgy than a war. Under Caracalla's orders, the soldiers committed the outrage of entering the tombs of the Parthian kings and scattering the royal ashes to the winds. That was Caracalla's Parthian victory. He did not gain the princess, but he gained a great deal to boast about.

The Osrhoënians occupied a part of Mesopotamia which had been restored to its rightful king by Severus. They were supposed to function as a buffer state between Parthia and the Roman portion of Mesopotamia, helping Rome whenever help was required; and Osrhoënian bowmen served in Caracalla's army. But Caracalla apparently distrusted the king, Abgar. Perhaps Abgar had been conspiring with the Parthians against Rome, or perhaps he had been accused of doing this; or perhaps Caracalla simply thought that his kingdom should belong to Rome. Its principal city, Edessa, was not only on a lucrative caravan route but was strategically located for purposes of defense, and it would certainly be safer in Roman hands than in the hands of undependable Osrhoënians.

Whatever the reason might have been, Caracalla invited King Abgar to come to him, shut the monarch up in prison, and declared Edessa a Roman colony. He took up quarters there himself in the winter of 216/217.

But that was to be his last significant act of deception.

One of Caracalla's two Praetorian Prefects was a man from northern Africa named Macrinus. Whereas Severus had been of Carthaginian ancestry, Macrinus was a Moor; he even had a hole in his ear for a ring, as many Moors did. Intelligent and ambitious, he raised himself from the semi-obscurity of his birth by studying civil law. At Rome during the reign of Severus, he obtained the esteem of Plautian, who made him his steward. He gathered much money. In the shake-up following Plautian's assassination he was exiled to Africa, but by practicing both law and rhetoric he managed to keep himself prosperous and in the public eye. Severus, having pardoned him, put him in charge of superintending traffic on the Flaminian Way. Under Caracalla he was elevated to the order of knights, given other offices, and finally made Praetorian Prefect.

Being Prefect, however, had its disadvantages. Caracalla expected him to come along on campaigns, and Macrinus found a military life much less appealing than a civilian one. He liked to eat and dress well, possibly because he had not always been able to do these things; and Caracalla, reveling in the hard life of the common soldier, called him soft and ridiculed him. The other Praetorian Prefect, Adventus, was a much better soldier, said Caracalla, although anybody could see that Adventus was a fool in his dotage. Macrinus inwardly seethed. He may have wished then to be Emperor, but he probably had no intention of making his wish come true. It was circumstances that forced him to take Caracalla's place.

An Egyptian seer named Serapio told the Emperor that he did not have much longer to live and that he would be succeeded by Macrinus. Very much embarrassed, Macrinus persuaded Caracalla to throw Serapio to a lion, as a liar. The Egyptian would not withdraw his prophecy when faced with death, however, and the lion would not eat him. Serapio merely held out his hand and the beast became amicable. A man did the job which the lion would not do: Serapio was killed. But Macrinus knew how much importance Caracalla, who kept augurs, astrologers, and magicians around himself all the time, attached to prophecies. He suspected that Caracalla thought the seer had been telling the truth, and that consequently Caracalla was plotting his death. He would have to kill the Emperor to prevent the Emperor from killing him.

Caracalla had left at Rome an official named Materianus, with instructions to report information gathered from diviners in the city concerning affairs of state and in particular to report evidence of disloyalty. Materianus, either because he did not like Macrinus or because he had really heard something against him, wrote a letter stating that a prophetess in Africa had said Macrinus was destined to be Emperor. According to Cassius Dio, probably the most reliable historian of these dark and complicated matters, the letter was delivered not to Caracalla but to Julia Domna, who looked through the imperial mail at Antioch while her son was at Edessa in the Osrhoënian country. Meanwhile a friend of Macrinus in Rome got word of the prophecy and wrote to Macrinus himself, who consequently knew that he was about to be implicated in a design against the Emperor's life and that he would have to act quickly.

One of the horse guards, a man named Martialis, thought a great deal of Macrinus but hated the Emperor. Nobody knows for certain why he hated him; there is a story that Caracalla would not promote him to the rank of centurion, and there is another story that Caracalla had put the man's brother to death without justification. At any rate, Macrinus used him to commit the murder.

The winter was behind Caracalla and he was as restless as ever. In April of 217 he decided to travel from Edessa to the city of Carrhae so that he could sacrifice to Lunus the moon god, who had a great temple there. He took his horse guards along with him.

Prognostications of his death had been disturbing his mind. His father, with a sword on, had come to him in a dream and said, "Just as you killed your brother, I am going to kill you." His lion Rapier had behaved strangely. Although Caracalla kept a number of lions as pets, Rapier was his favorite; Rapier ate at his table and slept in his bedroom and enjoyed being stroked by the hand of his master; the Emperor did not expect Rapier to attack him. But the beast jumped at him one day and clawed his clothes. In addition, there were unfavorable words from the soothsayers, and of course there was the prophecy of Serapio. All this amounted to a great deal to worry about.

On the ride toward Carrhae Caracalla, finding it necessary to relieve himself, got off his horse. Martialis approached as if to address him, but mortally stabbed him with a dagger.

That was all. No final words, no heroic gestures, only a sudden thrust from a dagger. The prophecy had begun to be fulfilled.

# ❧ XI ❧

## *Macrinus: The Interlude*

Martialis did not long enjoy his revenge. He was foolish enough to keep the bloody dagger in his hand, and the soldiers quickly identified him as the killer. One of Caracalla's Scythian bodyguards impaled him on a javelin.

Macrinus' name was not immediately associated with the assassination; people ascribed the murder solely to a desire for revenge on the part of Martialis. For several days the Empire was without an Emperor, and Macrinus concealed the fact that he thought himself eminently qualified. He also shed many tears over the body of the would-be Alexander. He arranged for the funeral, had Caracalla's ashes enclosed in an urn, and sent the urn to Julia Domna at Antioch.

The troops were inconsolable. Hated though Caracalla had been by the upper classes at Rome and by all who had favored Geta, he had remained popular with the soldiers to the last, not only because he was solicitous about their financial and physical well-being, but also because he liked and admired them and because he was above everything else a military man himself like his illustrious father. He had left no children; now what would happen to the dynasty which Severus had worked so hard to establish? And what would happen to the poor forgotten soldiers? And where would they find another brave and generous leader with their interests at heart? Macrinus wailed along with them, partly in order to win them over.

On the fourth day after the murder the Praetorian Guard and the legionaries met to elect a new Emperor. They felt sure that the Senate would agree to their choice; otherwise the Senate would have to answer to them. The most obvious choice was an army leader, and the most obvious army leaders were the two Praetorian Prefects. Adventus, the senior Prefect, was probably offered the Empire first, but declined it on account of his very advanced age (some people called it his senility). The offer was made to Macrinus. He appeared reluctant, but he accepted. On April 11, he was hailed as the new chief of the troops and master of the Empire. He immediately conformed to expectation by distributing money among the soldiers.

An Emperor was sorely needed; the Parthian war, it seemed, was not yet over. Having recovered from the surprise attack, King Artabanus was advancing with a powerful army. He wished especially to avenge the carefree distribution of his ancestors' ashes to the winds. Caracalla had escaped his vengeance through death, but in the long run it did not make much difference: Romans were Romans. Macrinus would feel his ire.

At Antioch Julia Domna received the ashes of her son with desperate grief. Geta had been killed by Caracalla at the age of twenty-three; Caracalla had been killed at the age of twenty-nine; she had no children left, and no husband—only her sister and her two nieces and their sons, and she did not regard any of these relatives with great devotion. She sobbed in a fury of agony and frustration, and she screamed out her hatred of Macrinus, whom she suspected of murder. It was not that she had loved Caracalla abundantly, although her relationship with him of late had been gratifying enough. It was not even principally that her husband and the products of her womb had preceded her to death, although her aloneness sharpened her sorrow. It was that she had been Empress of Rome for twenty-four years, had for the past several years been at the summit of her authority, and had hoped for many more years of rule. Now she would have to give up her special complement of Praetorian Guards and her imperial retinue, and her power. Men would no longer fawn on her, looking as if they wanted to lick the ground under her feet. She would not be brought the official correspondence to examine and evaluate and answer with letters of her own dictation. Suddenly she had no claim to the Empire; she would be obliged to return to private life, and private life was an indignity for a woman fashioned as she was, a woman who bore the titles

Mother of the Camps, Mother of the Augustuses, Mother of the Senate, Mother of the Fatherland. She would rather die.

Perhaps she was dying slowly anyway; she sometimes thought that the pains in her breast would end with her death. So she would hasten the process; she was not born to be patient. She would starve herself.

But Macrinus changed her plans. The loathsome usurper acted toward her with unexpected kindness, sending her a message of condolence and making no move to deprive her of her retinue or her guards. She was still the Augusta and could hold her head high. She dried her eyes; grief was for private persons. The soldiers at Antioch were fond of her; many were devoted to her; she started scheming with them for the overthrow of Macrinus.

For the moment, Macrinus was too busy doing other things to pay much attention to Julia Domna. Being a lawyer by profession, he put a great deal of emphasis on legal matters. For example, he revoked all the condemnations for treason handed down during Caracalla's reign, and there were many of these. (One young man, it is said, had been condemned to death for the treasonable offense of carrying a coin which contained Caracalla's portrait when he went into a brothel.) He reduced the taxes on inheritance and on manumission of slaves to what they had been before Caracalla raised them, annulled pensions paid from the public treasury to men unworthy of receiving them, and in general did what he could to ingratiate himself with civilians, as well as with soldiers.

In his letter to the Senate he was careful to disclaim any part in Caracalla's murder and to say nothing extremely derogatory about his predecessor (except that he did blame Caracalla for the Parthian war). He knew that the senators would not mind hearing Caracalla damned, but the army would learn of the contents of the letter too. With a semblance of humility he asked the Senate to confirm the honor which the troops had bestowed on him, and he promised to be a good Emperor, not a tyrant but a man who would always keep in mind the prerogatives and well-being of the citizens. In contradiction to his apparent modesty, however, he signed the letter with the imperial titles that he was asking the Senate to confirm. This offended the senators slightly; he could have had the decency to wait, even if he did not consider their confirmation highly important; but they gravely acceded to his wishes, partly because they had neither the strength nor the originality to initiate any other course of action.

Besides, on the whole they were glad to see him their Emperor. It was true that he had held the post of Praetorian Prefect, but he was much more a lawyer than a soldier.

Furthermore, almost anybody was preferable to Caracalla. The Senate vented its fury on the dead Emperor by listing the people whose deaths he had contrived, equating him with the most despicable tyrants in the history of Rome, abolishing the chariot races customarily held in celebration of his birthday, stipulating that gold and silver statues of him should be melted down, and demanding the punishment of the unconscionable opportunists who had acted as his spies and informers. The Senate did not, however, declare him a public enemy; there were soldiers in Rome.

Perhaps it was to forestall accusations of unfairness that Macrinus lavished favors on old Adventus, his colleague in the Praetorian prefecture, who probably did not want them any more than he had wanted to be Emperor. Macrinus made Adventus a senator, sent him to Rome as Prefect of the City, and nominated him consul besides. The senators were as disgusted by the presence of Adventus in their midst as by anything in the new reign. The ancient man was not fit for office, being nearly blind—not that eyesight would have helped him a great deal in carrying out his duties, since he had never learned much from reading. What was worse, he had commenced his military service as a mercenary. Possessing no social polish and little knowledge of politics, he pretended to be sick so that he would not have to attend the ceremonies held for his installation as consul; he apparently had enough sense to realize that if he exposed himself in public the result would be grotesque. With this low-born incompetent in high office, and a man with a hole through his ear on the throne, the government seemed to be falling into the hands of the vulgar. The patricians kept relatively quiet but looked askance, and Macrinus, hearing about their unhappiness, had to appoint a replacement for Adventus as Prefect of Rome.

It did not take long for Macrinus to be informed that Julia Domna was conspiring against him with the soldiers in Antioch. Still anxious to be gentle with her, he simply ordered her to leave Antioch and proceed to Emesa, her home town, where her sister and nieces were also to move at his command.

The order was light enough, but to Julia Domna it sounded like the prelude to a long humiliation. She did not have the strength for more conspiracy; she felt sure that the cancer in her breast, perhaps aggravated when she struck it in her grief over Caracalla, was killing her. Of course it was a shame to die before she was old (she could not have been much more than fifty), but she had lost interest in life. She could look back on glory—the conversations with litterateurs and philosophers, the participation in the Empire, the military campaigns with her husband, the almost unlimited power she had exercised under Caracalla, the honors accorded her all over the Roman world (for inscriptions praised her, statues reproduced her likeness, and she saw her face on coins). She had to look back on horrors too—Plautian principally, and Geta's murder. But she had held her head high even when Plautian accused her of adultery, and she would hold her head high now. Although she was too tired and tormented with pain to fight, she would show Macrinus that an Empress does not submit. She would not obey his order to go to Emesa.

Instead, she resumed her original intention and ended her life by starving herself.

A greater menace than Julia Domna was King Artabanus of Parthia, who was coming to take revenge on the Romans. When he invaded the province of Mesopotamia the Emperor at the head of his armies felt reluctant to meet him; it was not that Macrinus was a complete coward, but he was not much accustomed to military matters and wanted to relax at Antioch or somewhere else that was pleasant. He sent Artabanus a conciliatory message, saying that the devastation of Parthia had been entirely Caracalla's fault and suggesting peace. He also returned the Parthians that Caracalla had taken captive. But Artabanus was not to be conciliated, probably evaluating the new Emperor as a weak man or in any case a man less ruthless than Caracalla. He demanded that Macrinus rebuild the forts which Caracalla had damaged, rebuild the cities which Caracalla had ruined, give Mesopotamia back to Parthia, and, above all, supply financial compensation for the scattering of the royal Parthian ashes to the winds.

The terms were hard, but before Macrinus had decided whether or not to swallow them an uncontemplated battle developed. The Parthian and the Roman armies were encamped near Nisibis, facing each other, with water between them. It was over the water supply that the two armies began fighting, and the fight went on for three days in the fall of 217—an inconclusive, enervating kind of warfare that gave neither army an advantage and procured glory for no one except the insignificant baggage carriers and armor bearers attached to the Roman force. These humble servitors saved the Roman camp by rushing out at the Parthians more bravely than the soldiers might have done and shocking them into retreat. At the end of the three days, however, neither force had really given up and everybody was dissatisfied. The Roman soldiers, in fact, acted surly and almost rebellious. Macrinus was no general: that was obvious. Caracalla would not have led them so hesitantly, and neither would Severus.

Realizing that the longer the war continued the less respect his men would have for him, Macrinus again suggested peace to the Parthians. This time they seemed willing (being exhausted), and the terms were not wholly disadvantageous to Rome, although they were expensive. Macrinus promised enormous sums of money to King Artabanus and the chief men of Parthia in expiation of the Roman insult—two hundred million sesterces, according to Cassius Dio—but Mesopotamia remained a part of the Roman Empire.

There was still Armenia to pacify, but money and negotiations solved the difficulties there too. The rightful Armenian sovereign ascended his throne with Roman approval, and Rome gave him back his mother, whom Caracalla had incarcerated. Macrinus expended sizable sums in reparation for the ravages committed by Caracalla's soldiers in Armenia. The East was now at peace, and he could go to Antioch.

Here he thought he lived like an Emperor—lavishly. His clothing was so gorgeous as to affront those Romans who still had some conception of the simplicity which had characterized the years of Rome's rise to power. On his head he wore a gold fillet set with jewels—not an extraordinary extravagance for an Emperor, perhaps, except that it suited some Oriental tyrant more than the first citizen of the Roman republic. To the more critical of the courtiers he seemed to be posing, with his carefully curled beard and his studiedly magnificent manner; and they remembered that Caracalla's affectation had been of a different kind, in the direction of military austerity rather than pretentious display. This man was vulgar; he did not know how to be an Emperor. In an attempt to imitate Marcus Aurelius, he paused at length before responding to questions and then spoke in a grave voice which was not his own (as everybody knew) and at such a low volume that people could hardly hear him. If he thought such antics imperial, he was a fool.

He attended shows at Antioch, listened to music, feasted, and had a rather enjoyable time, although he did not always feel quite secure in his rule. To have risen from his lowly origin to this supreme position was almost too much to believe. At least he could do his best not to incur the dislike of important people. The Senate had wanted Caracalla's informers prosecuted. If the informers were influential, if they belonged to Rome's proudest families, Macrinus tried to keep their names from being divulged to himself. In order to satisfy the Senate, however, he did allow three particularly heinous upper class talebearers to be tried, but he forbade condemning them to death. They were exiled to remote islands. It was, of course, a different matter with informers who occupied a lower station in society; they could be sacrificed to the senatorial demand for justice. Slaves who had betrayed their masters to Caracalla were crucified.

The population of the capital had not seen an Emperor now in several years; Caracalla had been on campaign continuously since 213, and Macrinus showed no desire to hurry to Rome. The citizens could judge him only from what they heard about him and from his actions —his appointment of ridiculous old Adventus, for example, or his appointment of others who were scarcely more deserving of governmental positions, or his response to the Parthian invasion. He had a son called Diadumenian, whom the Senate had proclaimed Caesar at his request. On September 14, 217, the boy's ninth birthday was celebrated with chariot races at Rome. The enormous crowd was in an ugly mood and felt free to indulge in self-expression because the Emperor was a long way off. "All nations have a leader," somebody shouted, "except the Roman nation." Somebody else took up the sentiment: "We have no leader, we have no leader." The senators and knights in the audience, who were loyally eulogizing Macrinus and his son, looked disturbed, but the populace paid no attention. Men called on Jupiter, or

Jove, king of the gods: "Only you are worthy to lead us. Father Jove, do not be angry at us any more. Father Jove, take pity on us." They raised their hands to the sky and hailed Jupiter as their ruler. That was how they celebrated the birthday of the son of the Emperor.

The Roman populace was terrified when the Flavian Amphitheatre (the Coliseum) was struck by lightning, the weapon of Jupiter and Minerva. The lightning started a ferocious fire that destroyed the topmost story and burned everything in the arena. It would take many years for the amphitheatre to be restored. What did all this mean? The event must signify that something calamitous was going to happen to the state.

But Macrinus was not worried about the opinions of the populace; it was the army, critical, foul-tempered, vaguely mutinous, and addicted to pleasure, that worried him. He had already tried to satisfy the troops by telling them that, with their consent, he wanted to give the boy Diadumenian the additional name Antoninus, which had, of course, been Caracalla's official name and which for that reason was beloved by the soldiers. They had received the suggestion enthusiastically, especially because Macrinus had promised them a bonus along with it. Perhaps they would follow a prince called Antoninus. He was only a child, of course, but he was tall for his age and would grow. They seemed to like him, their new Antoninus Diadumenian Caesar; they were lonesome for an Antoninus to serve. But the enthusiasm did not last long.

Macrinus thought he could satisfy them by stating that for all those already in the service at the time of his accession, the rights and privileges bestowed on the army by Caracalla would be continued; but he added that men entering the army during his own reign would be governed by the stricter standards that Severus had applied. His reasoning was probably sound: Caracalla had damaged the army by pampering it, and if Roman soldiers were to be Roman soldiers again they would have to submit to rigorous discipline; they could not expect the army to be a sinecure. He could scarcely hope to use stern measures with the old soldiers because they would probably revolt, but the fresh recruits might prove more malleable. There were not a great many of them so far, and by the time there were more, scattered over the Empire under stern commanders, the rigor might be too well established for a revolt to develop.

It soon became obvious, however, that nobody was satisfied. The new recruits, as he had feared, damned the unfairness of a double system, and the soldiers of longer standing suspected that as soon as he got the opportunity he would reduce them to the same condition as the levies. The rumor that this was his intention spread through the camps. The Parthian war, besides, had not provided anybody with very much booty or glory or pleasure; Macrinus' conduct of the campaign still rankled. The situation would have been better for Macrinus if the troops had already been dispersed to various parts of the Empire. Too many of them were still in Syria because of the Parthian crisis—at Antioch, for example, and at Emesa—so that seditious suggestions spread quickly among them.

He would have to brazen it out. A few soldiers carried discontent to the point of open rebellion; he gave them the execution that they deserved, hoping that his inflexible justice would deter others. They were beasts, these soldiers, demanding special treatment because they supposedly defended the Empire, ungrateful when a commander tried to act in their own best interests, insolent because they knew that they could make or break Emperors—uncultivated, most of them, wallowing in luxury, which the government paid for, and unable to enjoy the luxury with proper relish. He would show them what a real Emperor thought of them.

At Emesa there lived at this time a clever and very ambitious woman. Julia Maesa, sister of Julia Domna, had moved from Antioch to the city of her birth on Macrinus' orders, taking along her two daughters, both widows, and their two sons. But she was not finished. Like Julia Domna, she had become accustomed to the adulation of the great. Not that they had bowed and scraped to her as much as to Julia Domna, but as the sister-in-law of the Emperor Septimius Severus and the aunt of the Emperors Geta and Caracalla she had enjoyed prestige. Of course she possessed prestige at Emesa, since she was incredibly rich, but she wanted a great deal more than provincial honor. She wanted to see her dynasty on the throne again. Macrinus could be beaten. Her sister had not fought him, but her sister had been ill. Julia Maesa would use whatever means she could summon to get back to Rome in a position of authority. She had a candidate for the throne, one whom she could probably influence and control—her fourteen-year-old grandson, the only child of her profligate daughter Julia Soaemias. Named Varius Avitus, he was called Bassianus after his great-grandfather, high priest of the Sun at Emesa. Later he came to be known as Elagabalus, after his god.

In spite of his youth Bassianus now fulfilled the functions of high priest of the Sun; his grandmother Maesa had procured him that office already. It was an office which belonged to him by right of inheritance anyway; through the female side of his family, he was of course legitimately descended from the priest-kings of Emesa, who had retained their royal title until late in the first century, perhaps even the second century, and to whose progeny the priesthood still belonged. The god they served, Elagabalus (sometimes incorrectly called Heliogabalus), was the prime deity at Emesa. His magnificent temple shone with the gifts of gold and precious stones which Oriental potentates and affluent merchants or aristocrats had left there as offerings (the popularity of his cult in the East was, in fact, the principal source of the family's great wealth). In this temple stood a conical black stone, a meteorite, which was evidently associated with the phallus of the Sun God himself. This object was the focal point of the faith.

When the young Bassianus danced for the Sun God, attended by inferior priests in resplendent garments, Emesa crowded to watch, and if they had the chance, the soldiers encamped near the city watched too. People came from far away as the boy's reputation grew. He wore a diadem glittering with jewels, a tunic of purple and shimmering gold whose wide sleeves drooped all the way to the floor, and boots of soft gilded leather. Advancing, retreating, swaying, advancing, he danced extremely well, with the grace of a girl, to the music of flutes and cymbals. The god whom he adored was not a strictly local divinity, puissant only for Emesan votaries; under various forms the Sun was being worshipped by more and more people in the eastern half of the Empire, in Rome herself, and even on the barbarian frontiers, where recruits from the Orient had carried his religion. Although the ceremonies at Emesa may have impressed some of the soldiers as strange or exotic, quite a few of them probably felt religious stirrings of their own as they saw Bassianus dance. He seemed almost godlike himself, this beautiful boy-priest moving magically in honor of the Sun.

Maesa, noting her grandson's popularity among the troops, circulated the story that he was actually the illegitimate son of Caracalla.

His mother Soaemias did not contradict the rumor. For all she knew, he may have been Caracalla's son; her activities at Rome resolved themselves into a confused though colorful blur. At any rate, her character had been impugned so often already that calling her the mistress of her cousin Caracalla could not hurt it. Far from minding the imputation, she felt that if it helped to gain her son the throne it was worth a few long looks from the pure.

Bassianus even bore a facial resemblance to Caracalla, although the resemblance was probably due to a hereditary handsomeness of features in the Syrian family to which Caracalla and he both belonged, rather than to a father-and-son relationship. What was most important, the story satisfied the soldiers. Here was the son of their generous, murdered Emperor, the young prince they had been waiting for, the youth who should lead them and for whom they would willingly die. Here was the rightful Emperor of Rome.

The heavens helped Maesa. In April of 218 occurred an eclipse of the sun, and the daytime darkness, a thing whose eeriness chilled soldiers as well as civilians, could easily be interpreted as a sign of the Sun God's unhappiness with the reign of Macrinus. Not much later a comet appeared in bright day, and a comet meant the coming of a redeemer, someone to revive the dragging world. Maesa felt that it was time to act.

Other reasons besides celestial ones also convinced her of this. Since Rome was now at peace with Parthia and Armenia, the troops at Emesa could devote all their efforts toward defeating Macrinus. If she waited too long Macrinus would go to Rome, and he had to be conquered in person. In addition, the longer she waited the more time he would have to summon the military resources from the faraway provinces and send them against her.

On a spring night Bassianus was introduced into the camp outside Emesa by his elders, and the next morning at sunrise he was revealed. The troops cheered him lustily. They hailed him as Emperor.

In the midst of the delights of Antioch Macrinus was not extremely worried about developments at Emesa. The soldiers were much more a problem than a boy of fourteen, his promiscuous mother, and his middle-aged grandmother. Macrinus knew these people; they were eager for power, and of course they were displeased that he had become ruler of the world, but they did not represent a serious menace. Their whole military strength was the legionaries at the Emesan camp. They were foolish to contemplate open rebellion; he had credited them with more intelligence than that. Of course he would have to deal with them, but not in person. He would send his Praetorian Prefect, Ulpius Julianus, to defeat them and bring back young Bassianus' head.

In the meantime he could do something positive and constructive. He went to a camp of the Praetorians at Apamaea (not inconveniently far from Antioch) and had his own son Diadumenian, now called Antoninus, proclaimed co-Emperor there. If the troops at Emesa could have a boy Emperor, his troops could have one too—but a legitimate one, his son, whose very name would attract followers away from the dancing high priest. He promised each of the Praetorians twenty thousand sesterces for hailing his boy their new Augustus, gave each man a fourth of this sum on the spot, and restored privileges which he had taken from the soldiers—in fact, he courted the military in as many ways as he could reconcile with his contempt for them.

The nine-year-old Diadumenian probably did not have much conception of what was going on. He may not have wanted to be an Emperor, or, on the other hand, he may have liked the cheers and the subservience. He is little more than a name to us; we do not know. We know only that he fit into his father's plans.

Ulpius Julianus marched to Emesa and laid siege to the camp. Some of his soldiers were restless, discontented, and factitious, and obviously thought that the boy they were trying to conquer would make a better Emperor than the man whom they were defending. Others, however, being Moors like Macrinus, fought hard and succeeded in breaking open several of the camp gates; but then Julianus ordered his soldiers to withdraw for the night. Whether he was afraid that the Emesan troops would massacre his own army inside their camp, or whether he expected the Emesan troops to sue for peace, or whether he had some other reason, the decision was in any case unwise.

During the night some of Bassianus' soldiers fortified the gates of the camp. A few crept through the darkness to the camp of Julianus' troops, where they were admitted as friends and where they spread seditious sentiments in the quiet hours, calling Bassianus the son of the great Caracalla, talking about his gold, promising and cajoling, ridiculing Macrinus as a coward.

In the morning Julianus attacked the Emesan camp again, but Bassianus' soldiers defended it well. A number of them brought Bassianus himself up on top of the wall, together with effigies of Caracalla, and carried him and the effigies along the ramparts in view of Julianus' army, pointing out how much the boy resembled these images, trying to prove that he was Caracalla's child. Screaming down at the besiegers, they asked how anyone could make war on the son of the soldiers' friend, the rightful heir to the Empire.

He was surrounded by bags of gold, his grandmother's contribution to the cause. Not at all diffident on a day so significant to his fortunes, he made a speech to Julianus' troops. They could have the gold, he said, if they joined him. The men were easy to win over; gold and the idea of a new Caracalla proved irresistible. Most of the officers, however, seemed to be loyal to Macrinus.

That was how a kind of butchery which Julianus had not dreamed of began. His men mobbed his officers, swarmed all over them, yelping and murdering. An emissary from Bassianus' army spurred them on by promising that each soldier who killed an officer could have the dead man's rank and property. Julianus, deciding that it was the duty of a Praetorian Prefect to exercise discretion, ran away and looked for a hiding place; meanwhile the men stripped the uniforms from their officers' corpses. Bloody but exhilerated, they marched into the camp to shake hands with the rebels they had come to conquer.

At Apamaea, Macrinus waited for news of a victory. One day he feasted the populace at enormous expense; loyalty cost money. He said that the feast was to celebrate the elevation of his son to the rank of Augustus. He did not allude to the uprising at Emesa; there was no point in mentioning it if it could be stopped at its source.

A soldier was let in; naturally nobody tried to keep him out, since he wore a Roman uniform and came from Emesa. After reporting that he had brought something for the Emperor from Julianus, he hastily departed.

The package was covered with cloth and tied with cords, and the seal was stamped with the Prefect's own signet ring. Macrinus, very much delighted, expected it to contain the head of Bassianus; in fact, a laconic note to this effect was enclosed. The head, however, did not belong to Bassianus; it was the head of Julianus himself, who had not found a safe hiding place. The odor was already threatening to become offensive.

In spite of all the defections, Macrinus still had a large army composed of men who, perhaps seeing little hope of a victory for Bassianus, remained loyal for reasons of personal security. Bassianus' forces were, however, growing steadily, so that the Syrian family no longer hesitated to send them against Macrinus in a full-scale battle. The troops soon set off southward in quest of him.

Macrinus dispatched a letter to the Senate, calling Bassianus an idiot child. The senators, with the caution born of very justifiable fear, weighed the chances of the two contenders and decided that it was easier to hold on to the imperium than to grab it, especially if the would-be grabber was a teenager supported by two women. They did not wish to see a return of the oppressive Severans to the throne anyway, and this teenager was supposed to be Caracalla's son. In consequence they declared war on Bassianus, his mother Soaemias, his grandmother Maesa, his aunt Mamaea, and his cousin Alexianus, Mamaea's little boy. As Macrinus requested, they promised immunity to all who had defected to the Syrian cause but were willing to return to the side of "right."

Macrinus at length decided that he would have to go to war again, personally, at the head of his troops. His own position must be made secure once and for all, and the grotesque joke centering on the Prefect's head must be avenged. On the eighth of June, at a place called Immae, a poor little huddle of buildings less than twenty miles from Antioch, the battle occurred.

It certainly did not look as if the odds were in favor of Bassianus. His troops, being Roman soldiers, were well trained, it is true; but their leader was his tutor Gannys, who had led a soft life in the luxuries of the court and could not be expected to understand much more about how to win a battle than a bath attendant would. Bassianus himself was present—their Emperor, a boy of fourteen, a dancing high priest of a Syrian sun god. His mother and grandmother were there too, in their chariots—rich ladies used to the gorgeousness of Rome—neither one of them much of a Semiramis. This trio could not contribute physical help but was supposed to inspire the troops to victory.

Although Gannys may not have possessed experience as a military commander, he proved to be surprisingly competent. He chose an advantageous position for his army (where a pass led from the village), stationed the men in excellent order, and spoke to them reasonably about how necessary it was for them to win, since if they lost they would probably be executed as traitors. Macrinus' forces attacked. Once more it was Roman against Roman. Gannys succeeded in bottling up many of Macrinus' soldiers in the narrow streets of the village, where there was hardly room for a sword-arm. The hot sun burned relentlessly down as the armies fought in and around the village, and some men dripped sweat while others dripped blood.

In spite of Gannys' strategy it soon looked as if the fight was going against Bassianus. Macrinus, who had dreaded this day, watched his soldiers snap the lines of the usurper and saw his enemies turn their backs. Maybe it was only money that made his men loyal, but at least they were fighting well today.

Then Maesa and Soaemias got down from their chariots, and placing themselves in front of the fleeing men, screamed at them and pleaded with them to turn around, to fight some more, to fight harder this time for the sake of Caracalla's son—the hard grandmother and the voluptuous mother exhorting, entreating, crying, confronting group after group, wildly extending their arms, aware that if they lost this battle their lives were forfeited; but not stressing this, stressing only bravery and the urgency of winning for beloved Bassianus, their lord. And Bassianus himself whirled past on a war horse, brandishing his sword and encouraging his men—the young Emperor, the soldiers' Emperor, the son of Caracalla, inspired at this moment by some force outside himself, emanating courage, filling his men with the power to fight for his cause. They faced Macrinus' forces and went to work, and Macrinus himself turned tail.

If he had not fled, his soldiers might have won in spite of the histrionics of the Syrian family, even though a number of his troops defected to the enemy. As it was, his most loyal defenders, his Praetorians, fought on until messengers from Bassianus informed them that they were fighting for a coward who had already left them. If they gave up, Bassianus would pardon them and receive them as his own Praetorians. There was no reason to decline his offer.

Macrinus rushed pell-mell to Antioch, having sent messengers on ahead to tell the citizens that his troops had been victorious. For the moment, the city welcomed him. But stragglers from the battle came in with a different story—that the conqueror and new young Emperor was approaching the city with his army. The Antiochenes were a feverish, high-strung people, and the news resulted in riots between the pro-Macrinus faction and the pro-Bassianus faction. Macrinus realized that his own partisans were the underdogs. While the citizens of Antioch were shedding one another's blood he put his son Diadumenian in the care of people he could trust, instructing them to take him to King Artabanus of Parthia for safekeeping; now that there was another Roman Emperor, one claiming descent from Caracalla, Artabanus would surely be Macrinus' friend. Then he too fled, managing to get out of Antioch before Bassianus came in. He would try to reach Rome, where the Senate was favorable to him. Perhaps he could recoup his fortunes there.

He had shaved his head and shaved the long, curly beard off his chin, and had thrown a dark cloak over his robe of imperial purple. In his disguise, or disgrace, he rode through northern Syria with a few faithful attendants, and people thought he was an ordinary, everyday citizen, this Emperor driven off by a boy. In southeastern Asia Minor, at Aegae in Cilicia, he adopted a new disguise: he was now a soldier employed by the Emperor as a courier, and he was traveling on official business. In this role he commandeered a chariot. Northwestward he drove through Asia Minor, traversing Cappadocia and Galatia with their unpleasant hills. He felt relatively confident that his son was safe in Parthia by this time, out of reach of the priest-Emperor; perhaps at the end of his life he would be able to leave the Roman world to the boy; but first he must reach Rome, talk to the Senate, and gather the western armies. He skulked through Bithynia, avoiding Nicomedia, its capital, because he was afraid of the Bithynian governor. From the port of Eribolon he took passage on a ship to Chalcedon, still in Bithynia but looking toward the European shore. Sailing along the Bithynian coast, he felt, would be less dangerous than proceeding to Chalcedon by land.

At Chalcedon he made a mistake. He was short of funds and sent to one of the procurators for money. In this way he was discovered. A gale apparently rose up to prevent him from crossing the Bosporus to Europe; during the wait, he was seized by ambitious timeservers.

When the bloodhounds who had been trailing him through Asia Minor arrived at Chalcedon he was turned over to them. One of them, a centurion, officially arrested him in the name of the Emperor.

Then he had to endure the trip back—southeastward through Asia Minor, across Bithynia, across Galatia, and into Cappadocia. Far from being in disguise now, he was a common criminal, a felonious Moor with a hole in one ear. The soldiers did not bind him, but the knowledge that he was in their power was enough to crush him. For fourteen months he had commanded all the legions of Rome; now he had to wait for death at the hands of these military men.

While he was still in Cappadocia news came that his son had been captured and executed, the little boy who may never have wanted to be an Emperor but whose father was ambitious and cunning. Macrinus managed to throw himself from his chariot, hoping for death, but he just broke his shoulder.

He was sentenced to die on the road, without ever seeing Antioch again. In fact, he did not even get out of Cappadocia. Late in June, in a city about seventy-five miles from the Syrian border, he was executed.

# ❦ XII ❦

# *Beginning to Reign*

At the age of fourteen Bassianus was secure on the throne of his pseudo father. He had taken his pseudo father's official name; like Caracalla, he was called "Antoninus" on inscriptions and coins, in letters and other documents. The nickname Elagabalus, which he later acquired, was probably given to him by his enemies because of his notorious affection for his god. Antoninus was his political name, suggesting his relationship with Caracalla and, more vaguely, with the hero-Emperors of the golden second century, Antoninus Pius and Marcus Aurelius Antoninus. But the Syrian boy-priest was not very deeply interested in these hero-Emperors. His nickname, being far more appropriate than Antoninus, is the name by which he has come to be known.

Elagabalus enjoyed a triumphal entry into Antioch on the day after the Battle of Immae. His soldiers were, of course, eager to exercise the prerogative of soldiers by plundering the city; they could even find a kind of justification for looting it in the fact that it had, after all, been Macrinus' capital. The Emperor, however, perhaps on the advice of elders such as his grandmother Maesa, his tutor Gannys, and the soldier Eutychianus, prevented the opulent metropolis from being sacked. He promised to give each soldier two thousand sesterces instead. This money was to be provided by the Antiochenes themselves, but they were probably glad to furnish it if it meant that their city would not be violated.

Elagabalus paid less attention to the prerogatives of the Senate than to those of his army. A letter had to be sent to the Senate, of course, and one to the Roman people as well. In both these messages he assumed the various titles in which the honors and powers of the Roman Emperor principally resided, titles which the Senate was supposed to bestow. The senators were naturally insulted by so flagrant a disregard of their traditional function as the voice of the republic. Macrinus had shown a similar disregard only too recently; it was apparently becoming an imperial tradition. Perhaps this boy really was Caracalla's bastard; he seemed to have inherited Caracalla's disrespect for senatorial privileges.

As was to be expected, the letter to the Senate disparaged Macrinus in some detail. The usurper, said Elagabalus, had not held senatorial rank—had been only a knight—and knights were not even allowed in the Senate house. Elagabalus or his advisors had apparently forgotten that boys of fourteen were not found in the Senate house either.

The senators may have been insulted, but they realized that they had supported the wrong candidate and that their mistake must be remedied. They declared Macrinus a public enemy. They also started praising Caracalla, whose memory they found execrable, and expressed the hope that his son might resemble him, which would be almost unbearable.

One of Elagabalus' first acts as Emperor was to disperse the soldiers. He did not exactly distrust them, since some of them had made him Emperor, but he or his advisors did not like to see so many of them collected together in one province. Their enormous strength was a potential danger; if Macrinus had scattered them over the Empire at the conclusion of the Parthian war, the rebellion against him might never have occurred. Sending them back to their permanent posts was a wise move.

Macrinus' most faithful adherents had to be put to death; this was an understandable necessity, a safety measure. The governor of Syria died, as did the commander in Arabia, the governor of Cyprus, and several rich inhabitants of Rome who had been violently in favor of Macrinus. On the whole, however, the reprisals were light, and no inquisition was instituted in order to ferret out clandestine supporters of Macrinus.

In Alexandria there was trouble. The citizens would rather be

ruled by the most savage tyrant in history than by a boy who claimed
to be Caracalla's son. When Elagabalus' messengers arrived at Alexandria in the course of the rebellion, those in authority had them killed.
When the news of Macrinus' execution reached the city, riots started,
since the soldiers were as much in favor of Elagabalus as the citizens
were against him. As if there had not been enough unnecessary deaths
during Caracalla's visit to Alexandria, there were more deaths now.
Elagabalus, however, did not take revenge on the unquiet city for
opposing him; one of the authorities was chased to Italy and killed, but
private citizens escaped punishment.

Apparently not everybody believed that Elagabalus' power was
firmly established; several attempts to seize the throne had to be
quelled. A couple of the wishful usurpers were senators serving in a
military capacity—the tribune of the Third Gallic Legion and the
tribune of the Fourth Scythian Legion, both of whom were executed.
Other wishful usurpers occupied humbler stations; perhaps the rise of
Macrinus from obscurity to the imperium had inspired them. One was
the son of a centurion in the Third Gallic; another, a comber of wool;
another, a person of undistinguished status whose object was to con-
taminate the loyalty of the fleet stationed off the western coast of Asia
Minor, where Elagabalus would soon be coming in order to take up
residence at Nicomedia. All of these comparative nonentities lost their
lives.

Slightly more complicated was the affair of Paetus, a senator from
Galatia. The charge was that he had struck gold coins with his own
face depicted on them (which was, of course, an act of rebellion in itself, and a rather obvious one), whereas he had actually just stamped
his portrait on pieces of metal never designed as currency and then
plated the metal with gold. He affirmed that he intended to give these
gold-plated likenesses of himself to his mistresses so that they would
keep him in mind, but his accusers declared that he intended to distribute the gold coins in Cappadocia, the province bordering his own,
in order to finance a revolution. His defense of himself was not persuasive.

The court traveled to Nicomedia for the winter of 218/219—the young
Emperor, his mother Soaemias, his grandmother Maesa, his aunt

Mamaea, his cousin Alexianus (several years younger than he), his tutor Gannys, the military man Eutychianus, and a crowd of favorites, dependents, sun priests, and eminent Syrians, plus the Praetorian Guard. With the exception of his aunt (whose morality was a reproach to almost everybody that came near her) and possibly his grandmother (who was too busy planning to rule the Empire to have much leisure for love) and of course little Alexianus (who was too young), it was a gay and fast-living assemblage. The imperial mother, Soaemias, set the tone by living with Gannys. As a matter of fact, she had been doing that for a long time. He was evidently a very talented man; it is not every educator who can command an army and retain the affections of an oversexed Empress. He may have been ambitious too, since he broached the subject of marrying Soaemias. Elagabalus seemed willing to let him marry his mother and even talked about appointing him Caesar.

Nicomedia, a city of Hellenistic style, capital of what had once been the independent kingdom of Bithynia, was a pleasant place in which to pass the winter. Elagabalus watched chariot races and had an enjoyable time. His sexual interests, however, were developing in an embarrassing direction. It became increasingly clear to the courtiers that he preferred males to females, and that he had a tendency toward satyriasis, too. But these quirks might be corrected or counterbalanced; they were not anything to worry about immediately.

At least, that was how most people felt. Gannys seems to have felt differently. The records of the sojourn at Nicomedia are meager, but he apparently took to reproaching the Emperor for immoderate, imprudent living (perhaps on the instigation of Maesa), and Elagabalus must have decided that he would not like Gannys for a stepfather. (Gannys' own life was not, of course, an example of discretion.) Elagabalus, in his resentment of the tutor's reprimands, forgot that this same presumptuous pedagogue had had a great deal to do with his own elevation to the throne, not only at the Battle of Immae but also in the planning of the psychological campaign that preceded the battle. The specific occasion is not known, but one day Elagabalus, irate at something Gannys had said or done, rushed at his tutor with a weapon and drew blood. Gannys drew his sword in self-defense, but there were guards standing by and they murdered him.

The court of Elagabalus remained at Nicomedia until past the middle of May 219. That was longer than people had expected. Either Elagabalus was in no hurry to reach Rome or else, as is probable, he had a protracted illness. In any case, the citizens of Rome were eager for his presence; and Maesa, who knew that they had disliked Macrinus for not coming to Rome, was anxious to get started for the capital. But there were matters that presumably had to be settled first.

The most pressing one was the question of clothes. Elagabalus did not like the clothing of the Romans, considering it too plain. Wool, the material from which togas were made, displeased him; it was harsh, irritating, unluxurious. He preferred the dress of Syrian priests, and consequently acquired the nickname "the Assyrian." He would appear in public in silken robes of purple and gold ornamented with precious stones. Silk was at the time a textile of great rarity; occasionally a Roman lady of fantastic wealth would wear silk, but it was always considered ostentatious, and Roman men did not wear it for fear of incurring the jeers of their fellows. The Emperor's robes, besides, were of Phoenician cut, and in order to set off their effeminate splendor, he weighted himself down with precious bracelets, necklaces, and a tiara. Maesa was firm: he could not ride into Rome in that kind of costume. He agreed that it would constitute a shock for the Romans, especially if they were not prepared for him. The best course, he decided, was to send on ahead a full-length picture of himself in his priestly garments, standing beside the Sun God. He would also send orders that this portrait of himself and his god should be hung in the Senate house, where the senators could honor it with incense and libations of wine when they came in to transact their business.

His loyalty to his god was even stronger than his passion for sex— unreasoning and overwhelming. The conical black stone had been transported from Emesa to Nicomedia and would accompany him to Rome, where he would build a proper temple for it. When he was settled at Rome he would make the Sun supreme among the deities of the Empire. That was to be his policy.

# ❧ XIII ❧

## *Establishing a Religion*

Elagabalus with his entourage entered Rome in June or July 219. It was, of course, a very important occasion, and the citizens were out in throngs to see what kind of Emperor the gods had given them this time. If we are to believe the historian Herodian (who was not a contemporary), the young Syrian's clothes were silken and extravagantly Oriental, a pearl necklace gleamed at his throat, jewels glittered in his hair, his cheeks blushed with rouge, and his eyes sparkled as artificially as his cheeks blushed. Evidently grandmother Maesa had not prevailed. Since other historians do not describe his entry into Rome as in any way remarkable, however, it is possible that Herodian had abandoned truth for the allurements of fiction; there is no way of telling. But even if his entry into the capital was carried out in a decent Roman manner, Elagabalus soon enough became famous for his foreign taste in dress. Not that this was the only way in which he offended the sober Romans.

As soon as he could, he set about trying to establish the god Elagabalus as the foremost Roman divinity. What his grandmother thought at this stage about his plan to proselytize the Romans, or to force his god on them if persuasion failed, or to promote the Sun in whatever other way seemed necessary, we do not know. She probably applauded the intention; after all, the Sun God was the patron of her family, and her whole house was devoted to him, particularly Elagabalus' mother, Soaemias. But as a practical woman she may have disliked the plan.

A god associated with the sun was by no means unknown at

Rome, although most Romans who worshipped such a deity did not call him Elagabalus. Even aside from the Homeric Helios and the classical Apollo (not originally a god of the sun but confused with him), there had been sun gods adored at Rome for a long time. On the whole, the Emperors encouraged the sun cults because a certain connection existed between sun-worship and Emperor-worship. The crown of pointed rays which the Emperor wore on one of his coin denominations, and which would in time become almost inseparable from the idea of kingship, suggested that the Emperor was analogous to the solar deity, or at least that he was supported by this deity.

Among the varieties of sun god reverenced at Rome and in other parts of the Empire the most popular was undoubtedly Mithra. Having come from Persia, Mithra had reached Italy toward the beginning of the first century after Christ, if not earlier, and had been accorded official recognition toward the end of the second century by his convert Commodus. In his purest form, his original Persian form, he did not represent the sun but was rather the hero-comrade of the Sun God; but most of his Roman followers in the early third century, that age of religious confusion and amalgamation, had forgotten this distinction and would have identified him with Sol—the Unconquerable Sun, as he was often called.

Unlike the god Elagabalus, Mithra was almost exclusively a divinity for men. Women on rare occasions may have been admitted to his cult, but by and large his secrets were for male initiates only. As the Unconquerable Sun he appealed strongly to soldiers, and his religion was carried over the Empire by men who had entered the army in the eastern provinces. Wherever the soldiers from the East went, shrines to Mithra were built. Even in Britain the legionaries dedicated altars to the Persian god.

In Persian religion Mithra was much more than a mere superhuman warrior; he combated the evil principle, Ahriman, for the sake of the supreme god, Ahura-Mazda. He guarded the good, overcame demons, rescued the deserving, delivered humanity from malevolent forces. He was the savior god, and this conception of him remained one of the most fundamental aspects of his cult in the third century. Perhaps because the sun, which dies every evening, renews itself every morning, he also came to be associated with rebirth, with immortality. Like Serapis he promised everlasting life to his conscientious worshippers. This was probably one reason for his widespread popularity in the third century, not only among the military, who might expect to die at any moment, but also among others in an unusually death-conscious age. Through the adoration of Mithra the Conqueror, one could overcome death. Many of the poor, weak, and sick were attracted to Mithraism because of this promise, just as many were attracted to Christianity.

The cult of Mithra borrowed practices and concepts from non-Persian peoples. It acquired from the Babylonians the numerology and astrological lore they considered so important, so that each of the regions through which the soul was thought to ascend after death to Ahura-Mazda was conceived of as being ruled by one of the planets. From followers in the part of Asia Minor called Phrygia Mithra received his attire, particularly the Phrygian cap, a tight-fitting headpiece with a turned-over top, which he was usually shown wearing in sculptures. His religion resembled the other great creed of Asia Minor, the cult of the Great Mother, in the *taurobolium*, the participation in the blood of a bull. The bull was apparently slain on a platform above the believer, who let the warm blood fall into his mouth and all over him. In sculptures Mithra was often depicted slaying a bull—leaping on it, yanking back its strong neck, and stabbing it in the throat. His followers expected him to do this on their Doomsday, when mortal change would be ended; death would then be dead.

The early Christians objected that Mithraism was stealing ideas from them, and the Mithraists probably maintained the thefts were in the other direction. In any case, the two faiths had several elements in common. For instance, the Mithraists, like the Christians, named December 25 a feast day (because it marked the birth of the Sun), baptized with water, and celebrated communion, in which the higher grades of believers were given sacred bread to eat and watered wine to drink. In addition, there were the expectation of a Doomsday, the promise of the soul's immortality, and the conception of a savior from sin, a redeemer of mankind.

For all those reasons, Mithraism was apparently far different from the worship of the god Elagabalus. Although we know comparatively little about the Elagabalus cult, we do know that the conical black stone was essential to it, that an eagle was the god's own bird (as it was Jupiter's), and that the god in an early form had been the Baal, or Lord, of Emesa, one of many Baals adored in the East. We know also that his cult included women as well as men, and that its gorgeous rituals were at an opposite extreme from the solemn, secret ceremonies which took place in the grottoes or grottolike chapels dedicated to Mithra. We can assume that the emphasis on goodness was somewhat less important in the religion of Elagabalus than in Mithraism.

It must, in fact, have taken a very energetic syncretistic spirit to identify the two faiths. That such identification did occur in the minds of some Romans, however, especially members of the lower classes, is extremely probable. Mithra and Elagabalus and the other sun deities were evidently rolled together into one invincible Sun God, in the pious opinions of Romans who did not take the trouble to keep them separate, who thought they should not be separated, or who were not sufficiently subtle to see distinctions.

The immediate result was that a number of people at Rome were willing to pay homage to the new young Emperor's deity. Many of these, but not all, were unquestionably immigrants to the capital from the East. Significantly enough, half a century after the reign of the Syrian priest, the Emperor Aurelian was able to make the Sun God Elagabalus the foremost deity of the Empire, erecting a grandiose temple to him at Rome, creating a college of priests for him, and celebrating his birthday on December 25 with great joy. And the Unconquerable Sun probably continued to be unconquered into the reign of Constantine, who, like Aurelian, pictured the ray-crowned divinity on his coins. Constantine's recognition of Christianity as an allowable religion of the state in 313 certainly did the worship of the sun a great deal of harm, as did Constantine's own conversion to Christianity, but the Sun God took a long time to die.

Early in the third century, therefore, the Syrian boy might possibly have succeeded in establishing the worship of the divine Elagabalus at Rome if the boy himself had not been so objectionable and unRoman and if, in spite of the strong syncretistic tendencies of the age, the god Elagabalus had not at the time proved too much for most nonSyrians in the city to adore. He wore his Oriental origin too obviously to attract many devout followers in Rome. It may not be true that the Emperor sacrificed living boys to his god (although human sacrifice was reportedly common in the magical rites of the East), or that he shut a monkey, a lion, and a snake in the god's temple and fed them human testicles; these stories may be exaggerations or pure lies on the part of the historians Dio and Lampridius; but even so, the rites for the divine newcomer from Syria must have seemed to the more conservative Romans as extraordinarily outlandish and intolerably insolent toward the old religion.

In the view of these conservative Romans, Jupiter the Thunderer, king of the gods, demanded the religious respect of citizens of the Empire and especially of those residing in the capital. So did his matronly queen Juno, protectress of women in childbirth, and helmeted Minerva, the goddess of battle. So did deities such as Mars the Avenger, Venus the divine ancestress of Julius Caesar, Neptune the ruler of the sea, Apollo the lord of light and truth, and Vesta the goddess of the city's sacred hearth. The majestic temple called the Pantheon, with its coffered dome suggesting the dome of heaven, had been erected in a saner age to these and all the other national gods, and it stood as a reminder that none of them was named Elagabalus. By extending Roman citizenship throughout the Empire, Caracalla had, of course, opened the door to a wild assortment of divinities, but old-fashioned citizens of the capital felt that they at least must honor the true and ancient gods of Rome. Supreme Jupiter would thunder his wrath if the inhabitants of the sacred city abandoned the deities who had given Rome the world.

The old religion was in practice extremely dignified, consisting of sober rituals repeated by generation after generation of priests. It has sometimes been termed unemotional, and certainly its austere observances do not seem calculated to stimulate devotional frenzy. The Oriental creeds were of another kind—ardent, passionate, mystic. One tended to approach very close to the god one was adoring, which was not true with the Roman state religion. The Roman gods maintained an aloof distance from the priests performing their venerable rites. As for the body of the people, the nonparticipants, they seldom if ever felt that they loved a god, the way the Emperor Elagabalus loved his. This restrained aspect of Roman religion made some citizens of the capital turn to the excitement of Eastern faiths and no doubt helped the Emperor in his effort to convert the city to sun worship. On the other hand, it was the very emotionalism of Eastern faiths which conservative Romans found most repulsive. An emotional religion was, in their opinion, vulgar. The aloof distance of the old gods of Rome, the awesome formality of the rites, reflected the greatness of those gods and of the Empire which they favored. To abandon all that for some fanatic and gaudy Oriental cult would be foolhardy as well as horrible.

The temple to the Sun God on the Palatine, one of the projects that the Emperor was most anxious about, was apparently finished in the year 220. It was luxurious in an Asiatic manner, glittering with precious substances and exquisitely perfumed. Bulls and sheep in plethora were sacrificed on altars covered with spices, and the blood as it ran down was mixed with the finest wine. The Emperor, gorgeous in his Syrian sacerdotal robes, with paint above his eyes and vermilion on his cheeks, danced around and around the altars, graceful as he had been at Emesa, lithe and expert and ecstatic, attended by a pageantry of Syrian priests and priestesses, while the cymbals clashed and the flutes played. It was a spectacle of rare splendor, but it was not, in the old sense, acceptable.

It happened daily, and the senators resented it because they were expected to watch—arranged in a great semicircle, these guardians of Roman tradition, these successors to the powerful patricians who had guided Rome through the Punic Wars many centuries before. But most of the senators were more fortunate than the court officials, generals, governors, holders of high positions in the state. They had to wear garish Oriental costumes, it appears, and to participate in the rites. They had to carry off the entrails of the sacrificed animals in basins of gold.

Before the end of summer in the year 221, evidently, a suburban temple to the god was completed. Then occurred a great religious procession as the god's image was carried from the temple on the Palatine to its new house. Its chariot was encrusted with gold and precious stones, shadowed by umbrellas at the corners, and drawn by white horses in jeweled harnesses. The reins were so arranged that it looked as if the god himself were driving. Actually, the Emperor guided the horses—walking backward ahead of the chariot so that he would not have to turn his back to his god. Guards on either side of him watched closely to see that he did not get his feet twisted, but he was, as always, graceful. Statues of the old Roman deities were borne in the procession because these deities wanted to do honor to the Sun. Expensive offerings and the imperial insignia were carried along too. Members of the equestrian order marched in submissive worship, and the Praetorians also marched. Yellow sand and gold dust covered the streets. On the sidelines stood the people, among them those Romans most enthusiastic about the Sun, waving torches and hurling wreaths and flowers in front of the god.

# ❧ XIV ☙

# *The Daily Life of a Teen-age Emperor*

To find himself in control of a civilization is unbalancing to a man unless he has a stable character. Elagabalus was a boy, and his character was not stable. Overwhelmed with his own incalculable power, he went wild.

Although he was probably not as avid a charioteer as Caracalla, racing a chariot appealed to him and soon became one of his favorite amusements. One might have thought that he actually had inherited his love of the sport from Caracalla; with his Green garment flying out behind him (Caracalla had worn Blue), he thrilled to the speed, the danger, the competition, the applause of the crowd. The two Praetorian Prefects gravely presided at the races. Among the spectators were his vain mother, his worried grandmother, and his envious aunt. The senators had to watch these performances too, of course, but they minded them less than the terpsichorean exhibitions in the temple; under Caracalla they had grown used to applauding an imperial charioteer. In their own opinion, this boy demonstrated the same lack of dignity that his presumed father had shown: at the conclusion of a race he saluted with his whip the judges who were to give out the prizes, and reached up for gold pieces.

More artistically inclined than Caracalla, he excelled not only at chariot racing but at playing musical instruments. He performed on the flute, the horn, and stringed instruments, and also sang. It almost seemed that he was a young Nero, because Nero had also prided himself on his musical skill and had required the courtiers to admire it. But music sometimes proved insipid to Elagabalus. A more exciting diversion was to dress up in a disguise and wander through the slums, maybe hiring out as a barber's helper, or serving wine in some disreputable tavern, or hawking vegetables or perfumes in the crowded, filthy streets. This was a new kind of life for a youth brought up in elevated society. If he thought he deceived anybody by means of his disguises he was probably deceiving only himself, but at any rate the escapades entertained him.

Elagabalus disliked people who did not enjoy spending money. When he dismissed a courtier from an audience he customarily gave the man a gift, but any man who had a reputation for niggardliness went away emptyhanded. The Emperor himself spent money with a prodigality that scarcely anyone has ever been able to rival. He was a teen-ager at the summit of a civilization, and he could throw gold around.

Except, perhaps, for public appearances of an official nature, he still refused to wear the Roman toga, preferring either the luxury of silk or the magnificence of cloth of gold, heavy with emeralds, rubies, and sapphires. Jeweled bracelets dangled from his wrists, rings set with massive jewels added splendor to his fingers, a sumptuously jeweled diadem enriched his curls, and jeweled necklaces hung around his imperial young neck. Even the buckles of his shoes were garnished with precious stones engraved by skillful artists; one had to look rather closely to appreciate the miniature fineness of the workmanship, but it was there. He declined to wear linen that had been washed or shoes that had been worn once before, and it has been said that he did not even put on the same ring twice.

He sat, walked, ate, and slept in conspicuous consumption. His couches were of solid silver elaborately carved, and the purple cushions on which he reclined at meals were stuffed with fur from hares or feathers from the underside of partridge wings. The food for himself and his guests was, of course, served exclusively on gold or silver, and he liked to give a complete table service away to one of the guests after a banquet. Vessels of silver weighing as much as a hundred pounds were used at the meals; obscene pictures carved on them in high relief amused guests between courses. The fact that in cool weather the rooms were heated by burning Indian aromatics rather than coal was not extraordinary in a society that craved beautiful smells, but Elagabalus apparently went to an extreme in his fondness for fragrance, perfuming everything he could. It was also extravagant to have silver dust and gold dust spread on the floors of the porticoes through which he passed on the way to his horse or his carriage. He even deposited his excrement in pots of gold.

The more exotic his foods were, the more pleasure he took in them. He might delight his guests with the tongues of nightingales, the combs of roosters, or the heels of camels. His servants might feast on flamingo brains or pheasant heads heaped on platters. He was fastidious about sauces; at least Lampridius says that a guest who on command failed to invent a good sauce was ordered to continue eating his own poor product until he could devise a better one, and then he was rewarded with a robe of silk. According to report, the Emperor would surprise his guests by seeing to it that little bits of gold were mixed with their peas, amber with their beans, and onyx with their lentils; on other occasions the diners would have to dig through tiny pearls to reach the quail underneath. The lions in his menagerie ate parrots, and he fed his horses grapes.

Lavish expenditure was, of course, an imperial tradition of long standing, although some of the best Emperors did not follow it. Elagabalus might not have been conforming to the antique ideal of Roman simplicity, but he could point to Caligula, Nero, Vitellius, Hadrian, and several other Emperors as his models. Even in comparison with these gourmands and builders of priceless palaces, however, he was remarkably free with the revenue of Rome, so that he impressed his contemporaries (who were themselves not used to Spartan living) with his incredible love of costly comfort.

More difficult to understand than his mere taste for luxury is the seemingly frantic search for novelty and for exotic ways to dispose of money. He put rose water in his fish ponds; at the amphitheatre he had a naval spectacle performed on canals of wine. Wishing to see winter in the summer, he commanded snow to be brought from a mountain in buckets and piled up in his garden until he had a high hill of it there. He evidently offered prizes to his slaves for collecting spiders' webs; he wanted one thousand pounds, and when the slaves, eager for the prizes, managed to amass ten thousand pounds, he said, "That proves how big Rome is." All this straining for the new and rare makes one wonder whether Elagabalus, young as he was, had already become satiated with luxury; perhaps it surrounded him in such oppressive quantity that it just about smothered him, and its usual forms grew so cloying that he had to look for fantastic ones. On the other hand, perhaps he was merely enjoying to the full, with the immature joy of an adolescent, the fact that he was Emperor. He could expect his wishes to be obeyed no matter how bizarre they were. As long as the teen-ager had a civilization at his disposal, he would make colossal use of it. He would not be satisfied with the ordinary; he would experiment; he would live high.

Like a number of adolescents, children, and adults who never mature, he was fond of practical jokes. The parasites who received invitations to his dinners were, it seems, sometimes served wooden desserts, or ivory desserts, or desserts made of wax or marble or clay. He had what is often said to be essential to humor: a sense of what was not apropos. His gifts to his favorites were not always silver table services; sometimes he would give away dead dogs or jars of frogs, scorpions, or flies. Snakes in particular attracted him, and he used to let them slither among his dinner guests, without forewarning the guests. If one of his friends had indulged too avidly in scented wine and was borne off intoxicated to a bedroom, the inebriate was likely to wake up with a lion or a leopard staring him in the face. The animals were aged and innocuous, but their roommates were expected to discover this for themselves. It amused him exceedingly to invite to dinner eight bald men, eight one-eyed men, or eight fat men and to note their mutual discomfort as they looked at one another; or he would invite eight men who were hard of hearing and note their conversation.

All that was only mischief and did not hurt anybody. The mischief-making, however, could take a more serious turn. It appears, at any rate, that Elagabalus opened a convertible ceiling on his dinner guests one night and let down floods of flowers, tons of sweet-smelling suffocating blossoms, so that several people were smothered in violets.

His impulsive generosity was perhaps a strong antidote to this whimsical, fatal mischief-making. He would have his dinner guests draw lots for prizes which might consist of several pounds of gold. Fascinated by prostitutes, he is said to have donated to the whores and catamites of Rome the grain supply for the city for a whole year. There is a story that he gave each of the light ladies of the theatre, the amphitheatre, and the other places of public resort a piece of gold, enjoining

them not to disclose where the money had come from. There is another
story that he gathered together Rome's male prostitutes, delivered an
interesting speech to them (as he did also to Rome's female prostitutes), and gave each one three gold pieces.

He distributed lottery tickets which could be turned in for slaves,
ships, precious stones, or country estates. It is reported that on one
occasion, instead of donating money or grain, he set before the people
an assortment of camels, fat stock, slaves, asses, and other desirable
items. The people were greedy and disorderly, and they fought over
the gifts. On the whole, however, they liked Elagabalus for thinking of
them in a manner both beneficent and original, and his generosity did
a great deal to dispel the bad impression created by his efforts to promote his god.

The shows which he furnished were, of course, colossal and different. He liked chariot races in which the chariots were pulled not by
horses but by tigers, lions, camels, deer, or dogs. He would even tie a
team of naked girls to a chariot and drive it himself, as naked as they,
nipping their posteriors with his whip. But this kind of thing was
mainly for his private pleasure.

Dancing probably characterized him more than any other activity.
Whatever he was doing, he danced. He walked with a tripping motion,
offered sacrifices with a glide and sway, acknowledged greetings with a
graceful step; he even danced when addressing an audience.

After he grew old enough to have a noticeable beard, he plucked
it. His face was painted. Senators who came to consult him found him
lying on a couch in coy languor. All of this induced people to think of
him as a girl, and the impression was one that he did nothing to discourage. As a matter of fact, he reminded people to address him as if
he were an Empress.

He loved to dress in women's clothes, particularly the loose garments worn by prostitutes. In this attire, which made it difficult to conceal very much, he would pose as a courtesan, attempting to conceal
nothing, and talk in a feminine coo. People said that he was a man for
every woman and a woman for every man; the second half of the saying is the more easily verifiable. He may conceivably have been interested in both sexes—a bisexual teen-ager who was exploring the alleys
of love with the same whimsicality and exuberance that he showed
toward his other pleasures—but his courtiers and counselors realized

that his interest in males was predominant. The reason prostitutes fascinated him was evidently that he had a desire to be one of them himself. He lay with them at times, but according to Cassius Dio, it was so they could teach him the secrets of their profession, which he would later try on his male bedfellows. Although he spent an enormous sum for a concubine, he refused to touch her; she was his virgin, and it seemed likely that she remained one.

He used to stand naked in the doorway to a room in the palace which had been converted into his personal brothel. Gold rings hung from the curtains; he shook them softly, as a whore might do, and sweetly simpering, invited passers-by to come in. Many came; sex with the Emperor was a relatively small price to pay for advancement at court. He carried the pretense of harlotry so far that he would charge his patrons for the privilege of having relations with him, and then he would compare prices with the prostitutes, announcing that he had more lovers than they did and that his lovers paid better. He would also compare experiences with them, retailing and evaluating delights.

He was an Emperor who wanted to be a woman. His physicians, however, felt obliged to decline when he offered them a great deal of money if they would cut him open and insert a vagina. Even the lord of civilization could not have everything.

# ❦ XV ❧

# Six or Seven Marriages

For a transvestite, Elagabalus was married a surprising number of times. The chronology of these marriages and those of his god is confused. Although the order of events followed in this chapter seems the most defensible, the reign was so chaotic and is so chaotically recorded that some other order is certainly possible.

It would appear that the Emperor's first wife was named Julia Cornelia Paula and that he married her in the second half of 219—in other words, shortly after arriving at Rome from Nicomedia. Her age is unknown—she may have been twelve years old or she may have been in her thirties. In any case, she was of high birth and presumably was physically attractive. The wedding constituted an excuse for much magnificence, including a large donation to the senators, a lavish banquet for the populace, another lavish banquet for the soldiers, and the deaths of many gladiators, fifty-one tigers, and an elephant. At the public games Elagabalus surrendered to the taste of his subjects by wearing a purple-bordered toga rather than one of his Asiatic costumes.

At least, all this magnificence was probably in celebration of his first marriage; there is a possibility that one of his other marriages was being celebrated.

Perhaps it can be assumed that the marriage with Julia Cornelia Paula had been arranged by his grandmother Maesa. Since Elagabalus was only about fifteen at the time, it looks as if his elders were hurrying matters. The probable reason for the marriage was to connect the Syrian dynasty with the Roman nobility. Now that Septimius Severus and his sons were dead, many influential Romans resented the reigning family as a group of foreign opportunists, people who may have rightfully enjoyed high station in their own benighted country but who were not Roman enough to rule on the Tiber. Elagabalus himself, of course, did not worry about whether his subjects thought him a foreigner or what they thought him, but the more practical Maesa presumably saw the danger of alienating the upper class if not the common people. For the future safety of her family, an alliance with a Roman house of the first rank was almost a necessity.

There was, however, no issue, no child in whom the blood of Roman aristocrats and Syrian priest-kings could mingle—Maesa had been too sanguine. And late in 220 Elagabalus divorced Julia Cornelia Paula. She did not please him; besides, he wanted to marry somebody else. His second marriage was almost certainly his own idea rather than that of his elders.

The Vestal Virgins were selected from the noblest families in Rome. Since they took a thirty-year vow of chastity they were unmarriageable until after their physical appeal had considerably waned, and not many of them ever got married. Having been dedicated to Vesta as little girls, they devoted the first ten years of their vow to learning the duties of their order, the second ten to performing those duties, and the third to teaching others. The Temple of Vesta was perhaps the holiest spot in all Rome. In it burned the fire sacred to the goddess, the hearth-fire of the republic, which the virgins had to keep lit. Belief in the sanctity of fire was, of course, much older than Rome, and belief in a hearth-deity associated with fire had stirred the inchoate religious emotions of primitive peoples long before Italy had cities. This particular fire, it was thought, contained the greatness of Rome; to allow it to go out would mean calamity to the state. Revered national relics were also kept in the Temple of Vesta, and the priestesses were expected to guard them because on them, too, the well-being of the state depended.

These priestesses had to perform the Vestalic rituals: to offer a daily sacrifice on the hearth in the temple (a sacrifice of plain food in a rude clay container, reminding people of the virtuous simplicity of Rome's beginnings); to perform the daily rite of purification with running water carried from a sacred fountain; to send up daily prayers for the good fortune of Rome and special prayers when Rome was in dan-

ger; to lead worshippers in the Festival of Vesta on July 9; and to participate in festivals to other primal deities of the republic.

The virgins wore garments of pure white linen, and at the time of
the sacrificial rites they put on their heads purple-bordered white
woolen veils. Although their lives were to be blameless, they were not
cloistered. Men could enter all parts of the temple during the day except the portion where the relics were preserved; only at night was the
temple exclusively for females. The Vestals, besides, went out a good
deal; for instance, they occupied special seats at the public games, and
no lady who watched sweating gladiators kill one another could be
termed entirely otherworldly. Their chastity was taken for granted by
most people, but it was subject to doubt under certain Emperors, as it
had been once during the republic. The breaking of their vow was
punished by living burial.

Because of their incalculable importance to the welfare of Rome
and the antiquity of the worship to which they were dedicated, if not
because of their sexual innocence, they were accorded great honor.
When they appeared in public they were preceded by a lictor bearing
the fasces (the bundle of rods with an axe protruding that represented
authority). Even a consul had to give way to them. Since their integrity was supposedly beyond doubt, they were not required to take an
oath before giving testimony, and wills and other documents were
often put in their charge.

Early in the spring of 221, or at any rate soon after his divorce
from his first wife, Elagabalus married one of these ladies, Aquilia
Severa. Her vow of chastity did not deter him; as Emperor he was also
Pontifex Maximus, high priest of the state religion, and consequently
he could do what he wished with religious customs. Rome was, of
course, horrified at the sacrilege. It seemed as if Elagabalus, with a
perverseness for which no excuse was sufficient, was making an overt
and flagrant attempt to insult the ancient religion of the republic, to
publicize his disrespect for the national sanctities, to ridicule what Romans held most holy.

His actual motives, however, were partly religious and did not imply any gross impiety on his part. Aside from the possibility that he
really liked this virgin, perhaps better than he liked any other woman
and most men, he realized that it was his imperial obligation to carry
on the dynasty, and he could think of nobody better qualified to be the

mother of his children than a Vestal priestess. Other women were unworthy; only a Vestal was a suitable bride for the Emperor of Rome and High Priest of the Sun. The gods would smile on the products of their union, children who would themselves be godlike. He explained that to the Senate.

We do not know how Aquilia Severa felt about the marriage. She may have had an affection for this weird boy-Emperor; she may have reasoned that to marry the Pontifex Maximus was no offense against her goddess; she may have wanted to be an Empress; or she may have been coerced. In any case, the wedding seems to have been a quiet one; even Elagabalus evidently felt that to hold games and carousals this time would be in poor taste.

The god must have been married about the same time as the Emperor, but we are uncertain whether the divine wedding preceded or followed the human one. It is not exactly clear why the Emperor concluded that his god needed a wife. Carefully instructed in divine matters since childhood, however, he was probably enough of a theologian to see that a union with a powerful goddess would augment the powers of the god. On a more practical level he very likely hoped that the marriage would aid his plan to make the Romans sun-worshippers. The goddess-wife was to be Vesta herself, sometimes identified with Minerva, and the wedding would consequently present the opportunity to combine worship of the sun with an old Latin faith. The citizens could continue to worship Vesta, or Minerva, if they wished, but they might also feel obliged to honor her lord and master.

This was probably the period when the Emperor entered the portion of the Temple of Vesta where the relics were kept and had them carried off to the Temple of Elagabalus, together with sacred objects from other shrines. Among the holy things, essential to Roman religious and patriotic tradition, were the Palladium (the image of Pallas Athena which Aeneas had brought from Troy to Italy after Ulysses and Diomedes had stolen its twin, and to which the safety of the state was closely related), the stone of Pessinuntum (sometimes called the grandmother of the gods and responsible for driving the Carthaginians from Italy long before), and the bronze shield of Numa Pompilius (which had fallen from heaven to signalize the end of a plague that was devastating young Rome, and which the wise, pious, and peaceful Numa, Rome's first king, had interpreted as a symbol and promise of the city's future greatness). Elagabalus took the Vestal fire itself, the holiest thing of all, and transported it to the bright new temple of his interloper-god. The virgins in pure white linen, protectresses of the relics and the fire, could not protect them against the youth who was Pontifex Maximus. There must have been citizens who feared that Rome was doomed, that the nation could not survive such desecration. While some Romans trembled, however, others shouted their outrage, and drunken men in taverns cursed the foolish, impudent Syrian boy.

It was all admirably symmetrical: the Sun, the consort of Vesta; and the Sun's high priest, the consort of Vesta's priestess. It was a characteristically Eastern attempt to employ ritual for divine analogy; but it lasted about three months. Before the end of summer, 221, both the Emperor and the deity were divorced.

We know approximately as much about Elagabalus' third wife as we do about his first two, but there are more conjectures. Her name was Annia Faustina, and we can probably assume that she was even more illustriously descended than Julia Cornelia Paula or Aquilia Severa. One of her ancestors was Marcus Aurelius. Marrying her would ally the Syrian dynasty firmly with the aristocracy of Rome.

One supportable conjecture is that the marriage was engineered by Grandmother Maesa, tired of her grandson's embarrassing whimsies and alarmed by the attitude of the Roman people and the Senate. Elagabalus' feelings about the whole situation are, like so much else, a matter for guesswork. All we can be sure of is that he remarried his Vestal Virgin later on. It is possible that Maesa forced him to accept Annia Faustina as his Empress, that if he had had his own way he would not have divorced the Vestal.

Several questions revolve around the fact that Annia Faustina was not a maiden. Pomponius Bassus was her first husband, and Elagabalus had him executed. The questions are these: Did the execution occur toward the beginning of the reign or shortly before the Emperor's third marriage? Was Pomponius Bassus killed for actual treasonable activities, or was he killed on some pretext so that Elagabalus could marry his widow? Did Annia Faustina wish to see him killed? Did Elagabalus wish to see him killed? Was Maesa instrumental in his execution?

These questions are, in the weak light of the evidence we have, unanswerable. The only established facts are that Elagabalus accused Pomponius Bassus of making adverse comments about his reign and of plotting against him, and that Bassus' friend Messalla was executed at the same time (whenever that may have been) on the same charges.

Not quite as much darkness surrounds the second marriage of the god, which probably occurred shortly before or shortly after the Emperor's marriage to Annia Faustina. Elagabalus issued a statement to the effect that Vesta (or Minerva) was not a satisfactory spouse for the Sun and that she was consequently being repudiated. In place of her, the god would marry the primary goddess of Carthage.

This deity too had been much affected by syncretism. She went by a number of names—for example, Urania, Juno Caelestis, and Venus Caelestis. She was not Latin in origin. Like the Emperor's Sun God, she had risen in the Orient; the Phoenicians knew her as Astarte, the Hebrews as Ashtoreth, and the Babylonians and Assyrians as Ishtar. To all these peoples she was a goddess of sex, a fertility goddess, a patroness of the reproductive process, worshipped in picturesque, primitive ways; she meant the same thing to the early citizens of Carthage, who came from Phoenicia. Since the rain is necessary for the earth's fertility, she was also a rain goddess; and perhaps because the rain descends from the sky, she became a sky goddess too. She was associated with the moon just as Elagabalus was associated with the sun.

Septimius Severus, intensely proud of his Punic blood, had established her worship at Rome, and both Severus and Caracalla had put her image on coins. We cannot tell how large a following she had at Rome, but it must have been sizable. The reputation of her oracles throughout the Mediterranean world was very high, and that signified a great deal in an age when, after several centuries of comparative neglect, people began flocking to oracles again and inquiring about the future with superstitious awe. Her fame, therefore, made her a fitting bride for the god Elagabalus; she was, like Vesta, important. Furthermore, since she was originally non-Roman, the citizens of the capital could not object to the marriage. And in addition, it was suitable for the Sun God and the Moon Goddess to be husband and wife.

The Emperor enthusiastically sent to Carthage for her statue, which was transported to Rome so that it could function as a bride. A rich treasure was brought to Rome as her dowry. This treasure may have been another reason why the Emperor considered the marriage desirable.

Although the god stayed married to Venus Caelestis, the Emperor did not remain Annia Faustina's husband for long. It was probably early in 222 that, having divorced her, he remarried the (possibly still) virgin Aquilia Severa. His return to the Vestal offers an opportunity for further conjecture. It looks as though Grandmother Maesa had in the end failed to control him. If his divorce from Aquilia Severa and marriage to Annia Faustina indicate a retrenchment in his practice of alienating Rome—if they indicate that under the influence of Maesa he was trying to soothe the indignation of his subjects and tie his house in with the Roman upper class—then his divorce from Annia Faustina and remarriage to Aquilia Severa suggest a revolt on his part. We can conjure up emotional scenes at the palace—arguments, outbursts, cajolery, recrimination—grandson against grandmother, with the seductive mother Soaemias perhaps adding her own useless contributions and the moral aunt Mamaea indulging in pious sarcasm—but, as usual, we know nothing.

In addition to being a husband to several women, Elagabalus was a "wife." We are uninformed as to just when he married the charioteer Hierocles, but it was probably fairly early in his reign.

While the Emperor was watching a chariot race one of the chariots overturned in front of the imperial box, spilling out the young driver, who rolled toward him. The youth's helmet had fallen off, revealing yellow hair; he was apparently good-looking and well-built. Elagabalus, deeply impressed, had him taken to the palace.

Hierocles was probably a Greek from Caria in Asia Minor, and a slave as well. Whether he sincerely returned Elagabalus' passionate affection or whether he simply decided to profit by it is, once again, a matter for conjecture. We do know, however, that he loved his mother. She too was a slave, but after his fortune had been made he bought her from her masters and, with the Emperor's permission, had a company of soldiers escort her with great honor to Rome, where she was placed among the proudest ladies, the wives of former consuls.

Under the influence of Hierocles, Elagabalus took to spinning. The chariot driver stimulated the Emperor's wish to be female. Apparently there was a marriage contract, and the Emperor urged his courtiers to speak of himself as Hierocles' wife. He was, of course, egregiously unfaithful to his husband. Sometimes he contrived to have Hierocles discover him having sexual relations with another lover. Then there would be a domestic gale, in the course of which Hierocles would beat his wife enthusiastically. Elagabalus wanted to be beaten; he liked it; he would appear before his courtiers the next day with a black eye or some other bruise, and tell them that his jealous husband had given him this for flagrant infidelity.

Hierocles prospered from his association with Elagabalus indirectly as well as directly. Courtiers greedy for favors would come to him saying, "Please use your influence with the Emperor," and Hierocles would consent to do so if he was generously paid. He might speak to the Emperor concerning whatever it was that a particular courtier wanted—an administrative or military office, perhaps, or an estate—or he might not mention anything about the matter to Elagabalus. Later he would tell the courtier, "The Emperor will probably grant your wish," or else declare with a worried frown that the case was very doubtful. In either case, he accepted payment. This rewarding practice was known as "selling smoke."

Elagabalus may have been energetically adulterous, but he never tired permanently of Hierocles; the charioteer was the only spouse he did not divorce. Evidently he even planned to give his husband the rank of Caesar, with the implication of succession to the throne. Maesa, who tolerated a great deal because she could not do otherwise, raised vociferous objections to this intention, and Elagabalus did not carry it out.

Only one man ever seriously jeopardized the charioteer's ascendancy over the Emperor. This was a young Greek athlete named Zoticus, born at the city of Smyrna in Asia Minor and the son of a cook. Since his sexual organs were unusually ample, he was described in detail to Elagabalus by one of the people who drew an income from catering to Elagabalus' interests. It was not long before Zoticus' athletic career was interrupted; the youth found himself summoned to the court on the official pretext that he was to be *cubicularius*, or keeper of the bedchamber.

A less corruptible young man might have refused on the grounds that he was happy running and wrestling. Zoticus, however—a professional athlete of ignoble birth, doing his best at the games and trying to get ahead in life—did not. So he was brought from the games and ushered into Rome with tremendous fanfare, wearing

garlands and escorted by a huge crowd of attendants, like some victorious general. The palace glowed with torches as he came in, and the
courtiers stood wondering how the advent of this new favorite might
change their lives; and Hierocles was nervous.

"Hail, Lord Emperor!" said Zoticus.

Elagabalus saw that the athlete more than approached his physical ideal. He lowered his lead, lapsed into one of the graceful, feminine
postures that he had learned from the courtesans, looked up at Zoticus
with a soft expression, smiled sweetly, and said, "Don't call me that.
I'm a lady."

Zoticus, who would have called the Emperor a frog if that was
what the Emperor wanted, begged his pardon, and Elagabalus suggested a bath.

In the bath it was immediately evident to the practiced imperial
eye that Zoticus' generally concealed attributes were extraordinary, and
interest swelled into lust. When the two were clean, Elagabalus sat on
the athlete's lap and ate dinner.

But the indignant husband Hierocles realized that something must
be done quickly or he would find himself replaced. Fortunately, he was
on good terms with the cup-bearers. According to the story, he took
them aside and asked them to slip into the athlete's drink a potion
which would have an opposite effect from that of an aphrodisiac. That
night poor Zoticus was unable to perform as anticipated, in spite of all
the womanly charms which the Emperor displayed. It was extremely
embarrassing. It was also potentially dangerous. The Emperor, insulted
beyond the stretch of patience, reproached him, accused him, struck at
him with sarcasm. Zoticus had to lie quiet and listen—ineffectual, confused.

Elagabalus relieved the favorite of his honors and emoluments and
sent him out of Rome in disgrace. For a while Zoticus continued to live
in Italy, close to his brief life of elevation, hoping that the Emperor
would relent. But Elagabalus could not even stand the thought that a
man of such insolence resided anywhere near him, and Zoticus was
told to leave Italy.

The happy husband, meanwhile, had returned to the pleasant
routine of smelling smoke by day and beating his wife at night.

# ⚜ XVI ⚜

# *Unwanted*

Not many of Elagabalus' accomplishments could be called solid or constructive, but there were a few. The temples which he built for the Sun God on the Capitoline Hill and in the suburbs were certainly worthy of note, buildings whose splendor suited this age of extravagance just as the enormous magnificence of the nearly completed Baths of Caracalla did. His donatives to the populace may not have been very constructive, but at least they were not injurious.

For his mother, Soaemias, whom politics bored, he revived an ancient Roman institution called the Senate of Matrons. Legend said that many centuries before, in the early part of the fourth century, a group of aristocratic women met in order to help the young republic out of difficulty and voted to relinquish their jewels in its service. A female senate of some kind did meet occasionally, even in imperial times, but had apparently not been heard of in quite a while before Elagabalus came to the throne. He gave the ladies a palace on the Quirinal Hill and made his mother their president.

Under her strong leadership the society debated questions of etiquette. Congregating at frequent intervals, the ladies issued decrees about the modes of conveyance proper for women of various ranks (who deserved a litter, for instance, and who could ride in state in a cart drawn by mules, and who might be pulled by slow oxen, and who could proceed on horseback), dress (for example, who could wear jeweled shoe-buckles without incurring the charge of vulgar display and status-jumping), salutation (when two ladies met, which one had the right to speak first), decoration (which ranks merited litters inlaid

143

with ivory or with silver), and similar considerations. The Senate of Matrons contributed all it could to the smooth, orderly functioning of Roman society.

The populace may have been somewhat amused at all this, but not really disturbed. A number of citizens were even disposed to find redeeming features in the reign of Elagabalus. He was generous, he sometimes remembered the poor in his extravagances, he was not really cruel or tyrannical, one did not feel that one was living under terror; there were few executions and no persecutions, and a man was not afraid to open his mouth. It could be called a crazy reign rather than a grim one.

Rumors of the goings-on at the palace, however, disquieted many people. The Emperor's unusual sexual activities were not kept secret, and neither was his lavish spending for the satisfaction of personal vagaries. A still stronger factor in the Emperor's disfavor was, of course, the blatant advertisement of the Sun God and the insults offered to Roman piety. The soldiers were especially disappointed. They had not expected the son of Caracalla, the boy who in a moment of glory had inspired his followers to victory at the Battle of Immae, to turn into this Emperor-Empress. The suspicion that he was not Caracalla's son at all was more and more frequently expressed. The troops had not asked to be ruled by a dancing boy and his grandmother. They wanted a leader. They could feel little loyalty toward these strange Syrians.

At one point, it is true, Elagabalus demonstrated interest in marching with his troops against the Marcomanni, the barbarians whom Marcus Aurelius had battled long ago, but nothing came of it. There had apparently been a prediction that an Emperor named Antoninus (still his official name, of course) would destroy the Marcomanni, and Elagabalus felt that some military glory might lie within his reach. When his advisors, who did not relish any unnecessary military projects, told him that Marcus Aurelius had conquered the Marcomanni with the aid of Chaldean magic, he tried to find a way to overcome this magic so that the barbarians would rebel and afford him a pretext for attacking them. But the Marcomanni stayed quiet.

The Emperor sometimes gave political posts to friends who had crawled out of the scum of Roman society, and both administrative positions and senatorial status to Orientals who had followed him from

Syria. His freedmen governed provinces; his palace officials came from the theatre and the circus; a professional dancer commanded his guard; a mule-driver held a post in the department of inheritance taxation; a rapacious barber called Claudius supervised the grain supply for his own financial profit. This kind of thing had gone on under other Emperors (for instance, Caracalla), but its prevalence under Elagabalus confirmed the Senate in their opposition to his government, displeased the soldiers bitterly, and did not please the poor, who resented the sudden advancement of their own unscrupulous brothers much more than they would have resented the advancement of the rich.

Elagabalus may have been aware that he had fewer and fewer adherents left—that his effeminacy, his extravagance, his lack of sympathy for Roman religious beliefs, his unmilitary behavior, his strong Syrianism, his favoritism, and his general tampering with imperial functions would in time destroy him. Religious men from Syria apparently told him that he did not have long to live. His reaction to this prophecy was unusual. Instead of surrendering to violent distress, he evidently made preparations for a gorgeous suicide. He intended to live until the rebellion came, but when it did come, he would have a rich choice of exits. He ordered silken cords to be provided so that he could strangle himself, swords with gold blades in case he preferred to stab himself, priceless gleaming vases from which he might drink poison. He also ordered the construction of a tower from which he might jump. The ground at the bottom of the tower was paved with gold and studded with jewels, so that when he made his death leap he would fall to magnificence.

It is not easy to suppose that in his late teens this master of Rome was ready to die, that he was so sated with the pleasures of civilization as to lay ardent plans for giving them up. Perhaps at times he had doubts about the prophecy of the Syrian seers, or perhaps he tried to forget their grim prediction in the diversions of the palace. If he believed the prophecy, or even if he only feared at intervals that it might be true, his reaction must have struck people as the greatest of all the examples of whimsy which he had furnished in the past several years. Yet the reaction may not have been whimsy at all; the cord, the sword, the vases, and the tower do not suggest the heroic in any ordinary sense, but they do suggest a proud defiance approaching personal heroism, supported by that strong sense of the histrionic that most of his actions revealed. He had played with the world and wasted it, and the world could come after him in revenge, but it could not force on him an ignoble end. He would not be killed according to the world's terms. He was Emperor and he would die imperially.

Mamaea was ambitious. She wanted to be more than an Emperor's aunt. She wanted the throne for her son Alexianus, and she wanted it fiercely. While Soaemias lay in languid pleasure, her less beautiful, less sensual sister campaigned. She was as friendly as possible with the senators, well aware of their inimical feelings toward Elagabalus. Perhaps she overestimated the importance of their support, but after all, they represented the most exalted families in the Empire and she retained a high respect for rank. This respect, however, did not lead her to undervalue what was certainly a more influential element in the state; she also campaigned with the soldiers, bribing them away from whatever loyalty they still felt toward Elagabalus. Like the other members of her family, she was extraordinarily rich; and unlike her nephew, she did not enjoy spending money except for some expedient purpose. She thought that giving money to the soldiers would admirably serve her goal.

Mamaea aimed her third campaign at her mother. This campaign was relatively easy—not because old Maesa lacked the shrewdness to discern her daughter's design under all the verbiage with which she deprecated Elagabalus and praised her own son, but because Maesa had come to feel that the plan might possibly have merit. It seems to have been soon after the Emperor's first marriage to the Vestal Virgin and the Sun God's first marriage to the virgin goddess—in other words, in the spring of 221—that Maesa first seriously regarded little Alexianus as a successor to Elagabalus. She probably did not view Elagabalus' death as necessary or even as highly desirable, but there was no telling what might happen, and having a good replacement in readiness was obviously much better than being unprepared. A rebellion might come—if not soon, then later, since Elagabalus showed no convincing signs of reform—and Maesa had to provide for her house. It was extremely important to her that her family remain on the throne; her dynastic feeling was as strong as that of her brother-in-law, Severus. It was also important to her to remain in the palace; she did not intend to end up dispossessed like her sister Julia Domna. She had been mistaken in depending on Elagabalus; since he had proved unreliable, he did not deserve her help any longer. Her other grandson evidently deserved all the help she could give him. Little Alexianus, about four years younger than Elagabalus, was a very good boy; his mother had brought him up properly; he would not go cavorting around in an indecent manner; he would not even try to promote the worship of the Sun; if anything happened to Elagabalus, Alexianus should occupy the throne.

Mamaea was also a much less reproachable mother for an Emperor than her sister, Soaemias, was. Maesa realized that. Soaemias had never taken her position seriously enough. She had, it was true, done a commendable job as president of the Senate of Matrons, but in other respects she was far too frivolous. Maesa did not discountenance a little sexual activity now and then, having had a sufficient amount of it in her own day, but Soaemias displayed herself in too public a manner. Mamaea had a dependable sense of dignity and understood politics. If her son became Emperor, she would know how to act.

As popular indignation against Elagabalus grew and as Mamaea continued talking, Maesa's preference for Alexianus must have matured. But she could not yet have regarded Elagabalus as totally unreformable, and in a way he answered her dwindling faith in him. Interspersed among his pleasures he may have glimpsed the dangers in which he lived. Something, at any rate, made him cooperate with the wishes of his elders. He did even more than divorce the Vestal, make his god divorce the unsatisfactory Vesta, and marry the well-connected Annia Faustina. Around the middle of 221 he nominated Alexianus as Caesar and adopted the boy as his son. He also changed the boy's name to Alexander (for reasons that are not known).

Grandmother Maesa, not Mamaea, had done the persuading; he would not have listened to his repellently chaste aunt. Convincing him to adopt his strait-laced little cousin and to name the boy to the illustrious rank of Caesar, with its implications of his participation in the government and perhaps of his eventual succession to the throne, required tact. But Maesa had the tact; she simply suggested that if Alexander took over some of the duties of government—some of those boring chores that even a fun-loving youth had to perform in order to rule the Empire—Elagabalus would have more time to devote to his priestly duties. Very little more needed to be said; it is even possible that

Maesa felt contempt for Elagabalus for being so easily duped. The fact that Alexander was thirteen years old, whereas his new father was only seventeen, did not bother anybody. Adoptions often had little relevance to age in the Roman state.

The new arrangement was, for Mamaea, the thin edge of the wedge. For Maesa it constituted a fairly strong guarantee that her own house would continue in possession of the Empire. Alexander's partnership with Elagabalus might pacify the people, so that objections to the reign would die down; as long as the virtuous, well-motivated boy was there to see that his novel father did not go too far, the citizens might feel that the Empire was in safe hands. And if they did not feel this way—if the rebellion which she anticipated actually occurred—the Empire would, she hoped, still be in the hands of her family and especially in her own competent grip. There is little reason to believe that at this stage Maesa was actively plotting the death of her older grandson, but she would not have minded it.

In any case, when she looked at Alexander, a paragon of princely virtue, she felt that the future was not gloomy. A revolution was, of course, a potential danger—one could not be sure just how it would turn out—but she did not think there was much likelihood that the throne would go to anybody except Alexander. He was the most obvious candidate by far, and the way was being prepared for him.

The strains and irritations, tensions and abhorrences and machinations within the family have to be imagined, since no satisfactory record of them has survived. Whether Elagabalus had come to hate his grandmother; whether he suspected her of wanting his death, or hoped his apparent reform would dilute her anger, or made fun of her, or tried to avoid her; whether there were hot words between them, tearful reconciliations, or cold silences; whether he laughed secretly, believing that he had tricked his grandmother and his aunt into putting his young enemy right where he could watch him and govern him—at that, we can only guess. And we can only guess whether the two sisters were still speaking to each other, or were feigning mutual affection but nipping at each other with innuendoes, Soaemias implying that Mamaea was a prude and Mamaea suggesting that Soaemias was a prostitute. Perhaps the luxurious sister did not fully realize the acid envy of the pietistic Mamaea. Or perhaps their shrewd and domineering mother, who laid a great deal of stress on the importance of keeping up appearances, managed to keep them both under control, at least in public.

We know a little more about Elagabalus' relationships with his aunt and with his cousin-son. It is sometimes impossible to separate fact from fiction in accounts of these relationships, but at any rate we are not left entirely without hints as to what was going on.

Elagabalus may not have felt embarrassed by the difference between himself and Alexander, but he must have felt disgusted. Mamaea had taken great pains with her son's education. Alexander was not only trained in military and athletic exercises but was also exposed to the learning and literature of the past—especially the learning and literature of Augustan Rome and classical Greece. Horace and the Hellenic philosophers and poets were his daily companions; they caused him to ponder while Elagabalus indulged in practical jokes or merely played. Platonic concepts in particular appealed to him, and he studied how to be a philosopher-king. He was a boy of an unmitigatedly serious mind and, despite the examples of the court, a boy who wanted to remain virtuous. Like his master Plato, he placed little value on the everyday matters of life, being an idealist.

The Emperor evidently decided that Alexander needed a new kind of education—that the boy should learn the picturesque dances honoring the Sun God, that all his tutors were deleterious and should be driven from the palace, that in general his upbringing should be redirected along lascivious lines. The prig was too much under the influence of his mother for Elagabalus to entertain high hopes, but perhaps he was not entirely irredeemable. Mamaea, however, voiced objections, and, what was worse from the Emperor's standpoint, Alexander proved unresponsive.

Mamaea, meanwhile, did not relax her campaign. She smiled at the senators, whispered to her mother, and was prodigal toward the army. She also circulated the rumor that Alexander was the son of Caracalla, and Maesa seems to have helped her circulate it. Apparently Mamaea felt that her reputation for snow-white virtue was not too great a sacrifice for the attainment of her goal. If her sister could pose as the mother of an imperial bastard, so could she.

Elagabalus seemingly had no recourse. He saw his cousin and aunt in league against him—cousin and aunt and grandmother and Rome. It was probably at this point that he concluded reform was useless, flew in the face of his grandmother, almost suicidally went against everybody, staged his private rebellion, divorced Annia Faustina, and remarried the Vestal Virgin.

There is a slight possibility that Maesa, a very subtle mistress in the art of manipulation, encouraged him to reject the descendant of Marcus Aurelius and return to his Vestal. If she had by this time abandoned all hope for him, she might have been glad for anything he did that would prejudice people against him; the more foolish the actions he committed, the more likelihood that he would be removed from the throne.

That is a slight possibility but nothing more. Elagabalus was doing so many things to prejudice people against him that Maesa very likely felt he would be driven from the throne anyway, whether he remarried the Virgin or not. She was probably furious that he had opposed her wishes, had shown his independence, and had ignored her wisdom and authority. She was probably also angry because he was being more of an idiot than ever; after all, he was her grandson and his actions reflected on her house.

According to some accounts of his reign, he now tried to poison Alexander, whom he thoroughly hated by this time, or to arrange for the boy to be drowned in the bath, but the watchful Mamaea discovered his plots, supervised the preparation of her son's foods, and had the boy served by people she could trust. Whether attempts at murder actually occurred we do not know, but the situation at the palace must have been almost too tense for endurance—except for Maesa, who sat back to watch the unfolding of the tale.

Along the Danube rose up the spirit of Alexander the Great. It traversed the provinces of Moesia and Thrace on its way to Asia, accompanied by four hundred male attendants, each one wearing a fawn skin and carrying a thyrsus (a staff entwined with ivy and grape vines and topped by a pine cone). The fawn skin and thyrsus were attributes of the followers of the god Dionysus (Bacchus) and were appropriate to followers of Alexander, since the Macedonian king and the Phrygian god had both conquered India and were sometimes identified with each other.

Alexander's ghost was handsome, resembling what the great Greek must have looked like in the flesh and wearing similar armor. Its attendants—unlike the Dionysiac revelers of earlier ages, who had devoted themselves to divine madness and sex orgies—kept rather quiet and did not interfere with anybody. As the spirit and the four hundred men proceeded through Moesia and Thrace they were accommodated free of charge at the inns, and banquets were spread for them. Villages through which they intended to pass would wait in awe and impatience, the young men and maidens whispering, "Alexander is coming closer—Alexander will be here soon," and no soldier or governmental official would have dared to hinder the supernatural progress. The specter crossed from Byzantium to Chalcedon in Asia Minor; near Troy it offered a nocturnal sacrifice and buried a wooden horse. Having done that, it disappeared.

People asked one another what it meant, and some said that it betokened a change of reign, that the Greek Alexander had come to welcome his Roman namesake.

Elagabalus had had enough of almost everything. Totally surrounded, he decided it was time to act. He apparently instructed the Senate to withdraw the title Caesar from his cousin, also informing the army that the boy was no longer to be called Caesar, and let it be known that he wished statues and inscriptions honoring little Alexander in the Praetorian camp to be defaced.

The Senate, according to the story, did not react loyally to the Emperor's command; in fact, it did not do anything at all. The soldiers, when they saw Elagabalus' servants start to throw dirt at the statues of Alexander, contradicted the oath which they had sworn. The sympathies of most of the Praetorians lay with Alexander, partly because of Mamaea's generous wealth and partly because Elagabalus had disappointed them. Enraged at the Emperor, they staged a riot.

Accounts of just what happened then differ. The best account, however, is probably that of Cassius Dio, who reports that Elagabalus went to the Praetorian camp on his own initiative in order to find out what was happening there, and that he took his cousin along with him, suspecting that the boy must somehow be connected with the disturbances. When Elagabalus appeared at the camp, the Praetorians evidently complained about the favoritism in the government. They demanded that the Emperor dismiss from office his most outrageous favorites—the comedians, the chariot drivers, the sellers of smoke, etc.

They named several whom they particularly resented, and one of these was Hierocles.

At this, Elagabalus tried to put his foot down. He would dismiss the others, but not Hierocles. Making use of his lively dramatic instinct, he affirmed that he would rather die than give up Hierocles. "Leave me this one man," he pleaded. "Leave me my Hierocles, or kill me."

They apparently left him his Hierocles.

By fulfilling most of their stipulations he had appeased them, and it looked for a while as if the crisis was over. There was even a pretense of reconciliation with Alexander. The soldiers returned to their private thoughts, and Elagabalus returned to his pleasures.

They were, however, of short duration. On January 1, 222, he and Alexander were to receive the consulship together from the Senate. But the Emperor did not relish the thought of having Alexander as his fellow consul. Although he could not refuse the joint consulship, at least he would not comply with people's wishes to the extent of going with Alexander to the Senate house for the ceremony of installation. He would stay in the palace. Alexander was a moralistic hypocrite, and the Emperor hated him.

But Aunt Mamaea screamed and Grandmother Maesa urged; the senators were ready for the ceremony, and the soldiers might rebel if their own Alexander was badly treated. Elagabalus gave way. He put on his purple-bordered toga and stood with his virtuous rival in the Senate house. From there they were to proceed to the Capitol, since the sacrifices on the installation of consuls required the participation of the consuls themselves. But on this matter Elagabalus could not be persuaded. The Prefect of the City had to perform the sacrifices, and the ceremony was consequently not what it should have been.

According to one story, soon after this episode he commanded the senators to leave Rome at once, afraid that if they remained in the city they would elect an Emperor to replace him. Although he had inherited the contempt for the senators felt by Caracalla and Septimius Severus, he apparently feared their nominative power. Since this story is told by only one historian (Lampridius), however, it need not be accepted as fact. In actuality Elagabalus never worried much about what the Senate was going to do; it was the army that bothered him, just as the army had bothered Macrinus. On the other hand, he was certainly spontaneous enough to say to the Senate: "Leave town at once." In the squeeze and pressure of recent circumstances his reign was becoming crazier and crazier. There was no telling what he would do from one moment to another; he was irrational, inconsistent, bizarre. It seemed at times as if he courted calamity, defying life to do its worst. And then again it seemed as if he was naïve, only weakly aware of the perils of his position. He chased his fantastic pleasures with a relentless gaiety, since he could do anything he wished as Emperor of Rome.

Early in March, after he and Alexander had been sharing the consulship for a little over two months, he went again to the Praetorian camp. The reason he went is not clear. One historian (Herodian) says that in order to test the loyalty of the troops he had been circulating a rumor that Alexander was dying, and the soldiers, suspicious that the Emperor was trying to kill Alexander, had refused to send the usual guard to the palace and had demanded that the Caesar be brought to the camp so that they could see him. However, he may have gone to the camp simply because the soldiers were in a mutinous mood and he thought he could pacify them by talking to them. In any case, he intended to address them. Four years ago at Emesa he had stimulated intense devotion from the soldiers by giving them a speech. He could not hope for that now; these Praetorians were different, the year was different, and he was different too. But perhaps he could at least calm them down, as he had calmed them on the matter of favoritism. Appeasement was most necessary now. If he appeased them he could enjoy life again. He had better succeed, because by going to the camp he was putting himself in their power.

The ringleaders, however, must be punished. He would show that he still possessed imperial authority. These soldiers were presumptuous to interrupt the pleasures of an Emperor.

Presumably, Alexander rode with him, and presumably both mothers also proceeded to the camp while the grandmother stayed in the palace tending to her business—politics.

It was obvious to Elagabalus that most of the Praetorians could not easily be won over. They received him coldly; they were formal, wary, at times rude. But they greeted Alexander with loud and loyal cheers.

There is more than one explanation of what started the riot. If we are to believe Herodian, Elagabalus commanded that the most impudent Praetorians, the ones most zealous in their support for Alexander, be court-martialed, and the loyal officers who tried to arrest them met with a resistance that spread rapidly. If we are to believe Dio, however, Mamaea and Soaemias, unable to restrain their mutual abhorrence even in front of the soldiers, broke into a verbal battle, calling each other names, flinging vicious taunts and accusations at each other—stinging each other, like two rival queen bees fighting it out for a hive—and the unseemly sisterly row sparked a conflict between the two factions.

Elagabalus' party was so outnumbered that it could expect only defeat; the Emperor knew that. Whatever bravery he might have felt at the Battle of Immae had been dissipated in the interim. He had been young then, foolish and hopeful, trying to win the throne; now he was eighteen, satiated and supine, and totally afraid. With his mother, he ran from the riot, which was becoming a slaughter. They hid shivering in the camp latrine.

In the darkness, the insect-infested filth, and the smell that made one want to vomit, they sat terrified with their arms around each other, the lovely, luxurious mother and the son who used gold chamberpots. It had happened very quickly; it was almost over. Soldiers came in and ran them through.

Elagabalus never had the chance to choose among the cord, the sword, the vase, and the tower.

In the conventional Roman manner their bodies, naked, bruised, and headless, were dragged through the city for the people to hoot at and revile. Then the soldiers, tiring of the torso of the woman who had pleased so many men, tossed it aside. They heaved Elagabalus' body into the river. As it hurtled toward the water, they cheered.

# ☙ XVII ☙

## Trying to Be an Ideal Emperor

Although Alexander was not yet fourteen, people expected him to usher in a golden age. They saw in him a youth who would make the effort to be a good Emperor, a conscientious boy full of learning, piety, and high ideals. The army was for him, the Senate was for him, the populace was for him. The horrors of the past four years could be washed away; under Alexander the halcyon days of the Antonines would be revived. Of course he had been born in Syria, but he was more Roman than his cousin. It was true that he excelled at Greek and that in spite of his fondness for Horace and Cicero he did not seem to feel at ease with Latin, but he prided himself on the fact that he was a Roman. At his birth, people said, a star had shone above the house where he lay, and that was a sign that he would be a great ruler.

When he appeared before the Senate he was greeted with loud acclamations—resounding ovations and reiterated cries of "May the gods keep you safe," and other expressions of loyalty. This matter of acclamations was a formal affair, a custom dating from the republic, with a leader directing and the senators responding like a chorus in a kind of chant. It was a most impressive thing for a young Emperor to hear. The Senate immediately decreed him the imperial titles and prerogatives, naming him Augustus, Pontifex Maximus, and Father of his Country, and giving him the proconsular power and the tribunician power. The Senate also urged him to accept the name Antoninus and the surname the Great, but he modestly declined both these offers. The senators kept urging, and he kept declining. He said that he hoped he would be a better Emperor than his cousin (whom he deprecated in remarks that were largely true and sometimes understated), but that he had not yet done anything to merit the appellations Antoninus and the Great.

There may have been another reason why he did not want to be called Antoninus. Since Antoninus had been Caracalla's official name, to adopt the name himself might imply that he was entitled to it by right of birth. His strict conception of morality very likely found this implication revolting, even though it did not offend his mother. He did, however, adopt the name Severus, which connoted the triumphs of the reign of Caracalla's father.

Mamaea continued to supervise her son's education. She employed the finest tutors available—those most admirable for their virtue as well as for their learning—and kept away flatterers, who might make the youth conceited and autocratic, and tempters, who might corrupt his chastity (which she wished she could preserve inviolate). She had him attend courts of justice, so that he could see the laws of the Empire applied and rectitude rewarded. Under her guidance he enlarged his understanding of the great figures of the past, some of whom he came to idolize. His idealism was not destroyed by too much contact with the world, because Mamaea permitted him as little contact with the world as possible. In this great, cynical city, during a period when materialism and sensuality were rampant, he stayed pure and beautiful. The corrupt age in which he lived had, it is true, a certain spiritual hunger, often satisfied by the religions of the East, such as the Egyptian cults, Mithraism, and Christianity; many people were rebelling against cynicism, materialism, and sensuality. But with Severus Alexander, it seems, there was no rebellion; he would not have had a clear conception of what to rebel against. Given his environment, it seems unlikely that he was innocent, but perhaps it is possible for a person to be pure in Sodom, as long as he is puritanically reared.

Since he was too young to reign alone, a Council of Sixteen was formed to help him carry on the government. These sixteen were trusted senators, men of gravity, integrity, and intelligence. Their appointment suggested that among the innovations of this reign was to be a new attitude toward the Senate. It had been a long time since sixteen senators had been treated with as much respect by imperial personages as these men were treated by Alexander and his mother.

The contempt under which the Senate had smarted during the reigns of Septimius Severus, Caracalla, Macrinus, and Elagabalus was evidently relegated to the past; the Senate was in favor. Men wondered whether the army was consequently out of favor.

With the Council of Sixteen to advise Alexander, and with Mamaea and Grandmother Maesa to advise him as well, the administration began very well. One of Alexander's earliest acts was to ship the Sun God back to Syria. The symbols of piety which had been stolen from Rome's ancient temples and collected in the temples of the Sun were put back where they belonged, with the enthusiastic approval of most of the populace and all of the Senate. Roman religion was to be resuscitated; the tyranny of the god Elagabalus was over.

Another early action on the part of the Emperor was to clear the palace of Elagabalus' favorites and dependents. They were a curious and colorful throng—dwarfs, acrobats, male prostitutes, female prostitutes, singers, buffoons, pimps, mimes, eunuchs. The most unprincipled purveyors of debauchery were deported. Alexander is said to have felt a particular animus toward the eunuchs—and with reason—since they tended to be disorderly and to usurp authority. He would not retain any of them as his own servants, except for the care of the women's baths in the palace.

The Emperor dismissed from office the unworthies whose cleverness, brashness, or absence of conscience Elagabalus had rewarded with political posts. The vacated offices were filled with sane, serious men. The greatest office of all, that of Praetorian Prefect, Alexander bestowed on Ulpian, one of the most illustrious names in the history of Roman civil law.

During the reign of Septimius Severus, Ulpian had served as assessor under the great Papinian and had counseled the Emperor. He had been master of the records for Caracalla. It appears that he had occupied a place at court as tutor or guardian for Alexander (then little Alexianus), and the prince had come to love his mentor beyond perhaps everybody else except his mother. But Elagabalus, who hated his incorruptibility, had evidently removed him from office. Now he seems to have resumed his place as Alexander's guardian as well as fulfilling the duties of Praetorian Prefect. Mamaea was at first jealous of his enormous influence over the young Emperor; it was her belief that Alexander should be entirely in her control. Ulpian, however, had so much courtliness and was so wise, just, and valuable that he gradually won the esteem of even the jealous mother.

But what would succeed with Mamaea would not succeed with the army. It happened that the Praetorians already had two Prefects when Ulpian was appointed. Their names were Flavian and Chrestus, and they had probably been implicated in Elagabalus' murder. Flavian and Chrestus were very unhappy about Ulpian; so were the Praetorians. Not only was it irregular for the Praetorian Guard to have three Prefects, but Ulpian was not even an army man. Of course he could argue that certain predecessors, such as Papinian and Macrinus, had also been trained for law rather than for military service, but that was not the point. The Praetorians thought that the Emperor was trying to exalt the civilian over the military, and their objections cast a shadow on the commencement of this reign from which so much was hoped.

Just exactly what happened is not clear, but it would appear that Flavian and Chrestus incited the Praetorians to revolt, and that when the mutiny was crushed Flavian and Chrestus were executed by order of the Emperor. Then Ulpian was perhaps sole Prefect; at least, we do not know the name of anyone who shared the office with him. The soldiers continued to feel abused, with the result that there were disorders from time to time in the camp, causing the young philosopher-Emperor to worry and to wonder what Plato would have done. But Ulpian would remain Prefect; that much was certain.

The Praetorians, however, provided only a small part of the business of the day for Ulpian. His realm, in addition to law, was affairs of state. In large measure he was the master of the Empire. He certainly possessed as much power as the infamous Plautian had possessed under Septimius Severus, but he exercised it more modestly and more beneficently. Alexander, with his tendency to idolize people, called him "my friend" and even "my parent," consulted him about everything of importance, confided his adolescent fears and troubles to this kind old prime minister and guide. Letters and other papers which required the Emperor's consideration were examined first by Ulpian, who separated the essential from the decorative, applied his judgment to the questions involved, and then reported to Alexander. When a subject had an audience with the Emperor, Ulpian would be present throughout the conversation—respectful, attentive, protective. When Ulpian had a conference with the Emperor, very likely nobody else was present; the

Prefect was the only man with whom Alexander spoke in private. The earnest, intellectual youth probably did not miss the companionship of people his own age, whose frivolity he would have found boring if not displeasing. With Ulpian, the companion of his leisure hours and sometimes his sole dinner guest, he could discuss statesmanship and philosophy, the noble odes of Horace, the eloquent orations of Cicero, and of course the inexhaustible dialogues of Plato. Ulpian could teach him to be an ideal Emperor.

He was already a conscientious one. He arose early in the morning, often before it was light, perhaps engaged in a little fishing or walking in order to clear his mind, and passed the remainder of the morning conferring with Ulpian and other counselors or influential senators on matters of urgency to the Empire. No matter what happened during these conferences his face appeared contented if not placid, and his big, serious eyes showed no anger. If he had time, he studied Plato or some Roman poet, or read about the life of his namesake, Alexander the Great. Then, paying attention to the precept *Mens sana in corpore sano,* he engaged in some exercise, such as wrestling or running. After that came a bath. His lunch was simple, perhaps just bread and milk and an egg or two. In the afternoon, back to business, with Ulpian near by. He had his secretaries read him the letters to be sent from himself to various parts of the Empire and beyond; he would correct them and sign them. It would, of course, have been a grievous offense for a secretary or anybody else to sit in his presence without being asked to do so, but if his secretaries looked tired he often invited them to sit. In this way he demonstrated his difference from most Emperors and especially from Elagabalus.

He demonstrated that difference in many other ways too. Elagabalus, for example, had required his subjects to prostrate themselves before him, as if he was an Asiatic autocrat rather than a Roman; coming from the Syrian environment and descended from priest-kings, he probably had not understood the disparity between an Oriental despot and a Roman Emperor; but Alexander discouraged all obsequious gestures. He also forbade his subjects to address him as "my lord," although some excellent Emperors, such as Trajan, had not disliked the title. People were to call Alexander by his name and nothing else; he was democratic. Those who wrote him letters were to include no adulatory titles in the superscriptions but to pretend that they were just writing to another private citizen. They had to add the term "Emperor," but no more. When senators came to see him, he almost invariably told them to be seated—an act of graciousness for which he was much complimented. When friends were sick he went to the trouble of calling on them, even if they were not of high rank. He dismissed superfluous servants from the palace staff. Rejecting foreign fashions as foppery and taking care to avoid clothes made entirely of the hated silk, he wore the unpretentious toga, like any other Roman gentleman.

His frugality may have been inherited from his mother, who was both acquisitive and economical—who, as was mentioned before, had lavished money on the soldiers only because the end in view was so attractive. The greatest expense he went to for his own amusement was for an elaborate complex of aviaries within the palace. Here he could entertain himself by observing the feathered world at work and play—pheasants, peacocks, partridges, doves, and ducks. But even this expense, it seems, was not carried by the treasury. When the hatched eggs developed into edible fowl he apparently had the squabs sold for a profit.

He was certainly different from Elagabalus. Although he did not allow himself much idle time, he loved to watch the peahens sit on their nests and the pigeons waddle past and the male pheasants fight. His other amusement was to watch a puppy and a baby pig have sport together.

He took care to let the common people know that he liked them, even calling them together and favoring them with orations, as consuls and tribunes had done centuries ago, before there were Emperors. The priests and augurs, too, received proofs of his high regard. But his treatment of the Senate was a more noteworthy aspect of his internal policy.

It seemed that he wished to give the impression of re-establishing the dyarchy, the joint rule by Emperor and Senate which had been a fiction even under Augustus. The fact that the army disliked the Senate, and that by catering to the Senate he was alienating the army, did not greatly disturb him. On the whole, his mother preferred the Senate, and his own preference probably reflected hers. He may even have felt that the army had grown too demanding and needed to be put down. In this attitude he was probably right.

At any rate, to some extent he revived and augmented senatorial prerogatives. Before raising a man to the rank of senator, he made certain that the man had the Senate's approval. He consulted the Senate regarding provincial matters which had only nominally been in the hands of that body since the reign of Augustus. In early imperial times the Emperor had presented the Senate with a sizable list of nominees for certain political offices, and the Senate had selected the magistrates from this list. In later times, however, it became the custom for the Emperor to list only as many nominees as there were offices to fill, so that the Senate's part in the whole business had become perfunctory. Alexander returned to the earlier practice.

He was naturally well liked by the Senate, which showed its affection by granting him favors. An Emperor, for example, possessed the right to make his wishes known to the Senate by means of a written motion which his own delegate would read aloud and which took precedence over all other business in front of the body. This right was especially valuable if the Emperor wanted his wishes acted on while he himself was away at war. The number of imperial motions that could be presented per sitting, however, differed according to the Senate's pleasure. Some Emperors were given permission to have only one wish read per sitting; others could have two motions presented for them; still others, three. Both Marcus Aurelius and Alexander were given the right to have five motions introduced per meeting.

In the warmth of Alexander's friendship the Senate could perhaps have become a forceful, active partner in the government if the Senate had felt inclined to be active and forceful. Unfortunately, it did not feel so inclined. During the Punic Wars the senators had experienced their great days, their days of tight-lipped courage and selfless glory and strong national leadership. But the Punic Wars were a dim, patriotic memory extending back four or five centuries.

Another of Alexander's projects was to try to rebuild Roman morality. To this end he wished to do away with the coeducational baths which seem to have become popular at Rome. Such baths had already been frowned on by Hadrian and Marcus Aurelius, but under Elagabalus they had evidently prospered. Severus Alexander would put a stop to them. He also apparently considered making the trade of male prostitution illegal, but decided that driving the vice underground would only serve to strengthen it.

Roman officialdom needed drastic reform; it must be cleansed of the laxity, cynicism, and opportunism which had characterized it under Elagabalus. Alexander attempted to purge the Senate, the knightly order, the army, and the provincial magistracy of egregiously impure elements. There were few persons he disliked so deeply as a corrupt official, a man who oppressed the populace for his own private benefit, or who grew rich on bribes. Even a corrupt underling was subject to his contempt.

Like Septimius Severus, he exercised extreme care in choosing men for public office. Not entirely naïve, he suspected a great many persons of place-seeking and announced that in his opinion the man who most deserved a high office was the one who did the least to obtain it—who, in fact, tried to avoid the appointment. This rule-of-thumb worked sometimes but not always; it occasionally resulted in the appointment of a very refractory magistrate.

Alexander is said to have borrowed from Christianity—like his mother, he was quite interested in it—a custom that the Christians had probably adopted from the Jews and which impressed him as being wise. When a Christian was about to be elevated to the priesthood his name was broadcast far and wide, so that anybody who knew anything bad about the man—anything which should keep him from being made a priest—could voice his objections. Alexander tried to apply a similar practice to the appointment of magistrates. Since he detested informers, however, he added that if a man who had denounced a candidate was unable to substantiate his accusation, he would be killed for false testimony. This provision effectively deterred people from saying a word against a candidate unless they had self-evident proof, so that the benefits of Alexander's system were more theoretical than actual. The system might have worked better if his subjects had been sure that a just accusation would always be believed, or if they had not been afraid of death.

In order to keep governors uncontaminated and yet permit them to hold office in a dignified Roman manner, Alexander provided them free-of-charge with horses, mules, silver table services, official and domestic garments, a cook, a muleteer, gold, and, if a man was unmarried and wanted one, a concubine. But the Emperor stipulated that if at the end of their administration it was found that the governors had been unworthy of office, they would have to pay four times the value of what had been given them. If they had been good administrators, they could keep everything except the cook, the muleteer, the mules, and the horses.

By punishing corrupt officeholders harshly, Alexander hoped to dissuade others from being corrupt. His severity extended even to low subordinates. For instance, when it was discovered that a clerk had knowingly presented the council with an untrue version of a certain case, the sinews of the clerk's fingers were cut in order to prevent him from ever writing another word, and he was shipped off to an island.

It also came to the Emperor's attention that a man of high station had obtained an important military post through the influence of some foreign monarchs who were at the time living in Rome, and that he was using his position to rob with greedy industry. Alexander, according to the story, had him watched, and arrested him when his criminality seemed obvious. After the heinousness of the man's activities had been proved beyond a doubt, there remained the question of punishment.

The Emperor asked the kings, "How do they punish robbers in your countries?"

"By crucifixion."

Alexander was glad that the kings were there to give this answer; otherwise he might have been blamed for inclemency. The man was crucified.

At the court of Elagabalus, Alexander had watched Hierocles and others sell smoke. Among the people who most disgusted him were those that used their influence with an Emperor to profit from others. He was highly justified; the selling of smoke had become one of the worst abuses at the imperial court. In spite of his disgust at the practice, however, it happened that one of his most trusted courtiers, a man named Turinus who had squeezed his way into the Emperor's good opinion, sold smoke as energetically as if Elagabalus were still alive.

Turinus gave courtiers the impression that his influence with the Emperor was second only to that of Ulpian—that Alexander would do almost anything he said—that, in a manner of speaking, he led the young Emperor around by the nose. Some of his income was apparently protection money; he threatened to disparage people before the

Emperor unless they paid him generously. Much of his activity, however, was confined to the more traditional aspects of smoke-selling: a man who yearned for an important appointment or some other favor would go to Turinus, who would promise to speak on his behalf to the Emperor in return for a healthy sum. Perhaps he spoke, and perhaps he neglected the whole matter.

For a long time Alexander was idealistically ignorant of the man's baseness. When the situation grew intolerable, however, someone decided to make a revelation. The Emperor, shocked at last, did not consider it beneath his dignity to participate in a conspiracy to trap the deceiver who had in some degree made a fool of him. He had someone ask publicly for a favor and then go privately to Turinus for help. Turinus, for an exorbitant fee, promised assistance, but, as the conspirators had hoped, he did not even mention the matter to the Emperor. After Alexander granted the man's request, Turinus took the credit and demanded payment. The man was careful to pay him in front of several other people who had been included in the conspiracy and who could act as witnesses. Then Alexander ordered a trial.

Turinus, of course, was without defense; he had been tricked with the contrivance of the young man whom he had scorned as a fool. With the Emperor against him, he had no chance. Alexander did not try the case himself but functioned as one of Turinus' accusers, revealing to the judges many other instances of Turinus' duplicity that had been brought to his notice. His last laugh was long and indignant.

The former favorite was taken to the market place, at Alexander's command, and tied to a post there. Green wood had been piled under the post. When ignited, the wood sent up thick clouds of smoke. Turinus coughed his way to death, and while he was suffocating the criers called out: "The man who sold smoke is punished by smoke. The man who sold smoke is punished by smoke."

Toward the public, Alexander endeavored to be generous in spite of the niggardliness which he shared with his mother. During his thirteen-year reign he made five distributions of grain or money. This by no means represented prodigality, but at least it was more sensible than the extravagant and eccentric distributions that had occurred under Elagabalus. Alexander also restored to its original condition a fund which Septimius Severus had established for supplying the populace with oil but which had suffered during Elagabalus' reign. If a flood or an earthquake occurred in some city of the Empire, he remitted the city's taxes and sent money for the repair of the buildings and (perhaps) for the care of the injured, although most of the injured could probably fare better at some temple of Aesculapius. If he heard of people whose rank obliged them to live in a rich style but whose income did not allow them to do so, he was pleased to relieve their position by presenting them with land, herds, slaves, and farm tools, which inspired them to work.

The encouragement of industry was, in fact, one of his favorite domestic policies; an ideal Emperor should not let his subjects become lazy any more than he should let himself become lazy. Sometimes Alexander lent money without charging interest, but then he stipulated that the sum should be spent for land and that he must be repaid from the profits made by working the land.

By promoting economic conditions favorable to business, such as smooth trade relations, Alexander tried to attract merchants to Rome from far parts of the Empire and the kingdoms beyond. The taxes which he imposed on glass-makers, tailors, linen-weavers, goldsmiths, silversmiths, and blacksmiths were designed to be just rather than oppressive. The populace, as usual, complained that prices were too high, and when the Emperor inquired which prices in particular were prohibitive he was told that beef and pork cost far too much. Instead of saying: "Then eat fish," as a less benevolent Emperor might have done, and instead of placing a ceiling on the prices of beef and pork, as the populace undoubtedly expected him to do, he ruled that no sows, suckling pigs, cows, or calves could be slaughtered. The ban stayed in effect for two years. When it was removed the slaughterhouses ran with the blood of accumulated cattle and of pigs overripe for the axe, and so much pork and beef were suddenly available that they sold for a great deal less than before.

The Emperor apparently made a serious attempt to reduce taxes and, so far as we can determine, drastically lowered harbor dues and tolls, customs duties, etc., again for the promotion of trade. In spite of all his efforts, however, the capital and the provinces were in a less flourishing condition during his reign than they had been earlier— under Severus in particular. Elagabalus' extravagances and, much more important, Caracalla's wars had taken their financial toll. The quartering of troops in the provinces and necessary requisitions by provincial officials also helped to drain the Empire financially. The currency was steadily deteriorating, with the result that faith in the economic stability of the government suffered and prices sharply rose and fell. It almost looked as if good times could not be brought back.

Alexander was almost as anxious to support learning as to support industry. He provided salaries for rhetoricians, physicians, mathematicians, grammarians, architects, teachers of the mechanical arts, elementary educationists, and even such men on the periphery of learning as augurs and astrologers. He furnished schools for eager teachers, and he enabled the quick-witted children of the poor to attend the schools. Quite probably he was responsible for founding at the city of Berytus (now Beirut) in Phoenicia the law school which in the late Roman period ranked as the world's greatest training ground for lawyers. In his munificence toward mental activity he was following the example of good Emperors of the past, such as Vespasian and Antoninus Pius. An ideal Emperor must do all he can to stimulate the intellectual interests of his subjects.

In contrast to this generosity was, of course, the economy illustrated by Alexander's alleged practice of having the young fowl from his aviary taken to the market and sold as if they belonged to some farmer. Whether his frugality was in the main dictated by his money-worshipping mother or whether it was inherent in his character, the fact remains that it was a quality badly needed after the outrageous expenditures of Elagabalus. Alexander was very careful not to fritter away the imperial income on private extravagances. He did not use gold plate on his table. Banquets for large numbers of people seemed to him a painful waste of money. It is said that when he did bring himself to hold a banquet he would not go to the cost of providing sufficient tableware or servants, so that guests had to furnish extra plates and spare slaves. His offerings at temples were, for an Emperor, paltry; he refused to give gold to the gods and did not think that they required much silver either. One of his favorite quotations was a line from Persius to the effect that gold is irrelevant to sanctity.

Despite his seriousness, he shared with many other Romans a taste for theatrical entertainments, which he often attended. Enthusiastic theatregoers in Rome had for a long time followed the custom of presenting their favorite actors with lavish gifts. Pantomimists particularly were rewarded for their cleverness and their satirical ability. Elagabalus had bestowed sumptuous garments on mimes who struck his fancy, but these theatrical people could expect no generosity from Alexander. A little money—a very little—was appropriate to men of their profession.

For a couple of years the Emperor was married. It seems that when his wife was given pearls of unusual size and luster by an official, he said that she could not keep them. Such remarkable pearls were luxuries, and it was indecent to indulge oneself in this manner; this young man shrank from luxury, believing that a Spartan simplicity best fit the imperial state. He tried to sell the pearls, but nobody would buy them; so he had them made into a pair of earrings for a statue of Venus.

He was more successful in his efforts to sell the crown jewels; people purchased these. But he did not keep the money; he put it in the treasury. An ideal Emperor is thrifty but not avaricious, realizing that the public good must always come first.

The most important maxim of government, he felt, was the Golden Rule. He had probably learned this precept in his investigation of the Christian religion, but he knew it in its negative form. "Do not do unto others what you would not have others do unto you"—that was a beautiful principle. He had it engraved in his palace; he had it inscribed in public buildings. If a man was executed for a crime which involved flagrant infringement of the rights of his fellow human beings, the crier would proclaim the Golden Rule for the edification of the bystanders. "Do not do unto others what you would not have others do unto you." If all governments followed this advice, he assumed, all governments would be ideal.

# ✠ XVIII ✠

# *Life at the Palace of Alexander*

Plato would probably not have approved of the extent to which Alexander let himself be directed by his mother. She apparently selected his bride, a lady of noble descent named Orbiana, the girl who was not allowed to keep the pearls. They were evidently joined in matrimony in the year 225, when Alexander was about sixteen years old. At approximately the same time Grandmother Maesa, having done her work and done it well, died. She left her daughter in efficient control of the situation.

Our knowledge of the marriage of Alexander and Orbiana is even murkier than our knowledge of Elagabalus' marriages. We are aware, however, that Orbiana's father was a gentleman of senatorial rank named Sallustius Macrinus, and that after his daughter's marriage he was given the title Caesar. It seems that Alexander was not disappointed in his bride, and there are even suggestions that he grew to love her. No children that we know of proceeded from the union, however, and it did not last long. It collapsed in 227.

Mamaea was evidently not happy with her daughter-in-law. Accustomed to governing people, she had expected to govern Orbiana and discovered that Orbiana had an independent mind. Mamaea did not relish the presence of another woman in the palace with the title Augusta. She may also have been jealous of the influence which Orbiana was exercising over Alexander; she considered her son her personal property, and a daughter-in-law was an intruder.

Orbiana's father may have complicated the situation by going to the Praetorians and complaining that Mamaea was mistreating his daughter and himself, that she was in fact persecuting them with all the malevolence of an envious woman. It is also possible that he nursed the hope of becoming Emperor himself, and conceivably he did more than merely nurse it. At least, those were the stories that were circulated. They must have combined with the animosity between mother-in-law and daughter-in-law to make the marriage unduly emotional. The emotionalism probably reached a climax when Mamaea drove Orbiana from the palace and brought the girl's father to condign or not condign punishment. Orbiana was banished to Africa and her father was executed for high treason.

The Emperor's reactions throughout these disagreeable proceedings are not recorded. He may have suspected that his wife and father-in-law were being sacrificed to his mother's need to dominate, and he may have been sorry about that, especially if he loved the girl. But he could also have felt that his mother's conduct was justified. We are not informed that he offered any objections, although of course our information is meager. Since no coolness developed in his relationship with his mother, the safest guess is that he felt his mother knew best.

There is no reason to think that he ever married again.

Married or single, Alexander stayed unexceptionable. Not only was he conscientious about being a good Emperor, he was also conscientious about being good in private life, probably because he thought private goodness essential to public excellence.

His ambition to improve his mind, and thereby improve his virtue, was insistent. In addition to reading masters such as Homer, Plato, Horace, and Cicero, he read moderns such as Serenus Sammonicus. He applied himself diligently to history and mathematics, learned how to play several musical instruments and to sing, and composed verses about the lives of the most exemplary Emperors. Although his intellectual capacities were not those of a genius, they were by no means inconsiderable; like other members of the Syrian family, he had intelligence and used it to advantage. When orators and poets recited their works in a lecture hall, he liked to join the fashionable crowd that assembled to hear them; he was particularly interested in hearing poems or orations on some heroic Roman of former times or some admirable monarch such as Alexander the Great (another of his idols). The Roman bar was among other things a kind of exercise in eloquence, and famous lawyers would polish their most successful speeches after a trial and read them to select audiences; the Emperor frequently came to listen to their rhetoric.

The company in which he took the greatest pleasure was that of a few men noteworthy for virtue and learning. With these estimable companions he would sit discussing philosophical tenets or political principles, much as his great-aunt Julia Domna had done, sometimes deferring to the opinions of his elders, or sometimes disputing, asking questions, and making pointed comments. But although he loved these men he also feared them; his future reputation, he suspected, lay in their hands, since they were the men who would write about him for posterity, and he placed great value on his posthumous image. He hoped that his friends would picture him as a moral and intelligent being. Not that he wished for unmerited praise, but he was conscious of his laudable qualities and did not want them misrepresented. His friends, he thought, should learn what he was like from his own conversation, not from the reports of others, who might engage in slander.

The Emperor's religion seems to have consisted partly in the worship of virtue. The men of the past who possessed his most fervent regard were those who had been, in his judgment, most virtuous. He collected together from all over the city the statues of the worthiest of the deified Emperors and put them in the Forum of Nerva, along with inscriptions setting forth their most distinguished accomplishments. The result was, in a sense, an exhibit of what the human character could attain, and of course it was hoped that the citizens would profit from the display. His palace had two *lararia,* or chapels to the spirits of the dead, one dedicated to men famous for military or literary talents, such as Achilles, Cicero, and Virgil, and the other one, which was perhaps more important, dedicated to men of surpassing virtue who had benefited mankind by means of their goodness and wisdom. In both these chapels he performed solemn rituals every day.

The chapel to virtue contained images of the good Emperors, of his own ancestors (in conformity with Roman practice), and of figures from the past whom he considered most deserving of adoration—for instance, Alexander the Great, Orpheus, Abraham, Apollonius of Tyana, and Jesus Christ. Apollonius of Tyana, the first-century miracle-worker and teacher who had been made into a god by believing multitudes, was the man whose biography Julia Domna had asked her savant Philostratus to write; the book was still quite new, and Alexander had almost certainly read it.

Long-bearded and shaggy-haired, wearing only linen clothing because he considered it evil to make clothes from the hide or hair of animals (such as sheep), wearing shoes of bark or no shoes at all, and declining to eat meat, Apollonius traveled over much of the known world with one or more disciples, particularly the faithful Damis of Nineveh. He was apparently a Pythagorean, but his Pythagoreanism was mixed with classical polytheism and with the Brahminism that he learned in India as a young man in search of wisdom. He could drive out demons and raise people from the dead and see into the future, and by the time he was incarcerated by the tyrannical Emperor Domitian it should have been obvious to everybody that he was divine and could not be executed. He was earnest, self-restrained, and intelligent (he could vanquish anybody in an argument, even the highly successful, perfumed Sophist Euphrates), and he fought evil in both theory and practice, as he made clear in lengthy lectures. It is not difficult to see why he appealed to Alexander.

After Alexander's death there arose a belief that Mamaea had been a Christian. Late in her son's reign, while she was at Antioch she apparently did send for Origen of Alexandria, probably the most eminent Christian then living, and received instructions from him; but that he converted her or that she was ever converted by anybody is extremely doubtful. As for her son, no evidence exists that he was a Christian either. Although both of them were very much interested in Christianity, they were interested in many other religions as well, and what probably attracted Alexander to Christianity was not its theological doctrines but its moral ones. He seems to have viewed Christ as an outstanding moral teacher, one worthy of rank with Orpheus, Abraham, and Apollonius of Tyana. He may even have thought Christ divine, but not to the exclusion of a large number of other figures.

At any rate, he was sympathetic toward Christianity and Judaism (they were still often confused with each other), and neither religion was repressed during his reign. The story that he intended to build a Christian temple probably has no validity, but he showed no hostility to the Christians in Rome. They could not worship in churches at the time, having none. Empty buildings and underground chambers, places where they would not be disturbed, held their congregations. One group of Christians, however, was involved in a dispute with sellers of wine over the occupancy of a certain building. Alexander ruled in favor of the Christians, remarking that the building would be put to better use as a center for worship than as an aid to drinking.

With regard to his other religious views we have only scanty information. He forbade worship of himself even in the eastern part of the Empire, where it was most enthusiastic; but this was probably not because he disapproved of Emperor-worship as such, but because adoration of the living Emperor had come to be associated with tyranny. The historians Herodian and Lampridius assert that he was a devout follower of the Great Mother, or Cybele, a goddess of Asiatic origin.

She had been introduced to Rome in 204 B.C. and shortly after that had been granted a home on the Palatine Hill, where she was a neighbor of Apollo. Her creed became very popular in the late republic and early Empire, although Roman citizens were for a long time forbidden to enter those cadres of her priesthood which required castration. In the age of the Syrian dynasty her cult grew more popular than ever. With a turreted crown on her head and a lion or two at her side, she must have been an imposing deity; and she was certainly an exotic one, accompanied by savage, part-demonic, frenzied beings, called Corybantes, who indulged in wild dances. From her rites the worshippers of Mithra had apparently borrowed the *taurobolium,* or purification in bull blood.

Cybele's story was both amorous and pathetic. She had fallen in love with a handsome youth named Attis, sometimes believed to be her son, but he disregarded her affection. Deeply hurt, Cybele evidently made him insane, and he tore off his testicles under a pine tree, and died. From his blood sprang violets which garlanded the pine, and the tree received his soul. Cybele carried the body to her cave, where she lamented. According to one version of the legend, in her anguish she asked Zeus to prevent the beloved body from decomposing. He not only granted her request; he even let Attis' hair grow and allowed the youth's little finger to move (the moving finger seems to have afforded her some solace, reminding her of the penis). Her story ended happily, because in time Attis was fully restored.

It was, of course, a primitive fertility myth, with Attis symbolizing the fruits of the earth, which die in the winter and are reborn in the spring, but it fascinated the sophisticated Romans; and Roman ladies, taking the tragic tale to heart, became Cybele's priestesses. As for Cybele's priests, they wore women's clothes and long hair sticky with sweet-smelling ointment. To the accompaniment of flutes, drums, and cymbals they performed barbaric, frenetic dances, like the Corybantes, and in their holy frenzy they scourged one another and lacerated themselves; and the young candidates for priesthood cut off their own testicles in enthusiastic imitation of Attis and threw them at Cybele's image.

What attraction the Great Mother held for Alexander is not easy to discern. Perhaps he loved her as a symbol of motherhood; perhaps as a child of the Orient he felt her Oriental appeal; perhaps he revered her as the greatest of the goddesses. In the minds of many of her worshippers she was identified with Rhea, wife of the Titan Cronus and mother of the Olympian deities—the Great Mother of Gods and Men, as she was sometimes called—and Alexander may have adored her in this connection. On the day in March when the resurrection of Attis was celebrated, he would demonstrate his joy by permitting a pheasant to be served at his simple table. But he observed the same relaxation of austerity on other feast days as well.

One other aspect of Alexander's religiosity was his addiction to astrology. Like Septimius Severus and Caracalla, as well as a large number of his Roman contemporaries, he had firm faith in those who predicted the future by means of the stars; and he allowed the professional astrologers—or Chaldeans, as they were called—to live unmolested at Rome, although they had been persecuted in earlier reigns as charlatans and practitioners of evil. The Emperor prided himself on his own acquaintance with the symbolism of the heavenly bodies; he studied astrology with minute attention, considering it a very necessary branch of learning.

He was also taught how to interpret lightning and earthquakes and how to read the entrails of sacrificed animals. This kind of knowledge was an important aspect of old Roman religion and carried a great deal more dignity than the astrological lore of the Chaldeans, although in his superstitious age astrology may have exerted a stronger appeal.

In 227 Mamaea received the official title Mother of the Augustus and of the Camps and of the Senate and of the Fatherland. Many other honors were accorded her—statues, inscriptions, flatteries. She was in her prime, secure in the station she had longed for, contrived for, schemed for; she could contemplate many more years of power, reigning in cold autocracy to the rear of the throne. Her son owed everything to her and he knew it; he placed her, unassailable, on a pedestal.

About the only source of friction between them was money. Mamaea could apparently not control her greed. With her, as with other members of her surpassingly rich family, acquisition was a way of life. Now that she was Mother of the Augustus, she saw many opportunities for acquisition not open to ordinary individuals. According to the historian Herodian (who, however, may have been greatly exaggerating), she even confiscated estates and inheritances, giving her son the excuse that money might be needed to pacify rebellious soldiers some day but actually putting the money into her own bottomless bag; and when Alexander reproached her for introducing the filth of avarice into his pure white government, she would employ the counter-reproach that he did not know how to live like an Emperor. Even though she hated to spend money needlessly and considered prodigality an unforgivable sin, she believed that imperial persons had to maintain imperial standards. When (according to Herodian) she had absorbed another fortune, she enjoyed spending a reasonable amount of it for personal pomp. Elagabalus had undeniably been a reckless fool with regard to finance, and so had Caracalla, but her son, she felt, went too far in the other direction.

If she had spent less money on imperial appearances and more money on keeping the good will of the army, her son's reign might have come closer to the ideal of which he dreamed. But with regard to the army, her economy paralleled his. She probably reasoned that she had given the Praetorians in particular enough money to have Alexander made Emperor. Neither Mamaea nor her son was actually very sympathetic to the requirements of the military, and neither of them was willing to admit that the army supported the throne and could upset it. Their trust in the Senate was, in the last analysis, unwise, not because the Senate was untrustworthy but because it was impotent. The army had the swords; the Praetorians also had a strong tradition of power.

These guards continued to demonstrate their unhappiness over the appointment of the lawyer Ulpian as their Prefect and the execution of their former Prefects Chrestus and Flavian. Sometimes they grumbled and sometimes they shouted. The Emperor may possibly have feared them, but he showed them only disregard. His mother was contemptuous of them. And the more honors Alexander and Mamaea bestowed on Ulpian, the more rebellious the Praetorians grew. They would have been quieted, perhaps, if they had received generous amounts of imperial money, and they might have been quieted if Ulpian had treated them leniently instead of exercising strict military discipline. He was a lawyer who expected conformity to the letter of the law. The relationship between him and his men became more and more strained. They sincerely hated him, and he had no patience with them. They rioted repeatedly, threatening him with death.

They were as arrogant as the Praetorians whom Septimius Severus had dismissed in 193, and a Severus was needed to humble them. They lorded it over the populace—the proud Praetorians, truculent and insolent to defenseless civilians, brutal when they had the opportunity. The indignation of the citizenry mounted to fury. In 227 a civil war broke out between the populace and the Praetorians. For three days the battle raged in the streets of Rome, the well-trained Praetorians slaughtering the populace with military precision, and the populace, indifferently armed but much more numerous, overwhelming the guards with the force of anger and driving them back, breaking their ranks, leaving them dead. While all this was going on the ideal imperial government sat dismayed. Plato had never had to contend with rebellious Praetorians. Gradually the soldiers were defeated, chased from the streets. As a last recourse, however, they set fire to the dwellings; and as the orange flames ate into the buildings and leaped onto fresh ones, and as the people ran screaming into the streets, the fear arose that the city would be destroyed. The populace therefore submitted. The Praetorians had not been humbled.

Perhaps because Ulpian treated his unruly guards with extra rigor for trying to burn down the city, or perhaps for some other reason, in 228 the Praetorians rioted against Ulpian again, more fiercely than ever, led by a man named Epagathus. The Prefect fled for refuge to the palace, where he had apparently fled for refuge in previous emergencies, but Epagathus and his mutinous mob of guards followed.

Ulpian's only hope was the authority of the agitated Emperor and of Mamaea. The three of them stood awaiting the Praetorians, who stormed into the room with swords drawn.

The Emperor, who was nineteen, commanded them to stop.

The guards came nearer, swords drawn.

Ulpian beseeched the Emperor to save him from them.

Alexander threw his purple cloak over his quailing old friend, the sober statesman learned in the law, the kind and brilliant man with whom he had discussed the *Republic*. The Praetorians rushed at Ulpian and ran their blades through the cloak. Falling at Alexander's feet, he died under the unprotecting purple slashed full of holes.

Alexander must have found it hard not to be able to avenge the death of his friend, his parent, his mentor, his murdered idol. But he was now very much afraid of these Praetorians. He did not even dare to execute Epagathus, because if he killed the ringleader he might have a full-scale revolution on his hands. When his tears had dried he made Epagathus governor of Egypt; that at least got the monster out of Rome. But the Emperor did not forget. Later he removed Epagathus to Crete, and there, after the Praetorians' memory of their champion had dimmed sufficiently, he had the man brought to justice. Epagathus was finally executed.

In spite of his lack of affection for the army, Alexander tried conscientiously to be a good Emperor toward the legions posted throughout the provinces. Night after night he sat studying the lists of officers, considering their pay, marking the names of men who had been promoted, making plans for the construction of conveniently located supply centers so that the soldiers would not have to carry heavy stuffed packs long distances. One of his favorite policies, and a very good one, though not original with him, was that of donating farmland on the frontiers to retired veterans, both officers and men. He stocked the land with cattle and provided slaves for the military settlers, and he promised that the soldiers' heirs could inherit the property if they also contributed military service to the Empire. By settling the frontiers with sturdy veterans, he was, of course, helping to protect the Empire against barbarian invasions, and by requiring military service for inheritance of the property, he was guaranteeing an influx of men into the army.

The legionaries under Alexander did not, then, suffer from oppression. They were provided with first-rate uniforms and equipment, their horses were fast thoroughbreds, their quarters were certainly more comfortable than military quarters had been during the republic or the early Empire. Wherever they went the soldiers of Rome could still expect deference. When they entered a town, the wine and the girls were theirs. They usually had enough money to spend (even though they thought otherwise), and they shone as they strode down the streets. Although Alexander did not adhere to the military favoritism of Septimius Severus and Caracalla, he was far from unfair; he even gave the troops liberal gifts. If the legionaries had not already been spoiled, they might have felt content. But they had learned not to be satisfied with fairness; they wanted more pay, more privileges, more amenities.

They also wanted an Emperor to lead them—not a Platonic boy who sat in a palace. Elagabalus had disappointed them enough as a leader; Alexander was becoming another disappointment. When he ascended the throne he was too young to command the respect of the army; he might command its loyalty (and he evidently did do that for a while, except in the case of the Praetorians), but the army needed a powerful man to follow. As he matured into an intellectual even the soldiers in far-off provinces realized that he was markedly uninterested in military enterprise. The legionaries might have been willing to do without a few favors under Severus or Caracalla because they knew that these Emperors were military men themselves, with a strong relish for a soldier's life. The bookish Alexander might try to understand them, but he need not make the effort. Without being told directly, they sensed that he was not of them.

And so there were revolts. Little is known about them except that they were widespread and violent. In Isauria the soldiers threw off the control of their superiors. In Mauretania extremely serious uprisings occurred. In Mesopotamia the troops killed the governor. In Osrhoëne a military leader tried to make himself Emperor. These insurrections were quelled, but lives were lost, prestige was injured, and in his palace Alexander felt unquiet.

The historian Cassius Dio had sat in the Senate, had governed provinces, and had served a variety of Emperors in a variety of ways with unimpeachable loyalty. In 227, at the age of seventy-two, he went to Upper Pannonia as governor. The troops were restless, undisciplined, greedy for outrageous concessions, foul-mouthed toward the government. It took Dio a few years, but he taught them to have proper respect for the authority that paid them. In 229 he returned to Rome to share the consulship with his Emperor. But the Praetorians, having heard about his severity toward the Pannonian legions, feared that this severity would spread and would eventually affect their own distinguished branch of the army. With almost unparalleled insolence, they demanded that the Emperor have him executed.

Alexander, however, would not be badgered, at least not immediately. He even promised Dio to defray the expenses which the consulship inevitably entailed. The Praetorians howled. In fact, they became so ugly that Alexander advised the consul to spend his term of office away from Rome. The Emperor himself had gone into temporary rustication in Campania, and Dio joined him there. For several days Dio stayed with him, showing no fear even if he felt it. There were of course Praetorians guarding the Emperor, or pretending to do so, but Dio did not shrink from appearing in front of them. The Pannonian legions had not intimidated him, and these arrogant Praetorians would not make him move a muscle. The murder of Ulpian, however, was still a fresh horror in Alexander's mind. The Emperor talked urgently with his consul; and Dio, saying that he had the gout, retired to his native country, Bithynia, in Asia Minor. There he passed the rest of his days in peace.

And back in the palace the Emperor, with his army at his heels and his mother at his side, soon found himself preparing for war.

# ✠ XIX ✠

## *Alexander's Two Wars*

The original kingdom of Persia came into being about 550 B.C. Until then the people called the Persians had simply inhabited a province in the Kingdom of Media. But Cyrus the Persian overthrew the Median king, captured the capital (Ecbatana), styled himself the Great King, and established the vigorous, warlike dynasty that was to give the Greeks so much trouble. Persia soon conquered the Near East, Egypt, and Asia Minor and became the most powerful kingdom. Although Cyrus' successors Darius and Xerxes were defeated heroically (and almost miraculously) when they tried to subdue Greece, the country as a whole did not suffer a great deal; it was vast, well organized, strong, and awesome. Only Alexander the Great could perform the almost impossible feat of conquering this immense nation on its own ground. In 331 B.C. the original Persia came to an end.

Alexander the Great died at Babylon as a partly Persianized Greek. For a while his Hellenic successors the Seleucids ruled the land, although their headquarters were soon moved to Syria. But the Seleucids were driven out by the Parthians, semicivilized horsemen and steppe-dwellers from Central Asia. The tremendous feudal kingdom which the Parthians founded on Persian soil lasted almost four centuries, superficially Hellenic during its early centuries but Asiatic underneath, chronically at war with the Romans from the time of Caesar on, rising to a peak of strength and glory about halfway through its history, and then degenerating at a fairly steady pace. When Septimius Severus defeated Parthia the country was visibly in a state of decline; when Caracalla defeated Parthia the enervation and demoralization were very noticeable. Parthia might still have gone on for a long while, however, if it had not been for Ardashir the Persian.

Within the Parthian domains lay the land of Persis, whose kings, of Persian blood, were subordinate to the great Parthian king. These vassal kings of Persis helped to preserve a great deal of Persian lore and tradition, and their priests carried on the ancient Persian religion of Mazda, which gradually became stronger and stronger and was even adopted by the Parthian rulers themselves when the Hellenic wash began to wear away. In 208 the King of Persis was overthrown by his younger brother Ardashir, Lord of Darabgerd, a violent, ambitious young man with an enthusiastic military following. For many years he remained apparently content as King of Persis, but early in the reign of Alexander he made war on his overlord the Parthian King of Kings, who happened to be Artabanus, old enemy of Caracalla and sometime enemy of Macrinus. Ardashir was shrewd, energetic, and inspiring, like Cyrus before him, and his desire to restore Persia to the Persians appealed to his nationalistic adherents. It was a war fought with emotions bordering on fanaticism. Artabanus was killed. Some of the outlying districts still had to be subdued, but their pacification was only a matter of time. About the year 226 Ardashir became King of Kings. Parthia was Persia once more. A nation had been reborn on the ruins of another.

This new young Persia, which was to be called Sassanid Persia after Ardashir's grandfather, was effervescently patriotic. Partly in order to strengthen the sense of nationality and partly out of piety, Ardashir made the old religion of the Persians the sole recognized religion in the state. The dualistic creed of Mazda, taught by the prophet Zoroaster, was based on the belief that the universe is under the dominion of two opposing principles—good, served by beneficent spirits and hero-gods such as Mithra, and evil, served by Ahriman and his dastardly legions. Ardashir augmented the power of the priests of this religion, the Magi, on whose altars the sacred fire always burned. He had the widely dispersed holy writings, the Avesta, collected in a new edition, which was to be the only official version. He claimed to be the deputy of the Good on earth—a kind of god incarnate. Religious freedom, which had existed under the Parthians, ceased; members of all non-Persian religions—Jews, Buddhists, and Christians—were persecuted.

Another important aspect of Ardashir's patriotism was his policy of making war on Rome. Ardashir had not willingly inherited a great deal from the Parthians, but he had gladly inherited from them a fierce enmity toward the Roman Empire. This animosity toward Rome was to live on in Persia for many centuries after his death. As long as Rome existed, Persia conducted periodic wars against her; when the Roman Empire of the East became the Byzantine Empire the intermitted warfare continued; when, at the end of four or five centuries of rule, the dynasty established by Ardashir was in its turn overthrown and Persia became part of Islam, the rivalry with the Byzantines did not end.

Ardashir affirmed that all the land possessed by old Persia was rightfully his. Mesopotamia, he said, should be his, not Rome's—and he invaded it in the year 230 and besieged the invaluable fortress-city of Nisibis. Asia Minor should be his, all the way to the Aegean Sea— and he sent his cavalry into the part of Asia Minor known as Cappadocia.

The Roman government had been watching developments in Parthia-Persia with unhappy eyes. Rome's armies in the East were unprepared, badly organized, and not entirely loyal. The Persians attacked and sacked their camps. Forceful action by Rome was in order. The situation, in fact, required the presence of the Emperor at the head of his troops.

Alexander, now in his early twenties, may not have been delighted at the prospect of going to war, but he knew that good Emperors must sometimes lead their armies to battle and he certainly resolved to be as conscientious a general as he was a monarch. Even Mamaea had to concede that it was necessary for her son to march to the East, especially after a peace-bearing embassy to Persia had failed, but she did not like the turn of events at all and declared that she would travel with him in order to help him keep safe and comfortable. Officially, the war was hailed at Rome as a good thing, a chance to teach these neo-Persians the lesson of humility that Roman legions had taught the Parthians many times before, and to add more glory to the Roman name; Alexander was praised as a great general (in embryo), who would give the spirit of his namesake cause to be envious. Despite all this enthusiasm in the capital, however, many Egyptian and Syrian troops deserted.

Throughout the Empire troops were raised, and men began marching to join the Emperor. Deciding to pattern himself after the Macedonian Alexander, whose biographies he had read with such care and devotion, he created a corps called the Argyraspides, which, like a corps created by Alexander the Great, carried shields of silver, and another corps called the Chrysaspides, whose shields were of gold. His resemblance to the great Greek ended there.

A couple of months before Alexander and Mother of the Camps Mamaea were to set out, the route which they would follow from Rome to Persia had already been planned in detail, and placards publicizing it were put up in the city so that the Romans would be able to see where the army would halt, at what places it would take on provisions, and so on. Sometime in 231 the elaborate expedition got under way.

On the march Alexander made a point of eating the same simple food that the legionaries ate. Since he preferred simple food to luxurious fare anyway, that was not difficult. He kept his tent open at mealtimes to give the soldiers a chance to behold his manly moderation. Like an admirable general, he demonstrated solicitude for the welfare of his men, furnishing them with mules and camels to carry baggage, if this was possible, and when a man became sick, visiting him in his tent, just as he used to visit his sick friends at their houses in Rome. If an indisposed soldier did not show signs of recovering quickly, the Emperor had him put up at a comfortable house and paid for his care and lodging.

When he, the army, and Mamaea arrived at Antioch, which was again to function as military headquarters, Ardashir still had not succeeded in taking Nisibis, and he now gave up the siege. Alexander hoped that his own imperial presence and the presence of the Roman troops had frightened the Persian off. Still eager to obtain peace if peace was obtainable, the Emperor sent another embassy to the King of Kings, suggesting in respectful language that Ardashir reduce his ambitions and stay in Persia. But Ardashir had no intention of avoiding a war with Rome. He dismissed the group, its mission unaccomplished. A short while later he sent his own ambassadors to Antioch. They consisted of four hundred of the tallest nobles of Persia, carrying bows, dressed in the splendor of gold and brilliant colors, mounted on horses magnificently caparisoned. These ambassadors were intended to represent the pomp and power of Persia, and they probably succeeded in that aspect of their mission; the Romans were sufficiently impressed to admit that Oriental barbarians could make a glorious appearance.

The main purpose of their visit was to demand that the Emperor relinquish to Persia all of Asia Minor and Syria. This demand was phrased as an order, and even the mild-mannered Alexander felt incensed. He would have liked to execute the four hundred ambassadors, but rather than completely violate "international law," he had them arrested, confiscated their jewels and gorgeous clothing, and sent them to Phrygia in Asia Minor, where he quartered them in various towns, denying them safe conduct back to Persia. The war was on.

Before marching off from Antioch Alexander presumably had trouble with the troops, who had been so seduced and softened by the city's sweet pleasures as to be incapable of heroic action. The story is probably false that Alexander imprisoned the ringleaders of one legion known for its lechery, and delivered to the legion an eloquently reproachful speech; that when the legion muttered mutinously he reproached it all the more and dismissed every member of it from the service; that the soldiers became penitent when they found themselves ignominiously cashiered by their Emperor; and that after a month he granted their meek request for reinstatement—but it probably reflects the kind of problem that the young Emperor faced. Antioch was no place to bring soldiers who were expected to endure hardships and perhaps die for Rome. Although it was convenient as a military headquarters, it was also morally dissipative, especially if the soldiers enjoyed much freedom.

Whatever difficulties arose, Alexander must have overcome them somehow, and the invasion of Persia commenced. The Mother of the Camps accompanied her son on the march.

In order to keep Ardashir worried, he attacked Persia from several quarters, obliging Ardashir to split his defending forces into several segments. Alexander divided his own troops into three bodies. One army was to approach Persia from the north, by way of Armenia, which was friendly to the Romans because its ruler was closely related to the dispossessed Parthian royal house. This division was to invade the outlying portion of Ardashir's dominions once known as Media. Another army was to travel south, through what had once been Babylonia, toward the confluence of the Tigris and Euphrates Rivers north of the Persian Gulf, perhaps with the ultimate aim of invading Susiana and the land of Persis itself. The third army, commanded by Alexander and including Mamaea among its *impedimenta,* was to take a middle route, marching eastward through northern Mesopotamia.

The strategy seemed excellent, but the results were not especially glorious for the Romans. We do not have a very clear picture of what happened, since accounts of the invasion differ, but it seems that Ardashir was too quick for Alexander. The King of Kings evidently began by defeating the Roman army of the north, which had come through the Armenian mountains intact and was winning battles and looting happily in Media. Then he whirled off to the south to attack the Roman troops in Babylonia. As for the middle army, the one headed by the Emperor in person, it intended to join the southern division but was marching very slowly, perhaps because Mamaea was reluctant to let her son become involved in a battle. We are of course unaware of whether Alexander himself felt courageous or cowardly at this point, but he certainly did not demonstrate any unquenchable thirst for military renown, or even any marked ability as a tactician.

Ardashir's forces, probably somewhat tattered from their successful encounter with the Romans in the north, waged a great battle, perhaps even a series of battles, against the Romans in the south. The Persians had several hundred elephants (animals which were awesome to the ancients and which sometimes brought about a victory simply because the enemy soldiers beheld them with such terror); they also had many chariots with scythes protruding from them to mow down and slice the opposition. Like the Parthians, the Persians did not fight on foot; according to Lampridius, who may have been exaggerating, Ardashir could count on 120,000 mounted men. We cannot even guess at the strength of Rome's southern contingent, but it was certainly well trained as a fighting unit. The battle, however, so far as we can tell, went against it. But for the Persians it was a Pyrrhic victory, since Ardashir's forces were too weakened to pursue the war; the Roman troops, adept at slaughter, had made them pay a high price for their triumph.

Lampridius would like us to believe that Alexander himself fought the Persians and did so as a hero, exposing himself to danger with reckless valor and shouting encouragement to his troops, but that is probably fiction. Ardashir may possibly have attacked Alexander's own division before or after the battle with the army of the south, but more likely he avoided it before the battle, and after the battle he just retired. Alexander retired too; his soldiers, large numbers of whom had come from the cold, rainy banks of the Rhine and the Danube, suffered extremely from the Mesopotamian heat and dryness, and a plague broke out among them; many died. The Emperor ordered the army of the north to withdraw from Media; sick, starving, and cold as they stumbled back through the mountains of Armenia, many of these soldiers also died.

Although the campaign seems to have ended in a draw, the Romans had actually come out ahead. They had not lost a foot of ground, and had delivered Roman Asia, for the time being at any rate, from the Persian menace. It is true that the troops did not pursue their advantage and carry the war farther into Persia and perhaps even conquer territory which Rome had never possessed before, but nobody expected them to do that. The days of confident Roman belligerence had long been over; in the third century the Empire was satisfied to protect what it already had. Mamaea could congratulate her son on a successful military achievement.

By the spring of 233 Alexander was back at Antioch, and later in the same year he returned to Rome, where he was greeted as a conqueror by the Senate and the people. There was a parade in which the spoils of the war were displayed, proof that the Romans had made great depredations among the Persians. The Emperor mounted the tribunal in the Forum and addressed a few words to the cheering populace, then proceeded on foot to the palace, with his triumphal car following behind, pulled by four elephants. The throng was so great and the enthusiam was so oppressive that it took him several hours to get to the palace. The next day he crowned his celebration with games at the circus.

Alexander would have been happy to stay at Rome, where he could read, discuss timeless questions, and regulate the Empire. But another emergency had arisen, and in 234 he was on the march again—this time against the Germans.

These tribesmen had been so quiet of late that there were only three or four legions stationed on the Rhine, whereas there had been eight in the early Empire. In 234, however, the Germans crossed the Rhine and ravaged Gaul, and they were apparently getting ready to cross the Danube and ravage Illyria. The Emperor's presence was needed again; the interlude was over. Those legions which had been left in the East in case of a renewal of the Persian war had hoped to be sent back to their permanent stations soon, but instead they were ordered to march north by west out of Asia through Europe toward the Rhine; Alexander with other soldiers would join them on the way. The veterans grumbled, but everybody came—even Mauretanian javelin men and dart-throwers, and Osrhoënian and Parthian bowmen. When Alexander joined his forces, he was accompanied by the Mother of the Camps.

On the march toward the Rhine Alexander prided himself on having placed a tribune named Maximin in charge of training the new troops, mainly Pannonians. He knew Maximin fairly well and esteemed him highly. The man had served him faithfully, had governed Mesopotamia during the Persian campaign, and had gained a reputation as one of the finest warriors in the Roman army.

Maximin came from Thrace and was of low origin. During his youth he had been a herdsman, and even then he showed qualities above the ordinary, leading a group of peasants against a robber gang. He grew to be not only a man but a giant—over eight feet high, it is said, and of muscular bulk. With a blow of his fist he could break a horse's leg or smash a horse's teeth; he could tear a young tree apart in a matter of seconds, and squeeze pumice stones to powder between his fingers. Men nicknamed him Hercules. He ate and drank with Herculean gusto—forty pounds of meat at a meal, apparently, and six or seven gallons of wine to wash it down. No wonder he found his way into the Roman army.

He entered it while he was still a young man, during the reign of Septimius Severus. According to Lampridius, the military Emperor, passing through Thrace in 197 on the way from Mesopotamia to Gaul for the war against Albinus, paused to hold games in celebration of Geta's birthday. These games consisted partly of wrestling matches, with articles such as bracelets and silver belts as prizes. Maximin liked to wrestle, and nobody had ever succeeded in throwing him—it would have been easier to throw a horse. Presenting himself before Severus, he asked permission to take part in the games. His Latin was limping and barbaric, but Severus, with his own Punic accent, did not mind. Looking up at the peasant-giant, the Emperor told him that he would not be allowed to wrestle the soldiers—the results might have proved embarrassing to Roman military pre-eminence—but that he could demonstrate his skill against the strongest sutlers.

Sixteen sutlers were chosen, and Maximin threw them all, without even breathing hard.

Severus, who recognized good military potential when he saw it, awarded Maximin sixteen prizes (they were less valuable than the prizes given to the troops, but that was as it should be) and invited him to become a soldier of Rome. Maximin joined the army immediately.

The Emperor was sufficiently interested in the young colossus to watch him showing off his strength on the parade ground several days later. Maximin looked awkward, still a peasant in his motions. Severus summoned the officer in charge; pointed out that Maximin was wasting his great body, moving like an impetuous bull; observed that the brute had the makings of an excellent soldier but needed civilizing; and instructed the officer to teach him how to be cunning and composed, how to conserve his strength, how to use it purposefully when he did use it—in other words, how to do things in an intelligent, Roman manner.

Noticing that he was the subject of the conversation, Maximin walked up. The Emperor applied his spurs to his horse, which began galloping. Maximin, who was by no means stupid, saw what was expected of him and ran alongside, keeping pace with the horse. Severus enjoyed the sport and rode for some time, occasionally shouting a comment or a jibe. The Thracian never lagged behind. At the end of the contest he did not even show strain.

Severus commented that Maximin had not done badly and inquired whether he felt like wrestling.

Since he was a soldier himself now, he could wrestle soldiers. The Emperor picked out the seven strongest, and one after another Maximin threw them. Delighted, Severus presented him with a collar of gold and enrolled him in his guards.

For the rest of Severus' reign Maximin was his very loyal guard. The officers found him a dependable, responsive soldier, and his fellow guards liked him and admired his physical power. They were careful not to cross him, however, because he was likely to fly into a foul rage and do harm; his training in civilized Roman ways had made him an effective fighting man but had not suppressed his inherent brutality. The Emperor continued to look on him with favor, although it was not until the reign of Caracalla, who also valued his services, that he was promoted to the rank of centurion. He married and became the father of a good-looking boy. On Macrinus' accession he seems to have left the army, refusing to serve under the man who had murdered the son of his beloved patron. Having bought some land near his home town in Thrace, he retired to it and carried on trade with his own people.

When Macrinus was overthrown Maximin offered his services to Elagabalus, whom he believed to be the son of Caracalla and the grandson of Severus. Elagabalus, pleased at seeing a bigger man than he had ever seen before, apparently responded with offers of his own. Maximin was insulted and stormed off, intending to go back to Thrace. According to the story, however, Elagabalus' friends apprehended that he would spread uncomplimentary rumors about the Emperor in the provinces and perhaps damage the Emperor's reputation with the soldiers, among whom Maximin was very influential. The giant was therefore reminded that Elagabalus was Severus' grandson. He was also promised a tribuneship. He stayed, accepting the rank of tribune, but he did no duty under Elagabalus and kept making excuses for not paying his respects to the Emperor in person.

Under Alexander he returned to active duty. Recognizing his merit, Alexander put him in command of a legion and even congratulated himself in front of the Senate for having acquired the services of so brave an officer. The name Maximin the Thracian was known to many people who had never seen him; as a giant, as a strongman, as a warrior, he was almost a legend with the soldiery and with civilians too. His physical vigor had not diminished perceptibly with advancing age. He could still throw five or six men without half trying, and he frequently fought his own soldiers in order to keep himself in form.

One day another tribune, also physically powerful, had the poor judgment to chide Maximin: "It doesn't do an officer much credit, you know, to beat his own men."

Maximin asked whether the tribune would like to fight.

The man nodded and stepped forward, but Maximin knocked him down with the first blow, which was to the chest. That was all. The legionaries cheered.

"I'm ready for another one," Maximin said, "but this time I hope he's a real tribune."

That kind of thing understandably increased Maximin's popularity with the Pannonians whom he was supposed to condition and turn into soldiers capable of defeating the Germans. His men idolized him, responding uncomplainingly to the strict discipline to which they were subjected. He trained them with great care; Alexander could not have chosen an officer better qualified to turn rough recruits into Roman soldiers. He personally examined their swords, spears, shields, helmets, cuirasses, and other equipment, and his parental solicitude and impatience with imperfection stimulated the men; not one of them could bear the shame of being accounted a slovenly legionary by a tribune of such heroic proportions. When the men tried to outdo one another at their exercises he watched with a rigorous eye, just as Severus had watched him on the parade ground when he was a young recruit.

But all of this militated against Alexander, who seemed less and less worthy compared with Maximin. We do not know when Maximin first conceived the idea of supplanting Alexander as Emperor. For quite a while he had probably despised the young man as a hypercivilized weakling under the governance of his mother. Life had been good during the reigns of the soldier-Emperors Severus and Caracalla, but their successors had disappointed Maximin—the cowardly lawyer Macrinus, the lecherous pervert Elagabalus, and now this twenty-six-year-old little boy. The Empire needed a man who could lead its armies. And nobody could do that better than Maximin himself. That was what Maximin thought.

His fatherly attention to his troops was not merely a matter of conscientiousness. He was trying to win them over from Alexander to himself. And in his disgust and in his ambition, he said things about the Emperor that a loyal subject should not have said. Not that he needed to say much, because the soldiers were already muttering among themselves. To go from one halfhearted war to another under the leadership of an imperial Platonist and his avaricious mother was almost more than a soldier could take.

Even Alexander's firmest adherents could not deny that the German war was, like the Persian war, conducted in a halfhearted way. The Emperor made a show of pugnacity by having a bridge of boats built across the Rhine so that the army could move into German territory, but at the same time he sent ambassadors to the tribes in case they were at all disposed toward peace. The soldiers regarded this conciliatory measure with contempt; the Emperor was betraying a pusillanimous heart. Besides, he did not understand barbarians.

Rumors circulated throughout the legions—that Alexander was trying to buy peace from the Germans with money which could be used to much better effect for soldiers' pay, that Mamaea wished her son to give up the German war and march his troops into Syria, where their number and splendor would serve to illustrate the pomp of the Roman Empress. The troops did not know which one they liked less, the mother or the son. Both were ungenerous—the pay should be increased, everybody agreed about that. At any rate, the choice between Alexander and Maximin was clear: on the one hand, an intellectual, an idealist with no sense to speak of, a young man who let his mother rule him, a column of vapor—on the other hand, a soldier's soldier, powerful, practical, self-made, brave. The rumblings turned into mutinous outcries; the Emperor had to disband the most unruly units. Another rumor went around the camps—that Mamaea had proposed a cut in the soldiers' pay.

We do not know to what extent Maximin was responsible for these rumors, but he certainly did nothing to discourage them, and it seems that he pointed out that when a new Emperor came to the throne a largesse was customarily distributed to the soldiers. There had been no new Emperor for thirteen years; Alexander had given largesses to the soldiers several times, but it was time for another distribution.

In March 235 the troops held a meeting on a plain close to what is now Mainz. It was a large and tumultuous meeting, and after the legionaries had damned Alexander they began shouting that Maximin should be Emperor. Although he pretended reluctance born of modesty (mentioning his vulgar descent), they overwhelmed him. When thousands of voices began to hail him as Emperor, he acceded to the will of the army.

Alexander knew enough about Roman history to expect death. It was just a question of time. He had tried to be a good Emperor, but he had apparently failed; he had studied and struggled to be an ideal Emperor, but he had failed. Plato had failed too, in Syracuse. And Socrates had drunk hemlock; but Socrates had been a better soldier. In his tent the young man waited, reproaching his mother for giving him unadmirable qualities and blind advice. The soldiers came in and murdered them both.

# ☙ XX ❧

# The Peasant and the Aristocrats

The senators confirmed the army's choice of Maximin as Emperor, but they were apprehensive. They could not expect the same flattering treatment from this new ruler that they had received from his predecessor; furthermore, they had liked Alexander. The Syrian dynasty might not have been perfect, but Alexander had at least been civilized and he had spoken Greek well. This new Emperor was a hairy, ignorant brute with a jutting chin. It was ironic that Septimius Severus' dreams and Maesa's machinations for the setting up of a dynasty should end in this oversized wrestler.

Maximin the Thracian was, in fact, the first peasant to become a Roman Emperor. Now that he was supreme, the upper classes suspected that the only things he really knew how to do were to wage war and to revile the rich.

A warrior was, of course, badly needed; the Germanic tribes had to be shown the might of Rome. The new Emperor fought the barbarian invaders under the trees and in the swamps, and the Germanic tribes learned that an oversized wrestler could defend the Roman Empire better than a cultivated Roman could. When he had won this war, however, there were others. After wintering at Sirmium, a bustling frontier town in southeastern Pannonia that was much more to his taste than Rome, he fought the unruly Sarmatians and Dacians.

The persecution of Alexander's adherents was not severe at first. Those who belonged to the upper classes were either sent back to Rome or appointed to offices in distant places, and these methods of getting rid of them were much more lenient than they might have expected. Maximin probably wished he could treat them more harshly, since he felt a peasant's resentment toward the upper classes—a resentment which his nomination to the imperium had aggravated rather than softened. He knew the Senate was against him, and he despised the senators—in fact, all the idle rich. This did not mean that he absolutely refused to ally himself with them; his son Maximus, a youth in his late teens whom he had had the Senate declare Caesar, and who had been given the education of a Roman gentleman, was contemplating marriage with an aristocratic lady, and Maximin saw that such a marriage would be an advantage. But by and large, to him aristocrats were loathsome.

Toward the officials of Alexander's household he was more rigorous. Realizing that they considered him responsible for their master's murder, he killed some of them; others he merely dismissed. Some of them were evidently Christians. For a religion that advised turning the other cheek, Maximin had no respect.

He dealt summarily with plots against his reign. For example, it was reported that a man of consular rank named Magnus considered murdering Maximin and making himself Emperor. This was not an unlikelihood; it seemed that the government of the Roman Empire had now become a chaos in which anybody strong enough could seize the throne. Maximin intended to have a bridge built across the Rhine. Magnus, by means of bribes, apparently made the guards promise to cut the bridge as soon as the Emperor had crossed into Germany. Those who crossed with the Emperor would be Magnus and other conspirators, and on the Germans' side, away from the main body of the army, they would kill him.

That, at any rate, was the story. When he heard it, Maximin did not bother to find out whether it was true. He put to death not only Magnus but, according to claims (possibly exaggerated), about four thousand other disaffected persons. Some died on crosses, some fought unfair fights against wild beasts, some were beaten to death, and some were sewed up alive in the bellies of dead animals.

Osrhoënian bowmen who had been brought from Asia by Alexander decided to support their own candidate for the throne. They hated Maximin for the murder of their patron and even more for his partiality toward the fierce Pannonian recruits, the men whom he had been training. In looking around for a new Emperor they discovered a serious and irreproachable ex-consul named Quartinus, who had been a friend of Alexander. He had no desire to be Emperor and tried to convince them of his unfitness for the role, but they would not listen; they defiantly declared him elected. Six days later, however, one of the conspirators, who had either undergone a change of heart or thought that a more munificent reward would be forthcoming from Maximin, killed the unwilling candidate in his bed and then went to Maximin to report what he had done. Maximin, however, knew that a turncoat who could kill his own choice for Emperor would be untrustworthy. The man was executed.

Maximin never visited Rome as Emperor. Although he had spent much time there in the past, he felt uncomfortable among the grandiose buildings and the highly educated people. The forests were his domain—and frontier towns, and military camps. He would pass the winters at Sirmium, receiving messengers from Rome and conducting state business, and with the coming of spring he would go on campaign again, through the thick forests, through the swamps, across the hills, after the barbarians. His world was war.

Once the Romans defeated a large number of Germans near a marsh, into which the barbarians fled in order to escape the wrath of their conquerors. The legionaries seemed reluctant to follow them into the muddy recesses, but Maximin made up their minds for them by plunging in ahead of everyone on his magnificent horse, which was soon up to its belly in water. Several barbarians turned around to engage him; he killed them all. His legionaries, thoroughly ashamed of their hesitation, plunged into the marsh too; the Germans rallied and a new battle began, a dirty fight in the water. Blood from the wounded, dying, and dead tinted the muddy bog. The casualties were heavy on both sides, so that bodies clogged the fen, floating on the surface, or lying tangled under the trees; but the Romans won.

Maximin considered the victory a great one, as it perhaps was. He had a description of the battle sent to Rome, and he had a picture of it painted, to be hung in front of the Senate house, so that the learned, polished, aristocratic cowards could see what kind of man they had for Emperor.

Roman historians who drew portraits of Maximin were strongly prejudiced against him, perhaps because they belonged to the strata of society that he despised. The portraits are consequently monstrous. Their ugliness, however, reflects a view of Maximin which was by no means confined to aristocrats. When the initial successes against the Germans had passed and the burden of taxation had not, many people below senatorial rank began to feel violently antagonistic toward the new regime. Maximin needed money for his wars; he had to squeeze the money out of an increasingly reluctant Empire. Although some of his subjects no doubt continued to look on him as a blessing—a soldier-Emperor who would lead Rome to new military glory—the cries against him rose in volume.

The ancient historians accuse him of following the principle that a ruler can preserve power only by means of cruelty, and of being rapacious to an unwarranted degree. Several instances of his reputed cruelty have already been mentioned. In his rapacity he is said to have been helped a great deal by informers, who would revive old charges against moneyed people or the people's ancestors, or invent charges, or report which owners of extensive property were most vulnerable. It seems that aristocrats who had held some of the most important offices in the state were carried off to Sirmium from Rome, and that at Sirmium they were fortunate if they were allowed to keep their lives. Those who most fondly remembered Severus Alexander appear to have stood in the gravest danger.

In addition to persecuting the rich and extorting heavy taxes from rich and poor alike, Maximin evidently confiscated the public funds of the cities—funds intended for distribution to needy residents, or for the purchase of food supplies, or the production of the games, shows, and festivals, which were the chief sources of popular pleasure. It is reported that he even showed disrespect toward religion, ransacking the temples for ornaments and images of the gods which could be converted into coins. Although stories of such outrages are surely exaggerated by the historians, they cannot be pure fiction; the reports must have been partially based on truth.

The Athenians, in a period of sad national necessity during the Peloponnesian War, had turned ornaments in the Parthenon into gold coins, but they had done so with the permission of Athena—for whose city they would very likely die—and that was sufficient extenuation. Maximin tried to extenuate his depredations by stating that the money was required for the soldiers of Rome, the valorous defenders of the

Empire, whose pay he had doubled. But this patriotic excuse, in large degree true, no longer sounded as impressive as it had sounded in the recent past. Too many Romans were wretched.

The discontent boiled over in March of 238 in Africa, where an unusually brutal procurator was oppressing the people, in the Emperor's name and for the Emperor's treasury. He apparently imposed fines on several young men of distinguished families, fines whose payment would have meant sudden impoverishment. The youths requested three days' grace. Instead of using the three days to obtain the requisite money, however, they talked their aristocratic friends into insurrection.

At the appointed time the young men appeared before the procurator, accompanied by their noble friends. In the background lingered the gentlemen's most trustworthy slaves, mingling nonchalantly with the crowd but keeping their eyes on their masters. Under their clothes the slaves carried staves, hoes, hatchets, equipment normally used in farming the great African estates.

The principal conspirators responded to the magistrate's demand for payment by falling on him and stabbing him to death. When his puzzled soldiers started to attack the assassins, the slaves brought out their farm tools and turned them into tools of murder—hewing and hacking, glad for the chance to chop away at anybody in authority. The soldiers ran.

Although the insurrection was a success for the moment, the well-born youths knew that imperial punishment would sweep down on them if they just sat back and waited. They realized that the best way to escape the vengeance of Maximin was to make some other man Emperor, and the obvious choice was the man with the greatest authority—the aged Gordian, governor of Africa.

Few eminent Romans in the early part of the third century could trace their pedigrees back very far; many of the great were newly rich, and even those whose families might be regarded as well established felt reluctant to look back more than two or three generations for fear of uncovering embarrassingly vulgar ancestors, possibly even freed slaves. Gordian, however, claimed descent on his father's side from the Gracchi, the popular heroes of the dimly remembered republic. On his

mother's side he was descended from Trajan, first of the great Emperors of the golden age. Appropriately enough, he had married a lady
who could call the Antonines her forebears.

His wealth was eminently suitable to his birth. People called him
the richest citizen in the Empire, a term which may not have been
much of an exaggeration. His estates constituted a small empire in
themselves; his house at Rome had once belonged to Pompey; his
whole mode of existence was one of lavish dignity. Like other aristocrats he had held the high offices of state; the expenses involved in
some of these offices had in the past depleted the fortunes of noble
Romans who thought more of their reputations than of practical considerations, but Gordian could spend princely sums without feeling any
strain. During his year as aedile he outdid previous aediles by providing an elaborate spectacle for the people every month, not out of
vainglory, evidently, but in the sincere belief that a great lord should
show munificence. Some months, as many as a thousand gladiators displayed their prowess on the sand of the arena; in one spectacle a thousand bears gave the crowd delight. For the August show he brought
into Rome wild horses, wild asses, Cypriote bulls, deer and chamois
and elands and ostriches—exotic animals, some of them—and let them
loose in the amphitheatre to be hunted for the people's amusement. He
occupied the consulship under Caracalla, and again the vulgar enjoyed an efflorescence of munificence. For the charioteers of the circus
he furnished a hundred swift Sicilian horses and a hundred choice
steeds bred in the hills of Cappadocia. Not only Rome but other cities
of Italy were also favored with free entertainment as the noble Gordian
distributed his blessings. Nobody excelled him in splendor.

Along with all this complimentary luxury he seems to have maintained a virtuous character, avoiding cruelty and excess, trying to lead
that life of reason which frequently proves attractive to members of the
upper class and which is beyond the grab of the hungry. As a son-in-
law, a father, and a husband he was irreproachable; as a private gentleman he led a quiet life seeking wisdom—cultivating his intellect in
hours of leisure, deriving principles of moral conduct from the perusal
of Cicero and Aristotle, Plato and Virgil. During his young manhood
he had engaged in literary endeavor himself, having written several
poems, one of them an epic about Antoninus Pius and Marcus Aurelius.
(We do not have it, but we are told that it consisted of thirty books.)

Now he no longer wrote; at eighty he governed Africa; but he retained a fine appreciation for the most instructive, eloquent, and edifying authors.

The conspirators, who had hurried to his palace in the city of Thysdrus, found him reclining on a couch. They told him what they had done and asked him to be their Emperor, together with his middle-aged son, also named Gordian. But he did not want the elevation. He implored them not to make him Emperor; they needed somebody more vigorous, a man not hungry for the comforts of retirement, a man not ready for the tomb. The leaders replied that if he did not fulfill their wish they would murder him immediately.

As they continued to importune and to menace, to flatter and to threaten, he realized that their request was inescapable. Maximin would kill any man who had committed the grave offense of being asked to become Emperor; it did not matter whether the man desired the eminence or not, or whether he declined such an offer—the request in itself was enough. The noble youths had virtually sentenced the two Gordians to death by so honoring them. If the Gordians accepted the imperium, at least they would have some chance to save their lives. Maximin's armies might be defeated, and Maximin himself might be killed.

Sadly, therefore, but with a modicum of hope, the old man consented to rule, and his middle-aged son followed his example. Outside the palace a large crowd hailed their new Emperors with noisy, demonstrative joy. The Gordians were proclaimed throughout Africa, and statues of the Thracian were pulled down.

Many people, apparently, did not take the time to reflect that even if the elder Gordian overcame Maximin he could not enjoy a very long reign; but to those who did realize this, the qualifications of the younger Gordian were in large measure acceptable. The middle-aged son had much to recommend him. He had already acquired political experience and shown outstanding administrative ability; under Elagabalus he had been a questor, and Severus Alexander, recognizing his comprehensive knowledge of law, had made him Prefect of Rome, which meant that the civil judicature of the capital was in his charge. Later he had functioned as a consul, and in recent years he had helped his father ably and compassionately in the governing of Africa. He resembled his father in an enthusiasm for learning, especially for polite literature, and even in attempting literary creation himself.

His taste for learning, however, was not stronger than his taste for lechery. A bachelor, he is said to have kept twenty-two carefully selected concubines and provided all of them, in time, with the responsibilities of motherhood. Although he evidently did not let his concubines or his bastards interfere with business, some of his contemporaries may have thought him a less ideal administrator than his father. He had not learned to forego any pleasure, to restrict himself in any way; he purchased whatever he wanted, exotic or otherwise; in the gratification of his tastes and whims he was passionately lavish. A few people may have remembered former insatiable men who had not made good Emperors.

It took about ten days for news of the events in Africa to reach Rome. The elder Gordian wrote a letter to the Senate announcing that his son and he had been hailed as Emperors and that they wished confirmation of their new condition. He reviled Maximin in the letter as a cruel tyrant and predicted that his own reign would be one of clemency. In proof of this clemency he ordered a review of proceedings against men who had suffered legal injustices and announced that exiles could come home. To the soldiers and the people he promised a generous distribution of money.

The senators rejoiced at this chance to get rid of the giant pig. Called together by the consul Junius Silanus, they assembled in the Temple of Castor and Pollux, listened to the letter from the elderly aristocrat, whom most of them knew personally and whom a few of them regarded as an old friend, and by a unanimous vote declared him Emperor. These senators might not have been fearless leaders, but they could still show spirit on occasion, and the removal of Maximin was the greatest occasion that they could imagine. They named him a national enemy.

Earlier that same day a less illustrious event occurred. Gordian had sent to Rome the questor of Africa, a young man on whom he could depend, together with a few soldiers. One of their assignments was to deliver Gordian's letter to the Senate; their other assignment was to murder Vitalianus, the Praetorian Prefect, who was incorruptibly faithful to Maximin and who, controlling both the Praetorians and the law, constituted the most serious menace to the Gordians' accession. If Vitalianus was allowed to live he would be able to intimidate the senators and the citizens. The older Gordian liked virtue well enough, but he was not impractical; his years in politics had taught him the lessons of prudence and expediency.

The young questor of Africa obtained a private audience with Vitalianus on the pretext of showing him letters important from the standpoint of Maximin's safety. While Vitalianus was examining the seals of the letters, the soldiers who had accompanied the questor stabbed the Prefect to death. The assassination of Vitalianus no doubt made it easier for the senators to declare in favor of the Gordians.

An edict to the people, informing them that they had two new Emperors, was posted in the Forum, and the questor and his soldiers even started a rumor that Maximin was dead. Although this rumor did not convince many people, the inhabitants of Rome felt reasonably sure that Maximin would be dead soon, since the Senate had sentenced both him and his son to execution. The sense of freedom came like a sweet, rare wine to the common citizens, and they swilled it and got drunk. In wild riots they fell on persons known to be informers for Maximin, tore them up, beat them to death, threw them into sewers. They sought out unjust magistrates and tax collectors, men who had profited from Maximin's rapacity, and dragged them through the streets and battered them into another world. The riots went on for days; Sabinus, the governor of Rome, tried to restore order, but a mob found him and murdered him. Since he was suspected of being a partisan of Maximin, his death disturbed no one's conscience. Some of the rioters took advantage of the frenzy to pursue their own private ends: defendants at law killed their prosecutors, and debtors disposed of their creditors in the name of freedom.

According to his biographer in the *Augustan History* (probably Capitolinus), when Maximin at Sirmium learned about the Gordians he banged his great head on the wall, bludgeoned the servants with his fists, waved his sword at imaginary senators, and got gigantically drunk. According to the historian Herodian, he fell into a mood of gloomy preoccupation, which he tried to conceal from those around him. In this case the less histrionic account sounds like the more reliable one. Whatever his initial reaction may have been, however, he was soon conferring with his supporters on a plan of action, and within a day or so he addressed his troops in order to inspire them to war against the Gordians. Unlike the soft and educated Romans, this man could not compose an eloquent oration; the speech, which rang with trumpet phrases, had to be written for him and he read it, as Othello might have done under similar circumstances. It would seem that he also sent a promise of amnesty to those Romans who would come over to him.

The senators, however, were not to be cajoled by such a promise; the idea of overthrowing the peasant was irresistible. Swiftly and efficiently, they made preparations for war. Since Maximin would have to invade Italy, for military purposes they divided the peninsula into twenty districts and put each district in charge of one of their own number. Troops were levied, and people braced for the invasion.

On the site of Punic Carthage (which the Romans had demolished in 146 B.C. in a merciless finale to the last Punic War), there had arisen the Carthage of Roman Africa, a vast and opulent capital, making up in luxury for what it lacked in Hannibalic stamina. To this city proceeded the Gordians, accompanied by guards, surrounded by the overwhelming pomp of the imperial office, and wreathed in the customary laurel. They would probably take up residence at Rome in time, but for the present, Carthage was safer.

One of the evil men whom the older Gordian disliked intensely was Capellian, governor of Numidia, an appointee of Maximin. Gordian had not been Emperor many days before he commanded Capellian to resign and sent a man of his own choice to govern Numidia. Capellian, however, refused to recognize Gordian's authority. Ambitious and desperate, he placed himself at the head of his legionaries and led them toward Carthage. His pretext was, of course, that of loyalty to the true Emperor, Maximin.

To the old man, nervously watching the approach of Capellian, the idea that he and his son would rule the Empire for any length of time seemed increasingly remote. The regular troops in Carthage were not numerous; the enthusiastic citizens, it was true, were arming themselves with whatever implements they could find, such as hatchets and poles sharpened at one end; but how could an undisciplined, citified rabble hope to frighten forces hardened on the wild Numidian frontiers? Gordian himself was too aged for battles, nor had he ever relished them. He would wait in Carthage for the outcome of this contest, while his middle-aged son faced Capellian. But even if, with the intervention of the gods, Capellian was defeated, there would be other battles, other strains and horrors. Life had become unrewarding for a venerable aristocrat who would have liked to finish it in peace.

Followed by his regular soldiers and the sketchily armed but very loyal mob, and wishing that he was doing almost anything else, the younger Gordian ventured out to meet Capellian. But it seemed as if the gods had decided to intervene on Capellian's side. A violent storm crashed down, frightening Gordian's defenders. When the pro-Gordians had been thoroughly terrorized by what they viewed as a portent, Capellian's men, to whom a storm was only a storm, attacked and slaughtered. It was not really a battle at all; it was a mass killing.

The middle-aged Gordian never lay with another mistress; he lay in some hill of dead men, and when the thing was over nobody could even find his body

Capellian marched in triumph into Carthage, intending above all else to do away with the old Gordian. But the patrician did not give his enemy the opportunity. If he had not already known, the tradition of his class would have told him what he must do in this kind of situation. Gordian retired to his closet and, using a cord which he liked to wear around his waist, hanged himself.

The Gordians had reigned about three weeks and were dead. The courage of the Senate seemed purposeless. Maximin advanced toward Italy.

# ❧ XXI ❧

# *The Substitutes*

The Senate had proceeded too far to back down: it must either carry through the revolution that it had undertaken, or suffer unspeakable consequences. Instead of wasting time in lamenting the deaths of the Gordians, it set about electing somebody to replace them.

The first senator that spoke proposed naming two Emperors rather than just one. A senator called Pupienus—long and grave of face, dignified and bearded—seconded the motion. The discussion proceeded. For the moment at least, two Emperors seemed preferable to just one; there was less danger of tyranny if the imperium was divided. The emergency called for two leaders anyway, one to deal with Maximin, the other to stay at Rome to pacify the citizens, who in the fervor of their confusion were likely to do almost anything. Vectius Sabinus requested permission to speak before his turn came. At a time like this, he said, every moment counted. Words were a foolish luxury. While the senators discussed, Maximin was marching ever closer and closer to Italy; soon it would be too late to do anything—except suffer cruelty and death. He proposed that Pupienus be elected one of the Emperors, and that Decimus Caelius Balbinus be made his colleague. The senators grew excited. "That's what we all want!" Pupienus and Balbinus were unanimously elected.

Pupienus, the man who had seconded the motion in favor of having two Emperors rather than one, and who had probably done so as part of a preconceived plan to get himself into office, was almost as unlikely a candidate for Emperor as Maximin, having had, according to report, a smith or a wheelwright for a father. He had, however, risen rapidly in the army, for which he showed great talent, until he was made a praetor. The praetorship entailed the expenditure of money which Pupienus did not possess, but a lady who evidently treated him as if he were her son paid his official expenses for him. Later he even became a consul, and after his consulship he successively governed Bithynia, Greece, and Gallia Narbonensis; led military forces against the Sarmatians in Illyria and against the Germans on the Rhine; and with inflexible justice (undue severity, in the opinion of his critics) filled the office of Prefect of Rome. The elder Gordian had held high offices with aristocratic nonchalance and magnificence, as his birth had almost required; Pupienus, one of the *nouveaux riches,* held high offices as prizes and did the best he could in them, and his best was evidently excellent. People might have grumbled about his austerity, but he commanded their respect. As co-Emperor he was to be in charge of the war against Maximin.

Fat-faced, clean-shaven Balbinus, his colleague, who would remain at Rome during the emergency, was rich and could trace his patrician ancestry back at least a century. He loved the pleasures of luxury, though not to any degrading excess, and valued himself as a connoisseur of wine. In the traditions of his class, he cultivated eloquence, tried his hand at poetry (and was apparently as good as many other poets of that age), and fulfilled important public functions. He held the consulship twice and headed the civil administration in Asia, Africa, Bithynia, Galatia, Pontus, Thrace, and Gaul. Although he commanded legionaries, his military abilities do not appear to have been remarkable; but his election was a guarantee that the imperium had not fallen entirely into the hands of the low.

The citizens, however, were not yet satisfied, and neither were the soldiers; at the very least, they wanted some member of the Gordian family as a Caesar. On the part of the soldiers the motive was not entirely one of affection for the family that had reigned for only three weeks. Those three weeks had not given the Gordians time to distribute the largesse which the troops had been promised; a new Gordian might be persuaded to make the distribution. As for the civilians, they feared the reputed severity of Pupienus and wished it to be tempered by a Gordian.

The joint Emperors acceded to the demands of the demonstrators. There was living in Rome at the time a grandson of the elder Gordian and nephew of Gordian II—a boy of twelve or thirteen whose name was also Gordian. Balbinus and Pupienus consented to the Senate's making him their associate with the title Caesar. The boy was sent for; he had a sensitive, innocent face—he was a true Gordian. If he was named Caesar, the people and the soldiers would agree to let Pupienus and Balbinus be Emperors.

Several days later, it seems, the people had still another demand. Of course they realized that their security and their lives were in grave jeopardy, that somewhere to the north the tyrant Maximin was on the march, and that the man most likely to defeat him was Pupienus. But before Pupienus set out from Rome, they must be entertained. In celebration of his election and as a prelude to the coming war, Pupienus must provide plays, chariot races, and gladiatorial combats. The citizens must have their customary circuses; then Pupienus would be permitted to go out and defeat the giant. Around the arena the people cheered and watched enthralled and bet on which gladiators would be killed, and they got drunk at the races, and the men lolled with the loose women who were plentiful there—and Maximin kept approaching.

He marched unopposed through Pannonia with his legions, heading toward northeastern Italy. When he drew close to Emona, the last city before the Italian border, a town in the foothills of the Alps, he sacrificed to the gods of the area in order to incline them toward his cause. Their help would be needed if he was to enter Italy successfully.

He was, however, by no means without supporters among the civilian population of the Empire. Officially at least, those border provinces that he had defended against the barbarians remained loyal to him, as did Spain, Dacia, and probably Asia Minor. Fear may have been an element in the loyalty, but hatred of Maximin was by no means universal, as the Roman aristocracy realized.

The Senate tried to anticipate Maximin's route and dispatched to the cities through which he would presumably pass experienced commanders, who were empowered to levy troops, rebuild dilapidated fortifications, and do whatever else in their opinion the military emergency required. The senators also issued proclamations to the effect that anyone in the provinces who provided Maximin's army with food or equipment, or, in fact, helped the Thracian in any way at all, would be

dealt with as a public enemy. Inhabitants of small towns were ordered
to evacuate their communities, which were incapable of defense, and
retire to the larger cities, taking their grain, cattle, and other belong-
ings with them, so that Maximin's soldiers could not forage en route.
Guards were put on watch along the Italian coasts and in the Italian
ports; the highways into Italy were barricaded; one might almost have
thought that the senators were the vigorous, self-confident nobles of
centuries ago, expecting the approach of a Hannibal.

Before reaching the city of Emona Maximin marshaled his forces.
In the vanguard he put his legionaries, among whom were the
Pannonians whom he had trained and who were still, he felt, his most
trustworthy men. Behind the legionaries came the baggage, and at the
rear rode the giant himself, surrounded by his Praetorians. The cavalry,
which was composed partly of Germans, occupied the wings, as did
also the Osrhoënian bowmen, Mauretanian slingers, and other light-
armed troops. Scouts who had been sent ahead returned with the news
that Emona had been abandoned; there was not a soldier in it, or a
citizen either. At first this news pleased Maximin greatly; it meant that
the senatorial forces were terrified of him, that they were running like
little animals. Soft Italy would probably prove an easy conquest. A little later, however, it appeared that the flight from Emona had been
anything but precipitate. All the farmlands around the city had been
systematically burned; no food could be found for Maximin's men or
horses, and the men grumbled. They grumbled louder when, having
entered the city, they discovered that there was nothing to loot; the
citizens had taken all their riches with them, and only empty buildings
awaited Maximin's army. Obviously the abandonment of Emona had
been carefully planned and carried out as a part of military policy;
the giant had been fooled.

On into Italy he marched. The first large Italian city he would
come to would be Aquileia, a busy, prosperous, and important place.
He received the report that it had locked its gates against him.

With the Emperor Pupienus on his way north to defeat the Emperor
Maximin, and with the Emperor Balbinus in charge of affairs in the
city, the people of Rome grew increasingly tense. While the sandal-
makers, stonecutters, vintners, merchants, and pimps went about
their daily business they could not keep their minds off the immediate

future, and in their apprehensiveness they cursed the great for causing so much trouble. But the great were agitated too. The senators would, of course, be the first objects of Maximin's revenge, and as they waited and deliberated, attempting to make preparations and trying to maintain a brave and calm demeanor, they became nearly frantic. They had gambled for the Gordians, and the Gordians had died; now they possessed as leaders an austere administrator who might soon lose his life in battle, a stout Sybarite who did not inspire unalloyed confidence, and a noble child of twelve.

Pupienus had left some Praetorians, veterans especially, behind at Rome. While the Senate was in session a number of these Praetorians, along with a mob of citizens, gathered outside the Senate house. Apparently no one intended to create a disturbance; but the times were unquiet, tense. When two or three of the soldiers pushed through the crowd and entered the Senate house, however, the fathers of the republic became alarmed. The soldiers were unarmed and out of uniform; they had probably been drawn simply by curiosity about what the senators were discussing, what steps were being taken for the national safety. They tended, nevertheless, to be noisy and arrogant, as Praetorians could be, and in their insolence they advanced past the altar of Victory. This was a great breach of decorum. In a moment the old enmity between the Senate and the military, the enmity that the reigns of Severus, Caracalla, and Alexander had fostered, flared into an ugly incident. An ancient senator named Maecenas and a colleague of his called Gallicanus, who had been a consul, pulled daggers from under their white robes, rushed at the Praetorians, and stabbed them to death. Gallicanus charged out of the Senate house, and, waving his bloody dagger at the mob below the steps, shouted that he had killed two spies of Maximin, that the other Praetorians were also Maximin's friends, that the Praetorians must be destroyed. The soldiers, who would probably have stood their ground if they had been carrying weapons, fled toward their camp.

Gallicanus may have had some personal reason to resent the Praetorians. At any rate, he did not allow the citizens to calm down. Playing on the tensions which sorely needed to be released, he incited the civilians to make an attack on the Praetorian camp. Most of them had no weapons, but he supplied them with weapons from the arsenals. A large number of gladiators joined them, not displeased at the prospect of a fight and perhaps thinking that in their own particular cases the best chance for safety lay in riot. Led by Gallicanus, this wild crowd assaulted the Praetorian camp.

The Praetorians, however, were ready now. They did not find it difficult to drive back the tumultuous, unskilled citizens, and even the burly gladiators did not present much of a problem. After the mob had been repulsed more than once, many people, their tensions eased, decided that it might be wise to leave war to warriors. They began to wander off.

But the indignation of the Praetorians could not be so easily appeased. Groups of soldiers ventured out of the camp, charged the civilians, and killed quite a few of them. The result was a state of civil war in Rome. The Senate, siding with Gallicanus, levied troops to oppose the Praetorians, and for several days the city was terrorized.

Meanwhile Balbinus endeavored to make peace. He issued statements, sent forth edicts, and promised the Praetorians that their violence would be forgiven. Who would have expected that his reign would be rent by such disorders?

Since the populace did not seem able to defeat the Praetorians by means of arms, it tried other tactics: it cut off the water supply to the Praetorian camp. The guards stood the thirst, however, and did not give up. Finally, almost crazed with want of water, they broke out of the camp and fought the people. It was the largest battle of the civil war, a wicked, screaming clash outside the camp, the Praetorians and the populace demonstrating their abhorrence of each other, as they had done under Alexander, by inflicting death. When the Praetorians had won they chased the people through the streets of Rome, exultant and vengeful, lusting to kill more. The citizens fled to the roofs of the buildings and threw down stones and tiles at their enemies, smashing an occasional guard in the skull or at least slashing a face. In retaliation, as much as in self-defense, the Praetorians set the buildings on fire, and citizens on the roofs were trapped by the flames. The fires spread; apparently, an entire quarter of the city was destroyed.

This did not end the civil war; sporadic fights kept occurring, and the people hoped to be victorious in another large battle.

Balbinus made a personal appeal for peace, but his auditors laughed at him. The mob signified its scorn for a weak leader by throwing things. According to one report, Balbinus was wounded by a stone; according to another report, he was wounded by a stick. We have no credible account of how the civil disturbances were stopped. Perhaps the people gradually exhausted themselves, having already exhausted their Emperor.

The senators had decided to make Aquileia their bulwark against Maximin. This populous city, having become rich through trade with both Illyricum and the Italian peninsula in times of peace, had let its fortifications decay, but under the auspices of the Senate they were repaired. A large number of soldiers were dispatched to the city, and two former consuls, both very competent military men, were put in command. As for the ordinary citizens, they could probably be depended on to do their part. After years of uninterrupted industry and the pleasures of wealth, they would not want to see their city fall into the possession of the tyrant and his ravenous army.

Maximin's Pannonians, having been sent on ahead, found Aquileia's ramparts lined with troops. The Pannonians scaled the walls in the name of the Emperor, but Aquileia's defenders knocked them off and killed a great many. The survivors returned to their leader and reported what had happened.

Since the city was obviously strong, and since he could not implicitly trust the loyalty of all his men, Maximin hoped to take Aquileia without a siege. One of the tribunes in his army happened to be an Aquileian; the man's wife and family were still inside the city, and so were many of his friends; perhaps if he spoke to his fellow citizens he could persuade them that the future lay with Maximin.

Accompanied by several centurions, the tribune rode to Aquileia and delivered his speech outside the city, shouting up to the residents who crowded the walls. He told his fellow citizens that Maximin was their true Emperor, that the Senate consisted of rebels, and that if Maximin was allowed to enter Aquileia he would pardon the city for having been temporarily in revolt, whereas if the gates were kept shut against him he would break in and wreak terrible vengeance. All of this sounded fairly convincing, and certainly the prospect of peace and forgiveness was attractive to a merchant community unused to war.

Before the Aquileians had made up their minds, however, Crispinus, one of the two ex-consuls sent by the Senate to take charge of the city, gave his own view of the situation. Maximin, he said, was an untrustworthy and greedy barbarian, a tyrant whose cruelty had already been demonstrated many times. The Senate had done right to declare him an enemy of the state, and the Aquileians would be committing a horrible error of judgment if they supported him. In the event that he won, his promise of pardon could not be trusted any more than his other promises; the city would be at his mercy; once his men had entered Aquileia they would surely not be so thoughtful as to leave its beauties unviolated and its women unspoiled. If, on the other hand, the Aquileians resisted this monster and saved Italy from his depredations, they would be the heroes of the age. There was, besides, no doubt that they would win; the entrails of the sacrificial victims had been in their favor, and the oracles of their tutelary god Apollo Belenus (an old Romanized Gallic deity) had declared that they would triumph over their enemies.

Crispinus was a better speaker than the tribune, and in addition, the sympathies of the Aquileians had never been with Maximin. The city prepared for a siege.

When Maximin approached the outskirts of Aquileia he discovered to his satisfaction that the citizens had not applied the policy that the people of Emona had applied to their environs. Fine houses and pleasant gardens provided almost the only amenities which Maximin and his men had encountered in a long time. The inhabitants had evidently not been able to bring themselves to destroy these things, but the invading army did the job for them, looting and burning the buildings, ripping up the vines, cutting down the trees in the gardens, and using the wood to construct siege engines.

There was a day of rest; then the assault began. Maximin's men moved their siege engines up to the walls, but the soldiers on top of the walls—the troops sent by the Senate and the native Aquileians who had enlisted for the defense of their city—kept the enemy out. Steaming pitch and rosin were dumped down on Maximin's soldiers, making them scream as they tore at their hair and faces. Military machines, their ropes reportedly woven from the hair of Aquileian matrons, shot darts at the invaders, who were unable to effect a breach in the walls. Maximin's men guessed that Aquileia was so plentifully supplied with food and drink that it could withstand a siege for a long time. The outlook for Maximin appeared dismal; the men grumbled as they had grumbled at Emona, and the more discontented they became, the more impatient Maximin grew. In his rages he called his soldiers cowards, called his officers traitors, singled out the officers whom he considered most responsible for the failure and rewarded them with death. The result was to spread further discontent among the men, which blossomed into bitter hatred. The Praetorians perhaps complained the loudest, since they were not accustomed to contemptuous treatment from an Emperor; the insults tore into them and made them furious. It seemed that this giant who had once commanded the respect and love of his soldiers, whose fame as an officer had swept through the Roman army, had forgotten how to lead. In addition to Maximin's harsh childishness the men of the Second Parthian had another reason for chafing—they had left their wives, children, and possessions at Alba, a city in central Italy and therefore under the control of the Senate, where the worst might happen to them. Even Maximin's favorites, the Pannonians, felt their devotion slip away as the siege dragged on from April into May.

Toward the middle of May, apparently, one day was designated as a day of respite. The soldiers lounged around the camp during the morning, feeling no happier when they thought that the siege was to be resumed the next day; and in the imperial tent Maximin and his handsome son Maximus, who at the age of approximately twenty-one had come along to help his father hold on to the imperium, rested from their labors and awaited a day they would not see. Around noon the angry members of the Second Parthian, carrying their weapons, proceeded to the imperial tent. They were evidently joined by other soldiers, and the guards at the tent removed from their standards the images of the Emperor whom they were presumably guarding. Maximin, hearing the commotion and of course realizing its cause, strode out of his tent, followed by his son, in the hope that he could shout and bluster these men down. The men, however, killed both him and his son.

The heads of Maximin and Maximus were cut off as presents for Pupienus; their bodies were left for the birds.

Maximin's troops, now an army of peace, unarmed and eager for reconciliation with the Aquileians, assembled below the walls of the city and explained that the Thracian and his son were dead. It immediately occurred to those in charge at Aquileia, however, that this might be a ruse on the part of Maximin. The effigies of the Emperors Pupienus and Balbinus and of the Caesar Gordian were therefore held out over the walls: if the soldiers demonstrated loyalty to them, then the assertion that they had killed their general must be legitimate. The soldiers without any hesitation recognized Pupienus, Balbinus, and Gordian as their sovereigns.

The siege was over, but the Aquileians were still cautious. They did not want even a friendly army rummaging through their city, perhaps taking booty, possibly taking revenge for comrades whom the Aquileians had killed. Aquileia was lovely and must remain lovely. The residents therefore did not open their gates; instead, they lowered food over the walls to their recent besiegers, who ate well for the first time in a long while.

It was apparently Pupienus' intention to let Maximin batter himself into exhaustion against Aquileia, and then overwhelm him. The co-Emperor was consequently biding his time at Ravenna when messengers brought him the two heads. In a few moments all Ravenna had heard the news and was rejoicing; at the temples the thick smoke rose up from animals sacrificed in gratitude to the gods. There was perhaps nobody, however, more grateful than Pupienus, who had not been looking forward with pleasure to an encounter with the giant, and whose position as Emperor was now certain. He dispatched the heads to Rome and set off for Aquileia.

When he reached this heroic city its gates were thrown open to receive him. Towns in the vicinity sent their magistrates to him to do homage; white-robed, crowned with laurel, and carrying the images of their gods and treasures from their temples, the magistrates professed their loyalty to the glorious Emperor. Many of Maximin's former followers, however, were not feeling quite so loyal. They lined up in front of him, bringing branches of laurel to signify peace, and they recognized him as their leader in a voice which they tried to make enthusiastic, but quite a few were now sorry that Maximin was dead. Many of these men had served under Maximin for several years, had hailed him as Emperor three years before, had fought beside him against the Germans, and had been inspired by his valor; it was not easy to pledge devotion to an Emperor handed them by the Senate. They had, besides, been rebels until very recently; even after the murder of Maximin, Aquileia had discriminated against them; there was no way of telling how this new Emperor or his colleague in Rome would treat them.

Fully aware of their dissatisfaction, Pupienus called them together on the plain outside the city and, having mounted his tribunal, delivered a diplomatic speech. They deserved congratulations, he said, on having resumed their lawful duties and associations and on having taken a solemn oath to serve the men whom the Senate and the Roman people had named Emperors, as the Senate and the Roman people certainly had the right to do. As for the late defection, the Emperor Balbinus and he would forget about that; an amnesty would be granted, and so would a generous donative. The promise of the money was perhaps the most politic part of the address.

Four days after the heads were presented to Pupienus at Ravenna they were presented to Balbinus and young Gordian at Rome. The Augustus and the Caesar were in the circus at the time (nervous Rome still demanded its spectacles), but they left immediately in order to share in the public pleasure. The news of Maximin's death circulated rapidly through Rome, as it had done through Ravenna; citizens flocked to the Forum; for the first time since Pupienus had left, a mob expressed joy. The temples were jammed with people come to offer thanks for the overthrow of terror. The senators, having hurried to their place of meeting, gave vent to their great relief in applause and acclamations, and in cries of detestation against Maximin. This was a great day for Rome, but it was a greater day for the senators: all at once the threat was lifted and they could look forward to living. They made provisions for sacrifices to the beneficent gods of the state who had put an end to their distress; and for the joint Emperors, triumphant without having had to fight a battle, they provided chariots, gilt-covered statues, and statues drawn by elephants. In the streets the two heads, rammed onto spearpoints, were carried around by the yelling rabble. The parade of the heads ended at the Campus Martius, where they were burned.

A committee of twenty senators, ancient holders of public office, among the most respectable men at Rome, was sent to Pupienus in order to escort him to the capital. His return through Italy resembled the advance of some conquering god. While he was still a distance from Rome he was greeted by Balbinus, the young Gordian, and all the other members of the Senate, plus a throng of ordinary citizens. They called him their savior.

The celebrations, however, soon began to pall for Balbinus, who—after the two of them were back at Rome, presumably acting in concert—did not hesitate to point out that Pupienus was not at all responsible for Maximin's overthrow, that he had sat at Ravenna while Aquileia was besieged, that he had issued forth only after being shown that the way was safe. Balbinus apparently mentioned these matters as often as he could, and the partial truth rankled. Pupienus retaliated by suggesting that Balbinus was fat, timid, and lazy; that he had been unable to check the war between the Praetorians and the people; and that he was obviously incompetent.

The Praetorian Guard meanwhile grew more and more uneasy. Pupienus had brought to Rome his German troops, who were his most ardent adherents, and his partiality to them was well known. He might even make them his Praetorians, just as Severus had done with his favorites, the Illyrians. The thought of such an eventuality was intolerable to the guards. Almost as intolerable, despite the promise of a donative, was the recollection that they had had no part in making either Pupienus or Balbinus Emperor, that their enemies the senators had done this on their own. They felt offended by Pupienus, by the Senate; they were dissatisfied. The reign was quickly drawing to a close.

Pupienus and Balbinus stayed in their palace while much of Rome watched the Capitoline games. Through the unusually quiet city the Praetorians marched. Warned that they were approaching the palace, fully armed and intent on murder, Pupienus ordered his Germans to come and protect him; and since these troops were faithful and fearless, they might have protected him very well. It seems, however, that they happened to be with Balbinus in another portion of the palace. Suspecting that Pupienus planned to instruct the Germans to kill him, Balbinus ordered them to remain where they were. The Praetorians consequently entered the palace without difficulty, and falling on both Emperors, ripped off their clothes, hauled them outside, and dragged them through the streets, pulling their hair and making them scream. The Germans set out to rescue Pupienus and, incidentally, Balbinus, but the Praetorians did not give them the chance; having lugged the naked Emperors around long enough, the guards murdered them.

# ☙ XXII ☙

## The Noble Youth

There was no need to look around for another Emperor, since the Praetorians had brought one with them. Partly in justification of the assassination and partly in a spirit of real affection, they announced to the people that young Gordian was the new Emperor and that good times had been restored. The Praetorians were finally satisfied. They had again created their own Emperor and had taught the Senate—the insolent Senate which had murdered several Praetorians a short time ago and had incited the populace to make war on the Guard—a much-deserved lesson.

The people probably felt that the best thing to do was to forget about the dead Emperors and hope that the new reign would be an endurable one. Hope, however, did not come easily. Elagabalus' effeminacy, Alexander's ineffectuality, Maximin's tyranny, the deaths of the first two Gordians, the terror while Maximin marched into Italy, the battles in the city streets under Balbinus, and now the brutal double murder had sharpened the cynicism of the Romans. It was July 238; the past few months had seen the close of Maximin's reign as well as the reigns of two pairs of Emperors; now a boy was back as nominal head of the state, and he too might not last long. The Senate, encouraged by Alexander to resume its privileges and powers, then insulted by the militarist Maximin, had finally reared up, stung into heroism by Maximin's scorn, and had fought out the war against him and elected successors to the Gordians; but since the war was over and the two candidates were dead, the Senate would not, or could not, do anything. To punish the assassins would be politically inexpedient. The

Praetorians were the real victors, the lords of the state; for all that the people knew, the Guard might kill the boy Gordian tomorrow.

Or, if he stayed on the throne, he might turn into a studious, timorous, strait-laced youth like Alexander, or into a monster like Elagabalus.

As for Gordian himself—apparently a carefree, fun-loving boy, although not even that is certain—we have no reliable record of his feelings during the early portion of his reign. He does not seem to have made any plans for the reorganization of the state; he probably did not understand what was needed. After all, he was only thirteen when he found the state in his hands. He certainly did not pattern himself after Elagabalus by indulging in one great splurge, or by trying to push a god into supremacy. His mother, unlike Alexander's mother, did not supervise his education along priggish lines, and yet he does not appear to have been stained by lasciviousness. He may have acquired from his aristocratic ancestors or patrician environment a certain good taste in conduct. During the first two or three years of his reign, besides, he was probably too innocent to have embraced the evils of the court even if he had been inclined in that direction. It is in his innocence, in fact, that he most resembled Alexander. He was called Gordian the Pious, and throughout his reign, so far as we know, he never did anything to make the name unsuitable.

In later years a story arose that unscrupulous courtiers, principally eunuchs, crept into the confidence of the young ruler for their own profit. However, this is unsupported by evidence, and it is much more probable that the boy Gordian was advised by prominent and competent members of the Senate. The early years of his reign were not at all noteworthy for corruption; much legislation was aimed at remedying abuses in the administration of the provinces. Besides, in 240 or 241 Gordian came under the strong influence of Timesitheus, probably of Greek descent, one of the most learned, distinguished, and eloquent gentlemen in Rome at the time, perhaps even comparable to the Ulpian who had guided Alexander. Earlier in his career various administrative posts had made him familiar with a large part of the Empire— Spain, Belgica, Arabia, Syria, Palestine, Germany, Bithynia, Pontus, Paphlagonia, Gallia Lugdunensis, and Aquitania. At Rome he had headed the office of the inheritance tax. According to ancient historians, he was not only extremely capable but also remarkably selfless, serving state and Emperor without trying to further his private interests.

Although his reported selflessness was probably authentic, Timesitheus did attain the honor of giving his daughter Tranquillina to the Emperor in marriage. If Tranquillina was no older than her husband at the time of the wedding in 241, she must have been an unusually young wife. There is no indication that the marriage was not happy, except that it produced no children. One would like to believe that Gordian and Tranquillina were two fundamentally fine people who enjoyed a pleasant connubial life.

Gordian had also made Timesitheus Praetorian Prefect. As Prefect, the statesman devoted much of his attention to the army. Since a soldier's profession tended to be very remunerative, boys would often join the army when they were actually too young to perform their duties properly, and men would remain in it after they had grown too decrepit to be of military worth. Timesitheus tried to make sure that only those who were fit for service received government pay and rations. He also saw to the repair of fortifications on the frontiers and at strategically located cities. If a frontier post was of particular importance, he equipped it with enough grain, straw, wine, and salt pork to last a year; less important posts were supplied with a sufficient amount of these for a month or two.

Military improvements were especially appropriate in the light of the new Persian threat. At the time of his assassination Pupienus had been preparing for war against Ardashir, who, with his well-trained, superbly equipped, and eager and courageous troops of Iranian horsemen, was menacing the Romans once again, as he had done during the reign of Alexander—he eventually took Carrhae (the city toward which Caracalla had been going when he died) and invaluable Nisibis. In 241 Ardashir died, but his son Shapur, young, confident, and highly competent, thirsted for personal glory and the aggrandizement of Persia. Almost immediately he began harassing the Romans, whom he was to continue to worry for more than thirty years. He proceeded into Syria, and although he could not enter Antioch, he cut off supplies to the great city and made its people tremble.

In the spring of 242 Gordian opened the doors of the Temple of Janus, which were closed only when the Empire was at peace. He is the last Roman known to have performed the ceremony. The tradition, like much else, may have been moribund; besides, in order for the doors to be opened again they first had to be shut.

On his way to Asia Gordian made war in the Danube valley, where barbarians—Goths and Sarmatians, apparently—had been raiding and killing since the beginning of his reign about four years before. He evidently succeeded in quelling them, with the help of Timesitheus, who had accompanied him partly in his capacity as Praetorian Prefect and partly as indispensable friend and guide. In waging war Gordian was simply performing an imperial duty; whether at the age of about seventeen he had a youthful enthusiasm for war or whether he did not enjoy it any more than Severus Alexander did we cannot tell. There are few Roman Emperors about whom less is certain. The most we can assume is that his efforts to reign, with the help of Timesitheus, were sincere, well motivated, and generally successful. If he had ruled badly, the record would be fuller.

On the march Timesitheus showed a personal interest in the men, sometimes making the rounds at night and talking with sentinels on duty at remote outposts. His motive, however, was probably a wish to make sure that the machinery of war was running smoothly rather than a paternal sympathy for the common soldier. Always on his guard and firm about discipline, he renewed the old Roman practice of surrounding even a very temporary encampment with a ditch.

Along with Gordian's army marched Plotinus the philosopher. About thirty-seven years old, Plotinus had spent the past eight or nine years at Alexandria studying principally under Ammonius Saccas, an erstwhile porter at the docks, a renegade Christian, and an obscure lecturer on Plato and spiritual truth. Having acquired much wisdom from this teacher, Plotinus had joined Gordian's expedition in the hope that it would give him an opportunity to study the wisdom of Persia, perhaps even of India.

He was a vegetarian like Apollonius of Tyana, a man indifferent to the state of his health, an amiable and unobtrusive but arresting man, one whose thoughts did not stay long in the world of the senses and appetites—a man who thirsted more for eternal verities than Shapur did for military victory.

Later he would go to Rome, where he would lecture for the rest of his life, largely about the soul and the spirit. He would tell his listeners that the soul is indestructible, that if it sins in the world of the senses and appetites it suffers by having to transmigrate into the body of a beast, but that its highest object, for which it struggles and reaches out through the hierarchy of experience, is union with the absolute spiritual oneness, the state of pure beauty or truth or good, which was his conception of God. The ascent to this union, he felt, involves the dropping off of all impurities from the soul, much as in Mithraism the soul sheds its earthly attributes in the climb toward Ahura-Mazda. The union itself is a mystical one—intuitive, ineffable, beyond description in human terms. The physical world should not be regarded as despicable, since the lower has proceeded from the higher; but it is the higher, the highest, the spaceless and the timeless and the incorruptible that one must yearn for and strive to reach.

This philosophy, which came to be called Neoplatonism, and which drew not only from Platonism itself but from other Greek systems of thought and from Oriental systems as well, was the last great intellectual endeavor of the classical world. In large degree it constituted a purging, since it discarded the crasser elements of the old religions—the plurality of particularized deities, their loves and jealousies, the superstitions and shibboleths, the bloody sacrifices and base beliefs of many cults. And, perhaps partly because it had divested itself of these, it did not disappear but became fused with Christianity. In the years after Plotinus was dead the Christian Neoplatonists of Alexandria exerted an important influence on the still-plastic church. Augustine, deeply impressed with Plotinus' writings as a young man, did not forget them after becoming Bishop of Hippo in 396.

But in 243 Plotinus marched with Gordian's army, amiable and unobtrusive, seeking wisdom.

In so far as the army was concerned, the march proved much easier than had been anticipated. Perhaps it was the presence of the extraordinarily efficient Timesitheus, perhaps it was the awe that was still aroused by the Roman name, but for some reason Shapur seems suddenly to have grown afraid. As the Roman forces advanced, he retreated, displaying more haste than valor, withdrawing his troops from their stations in Syria and then in Mesopotamia, evidently trying not to let the Roman army overtake him. Gordian, a young hero to joyful Antioch, crossed the Euphrates in pursuit of the King of Kings, defeated him near the city of Resaena, recaptured Carrhae and Hatra and Nisibis and in fact the whole of Mesopotamia. He looked forward to entering Persia itself and to sacking the capital, Ctesiphon. Timesitheus looked forward to a campaign in India. So, very likely, did Plotinus.

The boy was a conqueror, and the Senate, having received the news, ordered for him a procession in which his chariot was to be drawn by four elephants and Timesitheus' chariot by four horses.

The Emperor and his father-in-law, however, were not to return to Rome for the triumph.

First Timesitheus sickened and died. According to the official version his death was the result of influenza, but a few people whispered that his physicians had been bribed by an officer named Philip to administer too strong a laxative.

Marcus Julius Philippus, or Philip the Arab, as he was called, came from east of the Jordan. His father may have been a sheik. In his middle forties at the time of the Persian expedition—uncultivated, unscrupulous, shrewd, and extremely ambitious—Philip profited by the death of Timesitheus whether he had arranged it or not. Gordian named him a Praetorian Prefect in Timesitheus' place.

It is possible that Gordian liked Philip and admired his military skill; probably, however, Philip intimidated him. In spite of the fact that we know very little about Gordian as a person, the weakness of his character is not difficult to see. He was approaching twenty now; at the same age and under similar circumstances Caracalla would have acted with far more force. Gordian might have lived a quiet, inoffensive, kindly life if he had not had to be an Emperor. Deprived of the strong, intelligent leadership of Timesitheus, he could think of nowhere to turn and nothing to do. Philip probably took advantage of the paralyzing shock of Timesitheus' death in order to press his own demands.

In the face of Philip's ruthless cunning the noble youth had no more chance than a foolish finch stalked by a cat. Once he had become Praetorian Prefect, Philip apparently issued a secret order that the provision boats that followed the Roman army should follow it no more. On the march through the Mesopotamian deserts, far from any base of supply, the soldiers grew hungry and unhappy. Philip had his adherents insinuate that Gordian was to blame, that he was too young to command properly, that he might mean well but had unwittingly added to their discomfort; that they needed a hard, experienced commander, primarily a soldier like themselves, who would make certain that they were treated as Roman soldiers should be.

For more than one reason a campaign was a dangerous time in the life of an Emperor: Alexander had been killed on campaign by his own soldiers, and so had Maximin. When his troops began clamoring, Gordian may have sensed the deadliness of the situation. With the help of his friends, at any rate, he tried to act vigorously and to prevent the sedition from spreading; but apparently he was obliged to elevate Philip to the position of his colleague and tutor.

If he thought that this elevation would placate Philip and the army, he was excessively naïve. Without Timesitheus to stand between him and Philip, between him and the troops, he was insulted and reviled. The dramatic account which the historian Capitolinus gives of his ultimate reaction, however, is probably not to be trusted. According to Capitolinus, Gordian decided that he could no longer stand the insolence of his tormentors; they had finally driven him to firmness. He ordered his army to assemble and addressed it from the tribunal; in manly terms he complained of Philip's great offensiveness and ingratitude; but the troops only jeered. When he realized that they regarded Philip as his superior, his resolution faded. He asked to be allowed to keep the same rank that Philip held; the soldiers said no. He pleaded with them to let him be called Caesar; they refused. Sinking deeper in his humiliation, he said that all he really wanted was the office of Praetorian Prefect; they still refused. Perhaps too full of fear to be aware of his shame, he tried to wheedle them into promising him the title General and his life. Philip had been quiet all this while, indicating his views by means of signs, but now he spoke. At first it seemed that he would spare Gordian his life; then he ordered his soldiers to seize the young Emperor, carry him off, and kill him.

Capitolinus' story, however, is difficult to reconcile with the fact that Philip told the Senate that Gordian had died of a sickness: if the scene in front of the army had really taken place, there would have been too many witnesses present for Philip to send a false account to Rome. We do not know how young Gordian died, but his death was probably a private affair. Assuming sorrow, Philip arranged a funeral, had the ashes transported to the capital, and had his soldiers erect a cenotaph near Zaitha, the city where the youth died. He did not even object when the Senate raised Gordian to the rank of a god.

The year was 244 and Philip was Emperor of Rome. Although he made his son his colleague, the boy amounted to nothing. The time of the young Emperors was over.

# ❧ XXIII ❧

## *After the Young Emperors*

Things were to get much worse before they got better. During the reigns of Philip (244–249), Decius (249–251), Trebonianus Gallus (251–253), Valerian (253–260), Gallienus (253–268), and Claudius Gothicus (268–270), the barbarians made more vicious inroads into the Empire than they had ever made before, plundering and burning proud cities, giving Romans a preview of what their progeny were to endure two centuries later when the Western Empire was brought to an end. While the young Emperors were ruling, the danger from barbarians had not been acute. Many Romans would not live to see another period that was so secure.

In Philip's reign the Carpi played havoc in Thrace, Macedonia, and the Danubian province of Lower Moesia; and the Goths, the Vandals, and their savage kinsmen invaded the Danubian lands. The Emperor Decius died fighting the Gothic king Kniva. During the brief reign of Trebonianus Gallus the Goths and other wildmen raided the Empire again. Early in the reign of Valerian the Goths from the Black Sea region, taking to their ships, laid waste the coast of Asia Minor and devastated the old Ionian city of Ephesus, while more Goths spread death in Thrace. Valerian's gallant son and co-Emperor, Gallienus, fought the Germanic tribes for five years on various fronts, had to cede them part of Pannonia, and even took as a secondary wife the daughter of the king of the Marcomanni. In 256 the Goths coordinated a second maritime assault on Asia Minor with an assault on land, and wrecked such cities as Nicaea and Nicomedia, which had been great since Hellenistic times (it was in Nicomedia that Elagabalus had passed a pleasant winter on the way from Syria to Rome). Two or three years later the Alemanni, whom Caracalla had so fervently admired, broke into Gaul and Italy and even came close to Rome. In 267 and 268 the Goths swept over Asia Minor. They sacked Byzantium, the port which had held out heroically against Septimius Severus toward the beginning of his reign, and at Ephesus they burned to the ground one of the holiest buildings of the Empire, the great temple raised to Diana of the Ephesians. Bursting into Greece, Gothic tribesmen entered a terrorized Athens and roared on as far as the once-brave city of Sparta.

The cost of the barbarian invasions in property, morale, and life was terrible, but other factors also helped to make the second half of the third century one of the grimmest periods that civilization has ever suffered. A deadly plague which broke out in 251 shot through the Empire and ravaged it for fifteen years. The Persians, with whom Philip had concluded a peace, resumed their war against Rome in 252 under their ambitious king, Shapur, so that in the midst of the barbarian fury the Empire found itself assailed on still another front. Valerian, too old to have the necessary energy and not very competent besides, marched to the East in 256/257 but accomplished little against the Persians. In order to distract his subjects from these calamities, he instituted a persecution of the Christians in 257 and intensified it in 258, so that a sizable element in the Empire's population was exposed to another horror. In the year 260 he allowed himself to be taken prisoner by Shapur, and he was never heard of again.

The capture of the Roman Emperor by the Persians, coming in the wake of so many other disasters, demoralized the Empire as perhaps no other event had ever done. It sank the Roman name to a new depth of disgrace. The Romans watched while Shapur plundered Antioch.

Would-be usurpers took advantage of conditions to rise up against Valerian's son Gallienus. Not that these had been the first to try for imperial power since the advent of Philip; by the middle of the third century, in fact, the troops were proclaiming popular men Emperors at frequent intervals. The rash of attempted usurpations after Valerian's capture, however, was especially intense. The general Macrianus had his two sons named Emperors in the East; the Pannonian legions nominated the governor Ingenuus Emperor, and after his defeat, the governor Regalianus. Meanwhile an army man called Postumus had created his own Roman Empire out of Gaul, adding to it Spain and

Britain; and although Gallienus succeeded in stamping out the other
rebellions, he did not succeed in bringing Gaul, Spain, and Britain back
into the Empire proper.

Partly in consequence of the invasions and the plague, the population declined sharply. Cities in the European provinces shrank within
their walls, and fields were often left untilled. Trade dwindled, taxes
rose. Forced labor, which had originated much earlier, was now a customary imposition on the poor, and the rich were made to hold offices
that would oblige them to spend more than they could afford. Under
Gallienus, as the economic recession reached unprecedented depths,
the so-called silver coins became base metal plated with a thin silver
wash that wore off in dirty splotches.

But forces of revival were already in evidence. Odenathus, prince
of a vassal state whose capital was the rich desert city of Palmyra, defeated the Persians for Gallienus in 262, besieging Shapur in his own
capital, Ctesiphon. Claudius Gothicus (268–270), the soldier who succeeded Gallienus, demonstrated that Roman armies could still crush
Goths. Aurelian (270–275), a tough soldier like Claudius, subdued the
Vandals and Juthungi early in his reign and then turned east against
the Palmyrene state, which, noting Rome's weakness and its own new-
found strength, had occupied Asia Minor. Aurelian defeated a Palmyrene general decisively near Antioch, won another victory near Emesa
(with the help, as he later maintained, of the Sun God Elagabalus),
and took captive the imperious Palmyrene queen, Zenobia. Early in
274 he was in Gaul, where an inept man named Tetricus now reigned.
Tetricus abdicated and Gaul, Spain, and Britain were returned to the
Roman Empire. Aurelian celebrated his triumphs at Rome, where in
the most magnificent procession seen in many decades Queen Zenobia
had to walk in golden chains. He made an attempt to reform the coinage, he endeavored to unify the Empire through religion by establishing Elagabalus as the one great god, and in large measure he earned
the title which he bore, Restorer of the World; but in the spring of 275
he was murdered by his officers.

Although the barbarian invasions were slackening off now, Probus
(276–282) still spent much of his reign in the field against barbarians,
and so did Diocletian (284–305) and Maximian, whom Diocletian
made his junior Emperor. There were also, of course, more wishful
usurpers to deal with. On the whole, however, conditions improved. If

it had not been for men such as Claudius, Aurelian, Probus, and Diocletian, the Empire might not have been saved. These men, like Decius and Gallienus before them, realized that an Emperor in that harassed age had to be a hard military man, hurrying with his army from frontier to frontier, hitting barbarians and ambitious rivals before they hit him—almost a superman—trying to defend thousands of miles of border with insufficient troops, trying to put some fresh spirit into Romans, trying to reconstitute the old Empire (as Diocletian in a relatively long reign succeeded in doing), trying to hang on to a nerve-racked life and defying grossly unfair odds. These men accepted the fact that it was no longer possible, even for a few years, to pursue a life of luxury in a palace, as Elagabalus had done, or to sit in a palace studying Plato, as Severus Alexander had done. By virtue of their strenuous efforts, Romans could hope for safety again, perhaps for prosperity.

# ❦ BIBLIOGRAPHY ❦

## I. ANCIENT SOURCES

Aside from non-literary evidence such as coins and inscriptions, the three principal ancient sources for knowledge of the period dealt with in this book are the works by Cassius Dio, Herodian, and the so-called *Scriptores Historiae Augustae*, or authors of the *Augustan History*. Cassius Dio (less correctly, Dio Cassius), who was born at Nicaea in Bithynia about the year 155, is by far the most reliable. He occupied positions of responsibility under several Emperors. Unfortunately, his *Roman History* ends several years before the close of Severus Alexander's reign, and the portions pertinent to this book come down to us only in an abridged form. Herodian, possibly an Alexandrian Greek and Dio's junior by about fifteen years, carried his *Historiae* to 238. Since he was prejudiced and evidently given to invention as well, his account is not very trustworthy. The *Augustan History* is a compilation dating perhaps from the late third and early fourth centuries, quite possibly altered by an unknown hand at a later date. Six authors (only three of whom contributed material that is relevant to the period under consideration) presumably wrote the biographies of various Emperors in the *Augustan History*. The lives of Didius Julianus, Septimius Severus, Pescennius Niger, and Caracalla are usually attributed to a writer named Spartian; those of Elagabalus and Severus Alexander, to Lampridius; those of Maximin, the Gordians, Balbinus and Pupienus, to Capitolinus; that of Clodius Albinus, to either Spartian or Capitolinus; and that of Macrinus, to either Capitolinus or Lampridius. These three historians are probably even less trustworthy than Herodian.

**228**

When a reign is recorded by several historians, the accounts may be contradictory in many respects, even though they may agree on most major points. In cases of discrepancies, I have followed Cassius Dio in so far as it was possible. If no other evidence was forthcoming I have at times, and with due caution, accepted the word of Herodian or one of the authors of the *Augustan History*. If epigraphic or other evidence conflicted with such an author, however, that evidence was generally preferred. The epigraphic sources—the coins and inscriptions—are invaluable with regard to chronology, and sometimes they point to occurrences which none of the ancient historians thought worthy of mention.

*Coins of the Roman Empire in the British Museum*. Vol. V: *Pertinax to Elagabalus*. With an Introduction by Harold Mattingly. London, 1950.

*Coins of the Roman Empire in the British Museum*. Vol. VI: *Severus Alexander to Balbinus and Pupienus*. With an introduction by R. A. G. Carson. London, 1963.

Dio, Cassius. *Roman History*. With English translation by Earnest Cary. (Loeb Classical Library.) 9 vols. Cambridge, Mass., 1961.

Herodianus. *Historiae*. Edited by K. Stavenhagen. Leipzig, 1922.

Philostratus. *The Life of Apollonius of Tyana: The Epistles of Apollonius and The Treatise of Eusebius*. Translated by Frederick C. Conybeare. (Loeb Classical Library.) 2 vols. New York, 1912; London, 1917–21.

Plotinus. *Complete Works . . . With Biography by Porphyry, Eunapius, & Suidas*. Edited by Kenneth Sylvan Guthrie. 4 vols. London, 1918.

*Prosopographia Imperii Romani Saecula I, II, III*. Edited by E. Klebs, Hermann Dessau, and P. de Rohden. 3 vols. Berlin, 1897–98.

*Scriptores Historiae Augustae*. With English translation by David Magie. (Loeb Classical Library.) 3 vols. New York; London, 1921–32.

Tertullian, Quintus Septimius Florus. *Apology: De Spectaculis*. With English translation by T. R. Glover; and *Minucius Felix*. With English translation by Gerald H. Rendall based on the unfinished version by W. C. A. Kerr. (Loeb Classical Library.) London, 1931.

Victor, Sextus Aurelius. *Liber de Caesaribus*. Edited by Franz Pichlmayr. Leipzig, 1911.

## II. SUGGESTED MODERN READINGS

The following bibliography is intended merely to suggest further readings for those interested in the period either from the viewpoint of a layman or from a somewhat more technical standpoint. It is by no means intended to be complete. As one might expect from the conflicts among the ancient sources, recent historians of the period are sometimes in disagreement. There is, for example, no unanimous opinion about the date of Caracalla's birth. I have followed Harold Mattingly in *Coins of the Roman Empire in the British Museum* (listed above), who assigns Caracalla's birth to the year 188, rather than S. N. Miller, who in the *Cambridge Ancient History* prefers 186.

For the material on Antioch, I am largely indebted to the excellent works by Glanville Downey, and for the account of Alexandria, I have relied considerably on E. M. Forster's sympathetic treatment of that city.

Altheim, Franz. *A History of Roman Religion.* Translated by Harold Mattingly. London; New York, 1938.

Baring-Gould, Rev. S. *The Lives of the Saints.* 16 vols. London, 1898.

Blair, Peter H. *Roman Britain and Early England 55* B.C.–A.D. *871.* Edinburgh, 1963.

Brown, Frank E. *Roman Architecture.* New York, 1961.

Budge, E. A. Wallis. *The Gods of the Egyptians.* 2 vols. London, 1904.

Butler, Alban. *Lives of the Saints.* Complete edition edited, revised, and supplemented by Herbert Thurston and Donald Attwater. Foreword by Francis Cardinal Spellman. 4 vols. New York, 1956.

Butler, Orma F. *Studies in the Life of Heliogabalus.* New York, 1908.

*The Cambridge Ancient History.* 12 vols. Vol. XII: *The Imperial Crisis and Recovery,* A.D. *193–324.* Edited by S. A. Cook, F. E. Adcock, M. P. Charlesworth, and N. H. Baynes. London, 1956. Note especially the following contributions:

Bidez, J., "Literature and Philosophy in the Eastern Half of the Empire," pp. 611–45.

Burkitt, F. C., "Pagan Philosophy and the Christian Church," pp. 450–75, and "The Christian Church in the East," pp. 476–514.

Christensen, Arthur, "Sassanid Persia," pp. 109–37.

Ensslin, W., "The Senate and the Army," pp. 57–95.

Halphen, L., "The Barbarian Background," pp. 96–108.

Leitzmann, Hans, "The Christian Church in the West," pp. 515–43.

Miller, S. N., "The Army and the Imperial House," pp. 1–56.

Nock, A. D., "The Development of Paganism in the Roman Empire," pp. 409–49.

Oertel, F., "The Economic Life of the Empire," pp. 232–81.

Rand, E. K., "The Latin Literature of the West from the Antonines to Constantine," pp. 571–610.

Rodenwaldt, G., "The Transition to Late-Classical Art," pp. 544–70.

Carson, R. A. G. "The Coinage and Chronology of A.D. 238," *American Numismatic Society's Centennial Volume* (New York, 1958), pp. 134–57.

Carter, Jesse Benedict. *The Religious Life of Ancient Rome.* Boston, 1911.

*The Catholic Encyclopaedia.* Edited by Charles G. Herbermann *et al.* 15 vols. New York, 1934–40.

Collingwood, Robin G., and John N. L. Myres. *Roman Britain and the English Settlements.* Oxford, 1937.

Crevier, John B. L. *The History of the Roman Emperors, from Augustus to Constantine.* Translated by John Mill. 10 vols. London, 1814.

Cueleneer, A. de. *Essai sur la Vie et le Règne de Septime Sévère.* Brussels, 1880.

Cumont, Franz V. M. *The Mysteries of Mithra.* Translated by Thomas J. McCormack. Chicago, 1903.

———. *The Oriental Religions in Roman Paganism.* With Introductory Essay by Grant Showerman. Chicago, 1911.

Downey, Glanville. *Ancient Antioch.* Princeton, 1963.

———. *A History of Antioch in Syria: From Seleucus to the Arab Conuqest.* Princeton, 1961.

Duruy, Victor. *History of Rome, and of the Roman People.* Translated by M. M. Ripley and W. J. Clarke. Edited by The Reverend J. P. Mahaffey. 8 vols. Boston, 1883.

Edelstein, Emma J. and Ludwig. *Asclepius: A Collection and Interpretations of the Testimonies.* 2 vols. Baltimore, 1945–46.

Forster, E. M. *Alexandria: A History and a Guide.* Introduction to new edition by the author. New York, 1961.

Frazer, Sir James George. *The Golden Bough: A Study in Magic and Religion.* 12 vols. 3d. ed.; London, 1907–15.

Fuchs, Karl. "Geschichte des Kaisers L. Septimius Severus," *Untersuchungen aus dem Alten Geschichte* (Vienna), V (1884).

Harrer, G. A. "The Chronology of the Revolt of Pescennius Niger." *Journal of Roman Studies,* X (1920), 155–68.

Hasebroek, Johannes. *Untersuchungen zur Geschichte des Kaisers Septimius Severus.* Heidelberg, 1921.

Hastings, James (ed.). *Encyclopedia of Religion and Ethics.* 13 vols. New York, 1959.

Hay, John Stuart. *The Amazing Emperor Heliogabalus.* With Introduction by J. B. Bury. London, 1911.

Herzfeld, Ernest E. *Archaeological History of Iran.* London, 1936.

Hoefner, M. *Untersuchungen zur Geschichte des Kaisers L. Septimius Severus und Seiner Dynastie.* Giessen, 1875.

Hönn, Karl. *Quellenuntersuchungen zu den Viten des Heliogabalus und des Severus Alexander im Corpus der S. H. A.* Leipzig, 1911.

Hopkins, Richard V. N. *The Life of Alexander Severus.* London, 1907; New York, 1909.

Inge, William R. *The Philosophy of Plotinus.* 2 vols. 3d ed.; London, 1929.

Jardé, A. *Etudes Critiques sur la Vie et le Règne de Sévère Alexandre.* Paris, 1925.

Keyes, Clinton W. *The Rise of the Equites in the Third Century of the Roman Empire.* Princeton, 1915.

Kornemann, Ernst. *Grosse Frauen des Altertums.* Wiesbaden, 1952.

Lehmann, K. F. *Kaiser Gordian III.* Berlin, 1911.

Mattingly, Harold. "The Coinage of Septimius Severus and His Time," *Numismatic Chronicle,* 5th Series, Vol. XII (1932).

Moncrieff, Ascott R. H. *Classic Myth and Legend.* New York, 1934.

Murphy, Gerard J. *The Reign of the Emperor L. Septimius Severus, from the Evidence of Inscriptions.* Unpublished thesis, University of Pennsylvania. Philadelphia, 1945.

Nash, Ernest. *Pictorial Dictionary of Ancient Rome.* 2 vols. New York, 1961–62.

Pignatorre, Theodore. *The Ancient Monuments of Rome.* London, 1932.

Platnauer, Maurice. *The Life and Reign of the Emperor Lucius Septimius Severus.* Oxford, 1918.

———. "On the Date of the Defeat of C. Pescennius Niger at Issus," *Journal of Roman Studies,* VIII (1918), 146–53.

Reid, James S. *The Municipalities of the Roman Empire.* London, 1913.

Richmond, Sir Ian Archibald. *Roman Britain.* Rev. ed.; New York; London, 1964.

Rivoira, Giovanni T. *Roman Architecture and Its Principles of Construction under the Empire.* Translated by G. McN. Rushforth. London, 1925.

Robertson, Donald S. *A Handbook of Greek and Roman Architecture.* London, 1929.

Rostovtzeff, M. *The Social and Economic History of the Roman Empire.* Revised by P. M. Fraser. 2 vols. 2d ed.; Oxford, 1957.

Schulz, Otto T. *Der Römische Kaiser Caracalla: Genie, Wahnsinn oder Verbrechen.* Leipzig, 1909.

———. *Vom Prinzipat zum Dominat: Das Wesen des Römischen Kaisertums des Dritten Jahrhunderts.* Paderborn, 1919.

Seyffert, Oskar. *A Dictionary of Classical Antiquities.* Revised and edited by Henry Nettleship and J. E. Sandys. New York, 1956.

*Some Authentic Acts of the Early Martyrs.* Translated and with Notes and Introduction by E. C. E. Owen. London, 1927.

Starr, Chester G. *Civilization and the Caesars: The Intellectual Revolution in the Roman Empire.* Ithaca, N. Y., 1954.

Stuart, Duane Reed. "The Attitude of Dio Cassius Toward Epigraphic Sources," in *Roman Historical Sources and Institutions.* Edited by Henry A. Sanders. New York, 1904.

Townsend, Prescott W. "Chronology of the Year 238 A.D.," *Yale Classical Studies,* I (1928), 231–38.

Van Sickle, C. E. "A Hypothetical Chronology for the Year of the Gordians," *Classical Philology,* XXII (1927), 416–17.

———. "Some Further Observations on the Chronology of the Year 238 A.D.," *ibid.,* XXIV (1929), 285–89.

————. "The Terminal Dates of the Reign of Alexander Severus," *ibid.*, XXII, 315–17.

Wheeler, Sir Mortimer. *Roman Art and Architecture*. New York; London, 1964.

Whittaker, Thomas. *The Neo-Platonists: A Study in the History of Hellenism.* 2d ed. London, 1918.

Williams, Mary G. "Studies in the Lives of Roman Empresses: Julia Domna," *American Journal of Archaeology*, 2d Series, VI (1902), 259–305.

————. "Studies in the Lives of Roman Empresses: Julia Mamaea," in Sanders (ed.), *op. cit.*

Wirth, O. *Quaestiones Severianae*. Leipzig, 1888.

Wissowa, Georg. *Paulys Real-Encyclopädie der Classischen Altertumswissenschaft*. Stuttgart, 1894.

————. *Religion und Kultus der Römer*. 2d ed.; Munich, 1912.

# ✹ INDEX ✹